Concurrent Programming in ERLANG

Concurrent Programming in ERLANG

Second Edition

Joe Armstrong
Robert Virding
Claes Wikström
Mike Williams

Prentice Hall
London New York Toronto Sydney Tokyo Singapore
Madrid Mexico City Munich

First published 1993
This edition published 1996 by
Prentice Hall Europe
Campus 400, Maylands Avenue
Hemel Hempstead
Hertfordshire, HP2 7EZ
A division of
Simon & Schuster International Group

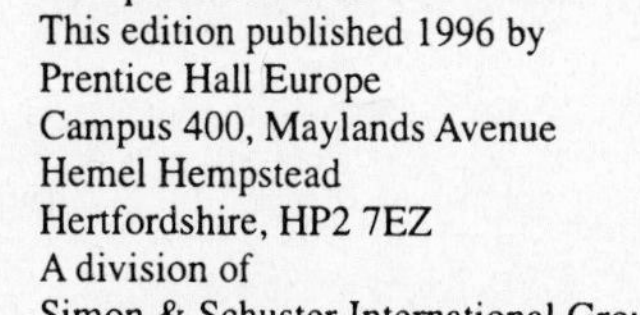

Printed and bound in Great Britain
by Redwood Books, Trowbridge, Wiltshire.

Library of Congress Cataloging-in-Publication Data

Available from the publisher

British Library Cataloguing in Publication Data

A catalogue record for this book is available
from the British Library

ISBN 0-13-508301-X

4 5 00 99 98

Contents

Preface

ERLANG[1] is a declarative language for programming concurrent and distributed systems which was developed by the authors at the Ericsson and Ellemtel Computer Science Laboratories.

The development of ERLANG started as an investigation into whether modern declarative programming paradigms could be used for programming large industrial telecommunications switching systems. It was soon realised that languages which were suitable for programming telecommunications systems were also suitable for a wide range of industrial embedded real-time control problems.

Many of the ERLANG primitives provide solutions to problems which are commonly encountered when programming large concurrent real-time systems. The *module* system allows the structuring of very large programs into conceptually manageable units. *Error detection* mechanisms allow the construction of fault-tolerant software. *Code loading* primitives allow code in a running system to be changed *without stopping the system.*[2]

ERLANG has a process-based model of concurrency. Concurrency is explicit and the user can precisely control which computations are performed sequentially and which are performed in parallel. Message passing between processes is asynchronous, that is, the sending process continues as soon as a message has been sent.

The only method by which ERLANG processes can exchange data is message passing. This results in applications which can easily be distributed – an application written for a uniprocessor can easily be changed to run on a multiprocessor or network of uniprocessors. The language has built-in mechanisms for distributed programming which makes it easy to write applications which can run either on a

[1]Agner Krarup Erlang (1878–1929) was a Danish mathematician who developed a theory of stochastic processes in statistical equilibrium – his theories are widely used in the telecommunications industry.

[2]This is very important in embedded real-time systems such as telephone exchanges or air traffic control systems – such systems should not normally be stopped for software maintenance purposes.

single computer, or on a network of computers.

Variables in ERLANG have the property of single assignment[3] – once a value has been assigned to a variable this value can never be changed. This property has important consequences when debugging or transforming a program.

Programs are written entirely in terms of *functions* – function selection is made by pattern matching which leads to highly succinct programs.

The ERLANG system has an inbuilt notion of time – the programmer can specify how long a process should wait for a message before taking some action. This allows the programming of real-time applications. ERLANG is suitable for most *soft* real-time applications where response times are in the order of milliseconds.

Current information about ERLANG can be obtained from the World Wide Web at `http://www.ericsson.se/erlang`, e-mail requests for information can be sent to `erlang@erix.ericsson.se`.

Commercially supported implementations of ERLANG can be obtained from Ericsson Software Technology AB. For information please send e-mail to `erl-biz@erlang.ericsson.se`.

Joe Armstrong
Robert Virding
Claes Wikström
Mike Williams
Computer Science Laboratory
Ericsson Telecommunications Systems Laboratories
Box 1505
S-125 25 Älvsjö
Sweden
`erlang@erix.ericsson.se`

[3]Also called write-once variables or non-destructive assignment.

Acknowledgments

The ideas in ERLANG are difficult to trace to a single source. Many features of the language have been influenced and improved as a result of comments by our friends and colleagues of the Computer Science Laboratory and we would like to thank them all for their help and advice. In particular we would like to thank Bjarne Däcker – Head of the Computer Science Laboratory – for his enthusiastic support and encouragement and for the help he has provided in spreading the language.

Many people have made contributions to this book. Richard Ehrenborg wrote the code for AVL trees in Chapter 4. Per Hedeland wrote `pxw` which is described in Chapter 17. Roger Skagervall and Sebastian Strollo provided the ideas behind the object-oriented programming methods described in Chapter 18. Carl Wilhelm Welin wrote an LALR(1) parser generator in ERLANG which generates ERLANG and provided the reference grammar contained in Appendix A.

Early users, in particular the first group of users (*ingen nämnd, ingen glömd*) at Ericsson Business Systems in Bollmora stoically acted as guinea pigs and did battle with many early and mutually incompatible versions of the ERLANG system. Their comments have helped us greatly.

We would like to thank Torbjörn Johnson from Ellemtel and Bernt Ericson from Ericsson Telecom without whose unfailing support ERLANG would not have seen the light of day.

This book was typeset in LaTeX with the macro package `ph.sty` provided by Richard Fidczuk from Prentice Hall. Comp.text.tex also helped answer our naïve questions.

Introduction

ERLANG is a new programming language which was designed for programming concurrent, real-time, distributed fault-tolerant systems.

Programming techniques for programming concurrent real-time systems have, for many years, lagged behind those techniques used for programming sequential applications. When the use of languages such as C or Pascal was standard practice for programming sequential applications, most programmers of real-time systems were still struggling with assembly languages. Today's real-time systems can be written in languages such as Ada, Modula2, Occam, etc., in which there are explicit constructs for programming concurrency or in languages such as C which lack constructs for concurrency.

Our interest in concurrency is motivated by a study of problems which exhibit a large degree of natural concurrency. This is a typical property of real-time control problems. The ERLANG programmer explicitly specifies which activities are to be represented as parallel processes. This view of concurrency is similar to that found in Occam, CSP, Concurrent Pascal, etc., but dissimilar to concurrent languages where the prime motivation for introducing concurrency is not for modelling real world concurrency, but for obtaining higher performance by compiling programs for execution on a parallel processor.

Languages such as Prolog [15] and ML [28] are now used for a wide range of industrial applications and have resulted in dramatic reductions in the total effort required to design, implement and maintain applications. We have designed and implemented ERLANG to enable the programming of concurrent real-time systems at a similarly high level.

Declarative syntax. ERLANG has a declarative syntax and is largely free from side-effects.

Concurrent. ERLANG has a process-based model of concurrency with asynchronous message passing. The concurrency mechanisms in ERLANG are lightweight, i.e. processes require little memory, and creating and deleting processes and message passing require little computational effort.

Real-time. ERLANG is intended for programming soft real-time systems where response times in the order of milliseconds are required.

Continuous operation. ERLANG has primitives which allow code to be replaced in a running system and allow old and new versions of code to execute at the same time. This is of great use in 'non-stop' systems, telephone exchanges, air traffic control systems, etc., where the systems cannot be halted to make changes in the software.

Robust. Safety is a crucial requirement in systems such as the above. There are three constructs in the language for detecting run-time errors. These can be used to program robust applications.

Memory management. ERLANG is a symbolic programming language with a real-time garbage collector. Memory is allocated automatically when required, and deallocated when no longer used. Typical programming errors associated with memory management cannot occur.

Distribution. ERLANG has no shared memory. All interaction between processes is by asynchronous message passing. Distributed systems can easily be built in ERLANG. Applications written for a single processor can, without difficulty, be ported to run on networks of processors.

Integration. ERLANG can easily call or make use of programs written in other programming languages. These can be interfaced to the system in such a way that they appear to the programmer as if they were written in ERLANG.

We have freely borrowed ideas from declarative and concurrent programming languages. The early syntax of ERLANG owed much to STRAND [22], though the current syntax is more reminiscent of an untyped ML. The model of concurrency is similar to that of SDL [11].

Our goal was to produce a small, simple and efficient language suitable for programming robust large-scale concurrent industrial applications. Thus, for reasons of efficiency, we have avoided many features commonly found in modern functional or logic programming languages. Currying, higher-order functions, lazy evaluation, ZF comprehension, logical variables, deep guards, etc., add to the expressive power of a declarative programming language, but their absence is not a significant detriment to the programming of typical industrial control applications. The use of a pattern matching syntax, and the 'single assignment' property of ERLANG variables, leads to clear, short and reliable programs.

ERLANG was designed at the same time as its first implementation, which was an interpreter written in Prolog [3]. We were fortunate in having an enthusiastic group of users who were, at the same time, developing a prototype of a new telephone exchange.

This resulted in an extremely pragmatic approach to language design. Constructs which were not used were removed. New constructs were introduced to solve problems which had caused our users to write convoluted code. Despite the fact that we often introduced backwardly incompatible changes to the language, our users had soon produced tens of thousands of lines of code and were actively encouraging others to use the language. Some of the results of their labours in producing a new way of programming telephone exchanges have been published in [2], [18].

The first Prolog-based interpreter for ERLANG has long since been abandoned in favour of compiled implementations. One of these implementations is available free of charge but is subject to non-commercial licensing. The present generation of ERLANG implementations meets our real-time requirements as regards speed and lightweight concurrency. ERLANG implementations have been ported to and run on several operating systems and several processors.

ERLANG is suitable for programming a wide range of concurrent applications. Several tools have been written to support ERLANG programming, for example, interfaces to the X Windows System, and ASN.1 compiler (written in ERLANG and generating ERLANG), parser generators, debuggers ...

Audience

This book is intended for people who are interested in real-time control systems and have some previous programming experience. Previous knowledge of functional or logic languages is not necessary.

The material in the book is loosely based on an ERLANG course which has been held many times in recent years at Ericsson and its subsidiary companies world-wide and at several Swedish universities. This course takes four days, which is more than sufficient to teach not only the language but also many of the paradigms used in ERLANG programming. The last day of the course usually has a programming exercise in which the students write a control system for a telephone exchange similar to that described in Chapter 15 and run it on a real exchange!

Summary

The book is divided into two main parts. The first part, 'Programming', introduces the ERLANG language and some of the most commonly used paradigms when programming in ERLANG. The second part, 'Applications', has a number of self-contained chapters containing case studies of typical ERLANG applications.

Programming

Chapter 1 is a tutorial introduction to ERLANG. The major ideas in the language are introduced through a series of examples.

Chapter 2 introduces sequential programming. The module system is introduced, as is the basic terminology used when we talk about ERLANG programs.

Chapters 3 and 4 contain examples of sequential programming with lists and tuples. Basic list and tuple programming techniques are introduced. Several standard modules, which will be used later in the book, are introduced. These include modules for implementing sets, dictionaries, balanced and unbalanced binary trees, etc.

Chapter 5 introduces concurrency. Sequential ERLANG needs the addition of a small number of primitives to turn it into a concurrent programming language. We introduce the primitives necessary to create a parallel process and for message passing between processes. We also introduce the idea of a registered process which allows us to associate a name with a process.

The basic ideas behind the client–server model are explained. This model is often used in later chapters and is one of the basic programming techniques for coordinating the activities of several parallel processes. We also introduce timeouts, which can be used for writing programs which have real-time behaviour.

Chapter 6 has a general introduction to distributed programming where we explain some of the reasons for writing distributed applications. We describe the language primitives which are needed to write distributed ERLANG programs and explain how sets of ERLANG process can be arranged to run on a network of ERLANG nodes.

Chapter 7 explains the error handling mechanisms available in ERLANG. We have designed ERLANG for programming robust applications, and the language has three orthogonal mechanisms for detecting errors. We take the view that the language should detect as many errors as possible at run-time and leave the responsibility for correction of such errors to the programmer.

Chapter 8 shows how the error handling primitives introduced in the previous chapter can be used to build robust and fault-tolerant systems. We show how to protect against faulty code, provide a fault-tolerant server (by extending the client server model) and show how to 'isolate' a computation so as to limit the extent of any damage caused if it should fail.

Chapter 9 is a collection of ideas and programming techniques not introduced elsewhere in the book. We start with a discussion of the last call optimisation. An understanding of this optimisation is essential if the programmer wishes to write correct code for non-terminating software. We then introduce references which provide unique unforgeable symbols. The next two sections in this chapter contain details of how to change ERLANG code in a running system (this is needed for writing non-stop systems) and how to interface ERLANG to programs written in other languages. Following this we discuss binaries which are used for efficiently handling large quantities of untyped data, the process dictionary which provides each process with simple destructive storage capabilities and the net kernel which is the basis of distributed ERLANG. Finally, we discuss efficiency, giving examples of how to write efficient ERLANG code.

Function calls can be nested:

```
> math2:double(math2:double(2)).
8
```

Choice in ERLANG is provided by pattern matching. Program example of this.

```
-module(math3).
-export([area/1]).

area({square, Side}) ->
    Side * Side;
area({rectangle, X, Y}) ->
    X * Y;
area({circle, Radius}) ->
    3.14159 * Radius * Radius;
area({triangle, A, B, C}) ->
    S = (A + B + C)/2,
    math:sqrt(S*(S-A)*(S-B)*(S-C)).
```

Program 1.3

Evaluating `math3:area({triangle, 3, 4, 5})` yields `6.0000` an `math3:area({square, 5})` yields 25 as expected. Program 1.3 intro new ideas:

- *Tuples* – these are used as place holders for complex data struct illustrate this by the following dialogue with the shell:

  ```
  > Thing = {triangle, 6, 7, 8}.
  {triangle,6,7,8}
  > math3:area(Thing).
  20.3332
  ```

  Here `Thing` is bound to the tuple `{triangle, 6, 7, 8}` – we s of `Thing` is a tuple of *size* 4 – it has four *elements*. The first el *atom* `triangle`, and the next three elements are the *integers* 6
- *Pattern matching* – this is used for clause selection within a func was defined in terms of four *clauses*. The query `math3:area({ci` results in the system trying to match one of the clauses defi with the tuple `{circle, 10}`. In our example the third clause `area/1` would match, and the free variable `Radius` occurring in the function definition is *bound* to the value supplied in the call to `10`).

Applications

Chapter 10 shows how to program databases in ERLANG. We start by combining the simple dictionary module developed in Chapter 4 with the client–server model of Chapter 5. This gives a simple concurrent database. We then show how to increase throughput in the database by representing it as a multi-level tree of parallel processes. We then add the notion of a transaction whereby several sequential operations on the database can be made to appear atomic.

Following this, we add roll-back to the database which allows us to 'undo' the effect of a transaction. The roll-back example provides a beautiful instance of the use of non-destructive assignment.

We discuss how our database can be made fault-tolerant. Finally, we show how an external database can be integrated with our database in such a way that the entire system presents a consistent interface to the programmer.

Chapter 11 introduces distributed programming techniques. We show how several well-known techniques used for writing distributed programs, such as the remote proceedure call, broadcasting, promises, etc. can be programmed in distributed ERLANG.

Chapter 12 examines the problem of distributed data. Many applications running on different physical machines may wish to share some comon data structures. This chapter describes various techniques which can be used for implementing shared data in a distributed system.

Chapter 13 is a discussion of the ERLANG operating system. Since all process management occurs within ERLANG we need few of the services of a traditional operating system. We show the main components of the ERLANG operating system which accompanies the standard distribution of the language. This operating system can be used as the basis of more specialised operating systems which may be required for a specific turn-key application.

Chapter 14 address two real-time control problems. The first is the well-known problem of controlling a number of lifts – here we see that modelling the system as a set of parallel processes provides a simple and elegant solution. The second section addresses 'process control' – in this case our 'process' is a satellite. The only way of 'observing' the satellite is by interpreting the data which comes from sensors mounted in the satellite. The only way of modifying the behaviour of the satellite is by sending commands to instruments on the satellite. While we have chosen a satellite control system in our example, the techniques are equally applicable to a wide range of control problems.

Chapter 15 is a complete example of a real-time control program for a small local telephone exchange. ERLANG was developed at the Ericsson Computer Science Laboratory and Ericsson is one of the world's major manufacturers of telephone exchanges – ease of programming telephony has always been (and still is) one of our principal interests!

The example in the chapter is only a 'toy' example. It is, however, fully functional and illustrates many of the techniques used in building telephony software in

How the code for **factorial** was compiled and loaded into
is a *local issue.*[1]

In our example, the function **factorial** has two definin
clause is a rule for computing **factorial(0)**, the second a
factorial(N). When evaluating **factorial** for some argum
are scanned sequentially, in the order in which they occur in t
of them matches the call. When a match occurs, the expressic
side of the '->' symbol is evaluated, and any variables occur
definition are substituted in the right-hand side of the clause b

All ERLANG functions belong to some particular *module.* T
module contains a module declaration, *export* declarations an
the functions which are exported from the module.

Exported functions can be run from *outside* the module. All
only be run from *within* the module.

Program 1.2 gives an example of this.

```
-module(math2).
-export([double/1]).

double(X) ->
    times(X, 2).

times(X, N) ->
    X * N.
```

Program 1.2

The function `double/1`[2] can be evaluated from outside th
`times/2` is purely local, for example:

```
> math2:double(10).
20
> math2:times(5, 2).
** undefined function: math2:times(5,2) **
```

In Program 1.2 the *module declaration* `-module(math2)` defin
module, and the *export attribute* `-export([double/1])` says
double with one argument is to be exported from the module.

[1] By 'local issue' we mean that the details of *how* a particular operation is
dependent and is not covered in this book.

[2] The notation **F/N** denotes the function **F** with **N** arguments.

- *Sequences* and *temporary variables* – these were introduced in the last clause defining **area/1**. The *body* of the last clause is a sequence of two statements, separated by a comma; these statements are evaluated *sequentially*. The value of the clause is defined as the result of evaluating the *last* statement in the sequence. In the first statement of the sequence we introduced a temporary variable **S**.

1.2 Data Types

ERLANG provides the following data types:

- *Constant* data types – these are data types which cannot be split into more primitive subtypes:
  - *Numbers* – for example: `123, -789, 3.14159, 7.8e12, -1.2e-45`. Numbers are further subdivided into *integers* and *floats*.
  - *Atoms* – for example: `abc, 'An atom with spaces', monday, green, hello_world`. These are simply constants with names.
- *Compound* data types – these are used to group together other data types. There are two compound data types:
  - *Tuples* – for example: `{a, 12, b}, {}, {1, 2, 3}, {a, b, c, d, e}`. Tuples are used for storing a fixed number of items and are written as sequences of items enclosed in curly brackets. Tuples are similar to records or structures in conventional programming languages.
  - *Lists* – for example: `[], [a, b, 12], [22], [a, 'hello friend']`. Lists are used for storing a *variable* number of items and are written as sequences of items enclosed in square brackets.

Components of tuples and lists can themselves be any ERLANG data item – this allows us to create arbitrary complex structures.

The values of ERLANG data types can be stored in *variables*. Variables always start with an upper-case letter so, for example, the code fragment:

```
X = {book, preface, acknowledgments, contents,
      {chapters, [
         {chapter, 1, 'An Erlang Tutorial'},
         {chapter, 2, ...}
         ]
      }},
```

creates a complex data structure and stores it in the variable **X**.

1.3 Pattern Matching

Pattern matching is used for assigning values to variables and for controlling the flow of a program. ERLANG is a *single assignment* language, which means that once a variable has been assigned a value, the value can never be changed.

Pattern matching is used to match patterns with terms. If a pattern and term have the same shape then the match will succeed and any variables occurring in the pattern will be bound to the data structures which occur in the corresponding positions in the term.

1.3.1 Pattern matching when calling a function

Program 1.4 defines the function `convert` which is used to convert temperatures between the Celsius, Fahrenheit and Réaumur scales. The first argument to `convert` is a tuple containing the scale and value of the temperature to be converted and the second argument is the scale to which we wish to convert.

```
-module(temp).
-export([convert/2]).

convert({fahrenheit, Temp}, celsius) ->
        {celsius, 5 * (Temp - 32) / 9};
convert({celsius, Temp}, fahrenheit) ->
        {farenheit, 32 + Temp * 9 / 5};
convert({reaumur, Temp}, celsius) ->
        {celsius, 10 * Temp / 8};
convert({celsius, Temp}, reaumur) ->
        {reaumur, 8 * Temp / 10};
convert({X, _}, Y) ->
        {cannot,convert,X,to,Y}.
```

Program 1.4

When `convert` is evaluated, the arguments occurring in the function call (terms) are matched against the patterns occurring in the function definition. When a match occurs the code following the '`->`' symbol is evaluated, so:

```
> temp:convert({fahrenheit, 98.6}, celsius).
{celsius,37.0000}
> temp:convert({reaumur, 80}, celsius).
{celsius,100.000}
> temp:convert({reaumur, 80}, fahrenheit).
{cannot,convert,reaumur,to,fahrenheit}
```

1.3.2 The match primitive '='

The expression `Pattern = Expression` causes `Expression` to be evaluated and the result *matched* against `Pattern`. The match either succeeds or fails. If the match succeeds any variables occurring in `Pattern` become bound, for example:

```
> N = {12, banana}.
{12,banana}
> {A, B} = N.
{12,banana}
> A.
12
> B.
banana
```

The match primitive can be used to *unpack* items from complex data structures:

```
> {A, B} = {[1,2,3], {x,y}}.
{[1,2,3],{x,y}}
> A.
[1,2,3]
> B.
{x,y}
> [a,X,b,Y] = [a,{hello, fred},b,1].
[a,{hello,fred},b,1]
> X.
{hello,fred}
> Y.
1
> {_,L,_} = {fred,{likes, [wine, women, song]},
   {drinks, [whisky, beer]}}.
{fred,{likes,[wine,women,song]},{drinks,[whisky,beer]}}
> L.
{likes,[wine,women,song]}
```

The special variable underscore (written '_') is the *anonymous* or *don't care* variable. It is used as a place holder where the syntax requires a variable, but the value of the variable is of no interest.

If the match succeeds, the value of the expression `Lhs = Rhs` is defined to be `Rhs`. This allows multiple uses of *match* within a single expression, for example:

```
{A, B} = {X, Y} = C = g(a, 12)
```

'=' is regarded as an infix right associative operator; thus `A = B = C = D` is parsed as `A = (B = (C = D))`.

1.4 Built-in Functions

Some operations are impossible to program in ERLANG itself, or are impossible to program efficiently. For example, there is no way to find out the internal structure of an atom, or the time of day, etc. – these lie outside the scope of the language. ERLANG therefore has a number of *built-in functions* (BIFs) which perform these operations.

For example `atom_to_list/1` converts an atom to a list of (ASCII) integers which represents the atom and `date/0` returns the current date:

```
> atom_to_list(abc).
[97,98,99]
> date()
{93,1,10}
```

A full list of all BIFs is given in Appendix B.

1.5 Concurrency

ERLANG is a *concurrent* programming language – this means that parallel activities (processes) can be programmed directly in ERLANG and that the parallelism is provided by ERLANG and not the host operating system.

In order to control a set of parallel activities ERLANG has primitives for multi-processing: `spawn` starts a parallel computation (called a process); `send` sends a message to a process; and `receive` receives a message from a process.

`spawn/3` starts execution of a parallel process and returns an identifier which may be used to send messages to and receive messages from the process.

The syntax `Pid ! Msg` is used to send a message. `Pid` is an expression or constant which must evaluate to a process identity. `Msg` is the message which is to be sent to `Pid`. For example:

```
Pid ! {a, 12}
```

means send the message `{a, 12}` to the process with identifier `Pid` (Pid is short for *process identifier*). All arguments are evaluated before sending the message, so:

```
foo(12) ! math3:area({square, 5})
```

means evaluate the function `foo(12)` (this must yield a valid process identifier) and evaluate `math3:area({square, 5})` then send the result (i.e. 25) as a message to the process. The order of evaluation of the two sides of the `send` primitive is undefined.

The primitive `receive` is used to receive messages. `receive` has the following syntax:

```
receive
    Message1 ->
        ... ;
    Message2 ->
        ... ;
        ...
end
```

This means try to receive a message which is described by one of the patterns `Message1,Message2,...` The process which is evaluating this primitive is suspended until a message which matches one of the patterns `Message1,Message2,...` is received. If a match occurs the code after the '`->`' is evaluated.

Any unbound variables occurring in the message reception patterns become bound if a message is received.

The return value of `receive` is the value of the sequence which is evaluated as a result of a receive option being matched.

While we can think of `send` as sending a message and `receive` as receiving a message, a more accurate description would be to say that `send` sends a message *to the mailbox of a process* and that `receive` *tries to remove a message from the mailbox of the current process.*

`receive` is selective, that is to say, it takes the first message which matches one of the message patterns from a queue of messages waiting for the attention of the receiving process. If none of the receive patterns matches then the process is suspended until the next message is received – unmatched messages are saved for later processing.

1.5.1 An echo process

As a simple example of a concurrent process we will create an *echo* process which echoes any message sent to it. Let us suppose that process `A` sends the message `{A, Msg}` to the echo process, so that the echo process sends a new message containing `Msg` back to process `A`. This is illustrated in Figure 1.1.

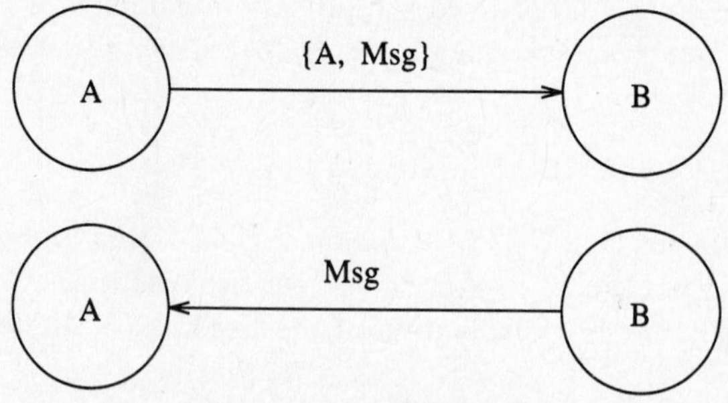

Figure 1.1 An echo process

In Program 1.5 `echo:start()` creates a simple echo process which returns any message sent to it.

```
-module(echo).
-export([start/0, loop/0]).

start() ->
    spawn(echo, loop, []).

loop() ->
    receive
        {From, Message} ->
            From ! Message,
            loop()
    end.
```

Program 1.5

`spawn(echo, loop, [])` causes the function represented by `echo:loop()` to be evaluated *in parallel* with the calling function. Thus evaluating:

```
...
Id = echo:start(),
Id ! {self(), hello}
...
```

causes a parallel process to be started and the message `{self(), hello}` to be sent to the process – `self()` is a BIF which returns the process identifier of the current process.

Chapter 2

Sequential Programming

This chapter introduces the concepts needed to write sequential ERLANG programs. We start with a discussion of the basic mechanisms by which variables acquire values and how flow of control is achieved. To do this requires an understanding of *terms*, *patterns* and *pattern matching*:

2.1 Terms

ERLANG provides the following data types[1] which are called *terms*:

- **Constant** data types
  - Numbers
    - Integers, for storing natural numbers
    - Floats, for storing real numbers
  - Atoms
  - Pids (short for 'process identifiers'), for storing process names
  - References, for storing system unique references
- **Compound** data types
  - Tuples, for storing a *fixed* number of terms
  - Lists, for storing a *variable* number of terms

2.1.1 Numbers

Numbers are written as in the following examples:

[1] Appendix A gives the formal ERLANG grammar.

```
123 -34567 12.345 -27.45e-05
```

The precision of integers is a local issue but at least 24-bit integer precision must be provided by any ERLANG system.

The notation **$<Char>** represents the ASCII value of the character **Char** so, for example, **$A** represents the integer 65.

Integers with base other than 10 are written using the notation **<Base>#<Value>** so, for example, **16#ffff** represents the integer 65535 (in base 10). The value of **Base** must be an integer in the range 2..16.

Floating point numbers are written in conventional notation.

2.1.2 Atoms

Atoms are constants with names; thus, for example, the atoms **monday**, **tuesday**, ... could be used to represent days of the week in some program which performs calendar calculations. Atoms are used to enhance the legibility of programs.

Examples of atoms:

```
friday  unquoted_atoms_cannot_contain_blanks
'A quoted atom which contains several blanks'
'hello \n my friend'
```

Atoms begin with a lower-case letter (a..z) and are terminated by a non-alphanumeric character – otherwise they must be quoted.

By enclosing the atom name in single quotes any character may be included within the atom. Atoms will always be printed in such a manner that they can be read back by the ERLANG reader. Within a *quoted* atom the following conventions apply:

Characters	Meaning
\b	backspace
\d	delete
\e	escape
\f	form feed
\n	newline
\r	carriage return
\t	tab
\v	vertical tab
\\	backslash
\^A .. \^Z	control A to control Z (i.e. 0 .. 26)
\'	single quote
\"	double quote
\OOO	The character with octal representation OOO

If a quoted atom contains the sequence `\C`, where the ASCII value of `C` is < 32, then the character codes representing `\C` are omitted from the atom (this allows long atoms to be split over several lines by terminating each line with a backslash followed by new line).

2.1.3 Tuples

Terms separated by commas and enclosed in curly brackets are called *tuples.* Tuples are used for storing a fixed number of items. They are similar to *structures* or *records* in conventional programming languages.

The tuple `{E1,E2,...,En}`, where $n \geq 0$, is said to have *size* `n`. The individual terms occurring in the tuple are referred to as *elements.*

Examples of tuples:

```
{a, 12, 'hello'}
{1, 2, {3, 4}, {a, {b, c}}}
{}
```

2.1.4 Lists

Terms separated by commas and enclosed in square brackets are called *lists.* Lists are used for storing a variable number of items.

The list `[E1,E2,...,En]`, where $n \geq 0$, is said to have *length* `n`.

Examples of lists:

```
[1, abc, [12], 'foo bar']
[]
[a,b,c]
"abcd"
```

The notation `"..."`, which we call a string, is shorthand for the ASCII representation of the list of characters occurring within the quotes. Thus `"abc"` denotes the list `[97,98,99]`. Within a string the quoting conventions used within an atom also apply.

When processing lists it is often convenient to be able to refer to the first element of the list and the remainder of the list when the first element has been removed. By convention, we refer to the first element of the list as the *head* of the list and the remainder of the list as the *tail.*

The notation `[E1,E2,E3,...,En|Variable]`, where $n \geq 1$, is used to denote a list whose first `n` elements are `E1,E2,E3,...,En` and whose remainder is the object denoted by `Variable`.

Note that the term following the '`|`' need not be a list but can be any valid ERLANG term. Lists whose last tail is the term `[]` are called *proper* or *well-*

formed lists – most (though not all) ERLANG programs are written to manipulate well-formed lists.

2.2 Pattern Matching

Patterns have the same structure as terms, with the addition that they can include variables. Variables start with an upper-case letter.

Examples of patterns:

```
{A, a, 12, [12,34|{a}]}
{A, B, 23}
{x, {X_1}, 12, My_cats_age}
[]
```

In the above `A, B, X_1`, and `My_cats_age` are variables.

Pattern matching provides the basic mechanism by which values become assigned to variables. A variable whose value has been assigned is said to be *bound* – otherwise it is said to be *unbound*. The act of assigning a value to a variable is called *binding*. Once a variable has been bound its value can never be changed. Such variables are called *bind once* or *single assignment*. This contrasts with conventional imperative languages which have *destructive assignment*.[2]

A *pattern* and a *term* are said to *match* if the pattern and term are structurally isomorphic and if, whenever an atomic data type is encountered in the pattern, the same atomic data type is encountered at the same position in the corresponding term. In the case where the pattern contains an unbound variable, the variable is bound to the corresponding element in the term. If the *same* variable occurs more than once in the pattern then all items occurring at corresponding positions in the term must be identical.

Pattern matching occurs:

- when evaluating an expression of the form `Lhs = Rhs`
- when calling a function
- when matching a pattern in a `case` or `receive` primitive.

2.2.1 Pattern = Expression

The expression `Pattern = Expression` causes `Expression` to be evaluated and the result matched against `Pattern`. The match either succeeds or fails. If the match succeeds any variables occurring in `Pattern` become bound.

In the following we assume that the pattern matching always *succeeds*. The treatment of *failure* will be discussed in detail in Chapter 7.

[2]Many people think that the use of destructive assignment leads to unclear programs which are difficult to understand, and invites obscure errors.

Examples:

```
{A, B} = {12, apple}
```

succeeds with the bindings `A` ↦ 12[3] and, `B` ↦ `apple`.

```
{C, [Head|Tail]} = {{222, man}, [a,b,c]}
```

succeeds with the bindings `C` ↦ `{222, man}` , `Head` ↦ `a` and, `Tail` ↦ `[b, c]`.

```
[{person, Name, Age, _}|T] =
        [{person, fred, 22, male},
         {person, susan, 19, female}, ...]
```

succeeds with the bindings `T` ↦ `[{person, susan, 19, female}, ...]}`, `Name` ↦ `fred` and `Age` ↦ `22`. In the last example we made use of the *anonymous* variable written '`_`' – anonymous variables are used when the syntax requires a variable but we are not interested in its value.

If a variable occurs more than once in a pattern then the match will only succeed if the corresponding elements being matched have the same value. So, for example, `{A, foo, A} = {123, foo, 123}` succeeds, binding `A` to `123`, whereas `{A, foo, A} = {123, foo, abc}` fails since we cannot simultaneously bind `A` to `123` *and* `abc`.

'`=`' is regarded as an infix right associative operator. Thus `A = B = C = D` is parsed as `A = (B = (C = D))`. This is probably only useful in a construction like `{A, B} = X = ...` where we want both the value of an expression and its constituents. The value of the expression `Lhs = Rhs` is defined to be `Rhs`.

2.2.2 Pattern matching when calling a function

ERLANG provides choice and flow of control through pattern matching. For example, Program 2.1 defines a function `classify_day/1`, which returns `weekEnd` if called with argument `saturday` or `sunday`, or it returns `weekDay` otherwise.

```
-module(dates).
-export([classify_day/1]).

classify_day(saturday) -> weekEnd;
classify_day(sunday)   -> weekEnd;
classify_day(_)        -> weekDay.
```

Program 2.1

[3]The notation `Var` ↦ `Value` means that the variable `Var` has the value `Value`.

When a function is evaluated, the arguments of the function are matched against the patterns occurring in the function definition. When a match occurs the code following the '`->`' symbol is evaluated, so:

```
> dates:classify_day(saturday).
weekEnd
> dates:classify_day(friday).
weekDay
```

The function call is said to *fail* if none of its clauses match (failure causes the error-trapping mechanisms described in Chapter 7 to be used).

Any variables occurring in the patterns describing the different clauses of a function become bound when a particular clause in a function is entered. So, for example, evaluating `math3:area({square, 5})` in Program 1.3 causes the variable `Side` to be bound to `5`.

2.3 Expression Evaluation

Expressions have the same syntax as patterns with the addition that an expression can contain a function call or a conventional infix arithmetic expression. Function calls are written conventionally, so, for example: `area:triangle(A, B, C)` represents calling the function `area:triangle` with arguments `A, B` and `C`.

The ERLANG expression evaluation mechanism works as follows.

Terms evaluate to themselves:

```
> 222.
222
> abc.
abc
> 3.1415926.
3.14159
> {a,12,[b,c|d]}.
{a,12,[b,c|d]}
> {{},[{}],{a,45,'hello world'}}.
{{},[{}],{a,45,'hello world'}}
```

Floating point numbers might not be printed out in exactly the same format as they were input.

Expressions evaluate to terms where the terms are isomorphic to the expressions and where each function call occurring in the expression has been evaluated. When applying a function its arguments are evaluated first.

The evaluator can be thought of as a function $\mathcal{E}$ which reduces an expression to a ground term:

$$\mathcal{E}(\mathrm{X})\ \texttt{when}\ Constant(X) \longrightarrow X$$
$$\mathcal{E}(\{t_1, t_2, \ldots, t_n\}) \longrightarrow \{\mathcal{E}(t_1), \mathcal{E}(t_2), \ldots, \mathcal{E}(t_n)\}$$
$$\mathcal{E}([t_1, t_2, \ldots, t_n]) \longrightarrow [\mathcal{E}(t_1), \mathcal{E}(t_2), \ldots, \mathcal{E}(t_n)]$$
$$\mathcal{E}(functionName(t_1, t_2, \ldots, t_n)) \longrightarrow \mathcal{APPLY}\ (functionName, [\mathcal{E}(t_1), \mathcal{E}(t_2), \ldots, \mathcal{E}(t_n)])$$

where $\mathcal{APPLY}$ represents a function which applies a function to its arguments.

2.3.1 Evaluating functions

Function calls are written as in the following examples:

```
> length([a,b,c]).
3
> lists:append([a,b], [1,2,3]).
[a,b,1,2,3]
> math:pi().
3.14159
```

The colon form of a function is explained in the section on modules. Calls to functions with no arguments must include the empty brackets (to distinguish them from atoms).

2.3.2 Order of evaluation

The order in which the arguments to a function are evaluated is undefined. For example, `f({a},b(),g(a,h(b),{f,X}))` represents a function call. The function `f` is called with three arguments: `{a}`, `b()` and `g(a,h(b),{f,X})`. The first argument is a tuple of size 1 containing the atom `a`. The second argument is the function call `b()`. The third argument is the function call `g(a,h(b),{f,X})`. In evaluating `f/3` the order of evaluation of `b/0` and `g/3` is undefined, though `h(b)` is evaluated before `g/3`. The order of evaluation of `b()` and `h(b)` is undefined.

When evaluating expressions such as `[f(a), g(b), h(k)]` the order in which `f(a)`, `g(b)` and `h(k)` are evaluated is undefined.

If the evaluation of `f(a)`, `g(b)` and `h(k)` has no side-effects (i.e. no messages are sent, processes spawned, etc.) then the *value* of `[f(a), g(b), h(k)]` will be the same no matter what evaluation order[4] is used. This property is known as *referential transparency*.[5]

[4]Provided that all functions terminate.

[5]Which means that the *value* of a function does not depend upon the *context* in which it is called.

2.3.3 Apply

The BIFs `apply(Mod, Func, ArgList)` and `apply({Mod, Func}, ArgList)` are functions which apply the function `Func` in the module `Mod` to the argument list `ArgList`.

```
> apply(dates, classify_day, [monday]).
weekDay
> apply(math, sqrt, [4]).
2.0
> apply({erlang, atom_to_list}, [abc]).
[97,98,99]
```

BIFs can be evaluated with `apply` by using the module name `erlang`.

2.4 The Module System

ERLANG has a module system which allows us to divide a large program into a set of modules. Each module has its own name space; thus we are free to use the same function names in several different modules, without any confusion.

The module system works by limiting the visibility of the functions contained within a given module. The way in which a function can be called depends upon the name of the module, the name of the function and whether the function name occurs in an import or export declaration in the module.

```
-module(lists1).
-export([reverse/1]).

reverse(L) ->
        reverse(L, []).

reverse([H|T], L) ->
        reverse(T, [H|L]);
reverse([], L) ->
        L.
```

Program 2.2

Program 2.2 defines a function `reverse/1` which reverses the order of the elements of a list. `reverse/1` is the *only* function which can be called from outside the module. The only functions which can be called from outside a module must be contained in the export declarations for the module.

The other function defined in the module, `reverse/2`, is only available for use *inside the module.* Note that `reverse/1` and `reverse/2` are completely different functions. In ERLANG two functions with the same name but different numbers of arguments are totally different functions.

2.4.1 Inter-module calls

There are two methods for calling functions in another module:

```
-module(sort1).
-export([reverse_sort/1, sort/1]).

reverse_sort(L) ->
        lists1:reverse(sort(L)).

sort(L) ->
        lists:sort(L).
```

Program 2.3

The function **reverse/1** was called by using the *fully qualified function name* `lists1:reverse(L)` in the call.

You can also use an *implicitly qualified function name* by making use of an `import` declaration, as in Program 2.4.

```
-module(sort2).
-import(lists1, [reverse/1]).

-export([reverse_sort/1, sort/1]).

reverse_sort(L) ->
        reverse(sort(L)).

sort(L) ->
        lists:sort(L).
```

Program 2.4

The use of both forms is needed to resolve ambiguities. For example, when two different modules export the same function, explicitly qualified function names must be used.

2.5 Function Definition

The following sections describe in more detail the syntax of an ERLANG function. We start by giving names to the different syntactic elements of a function. This is followed by descriptions of these elements.

2.5.1 Terminology

Consider the following module:

```
-module(lists2).                                       % 1
                                                       % 2
-export([flat_length/1]).                              % 3
                                                       % 4
%% flat_length(List)                                   % 5
%%  Calculate the length of a list of lists.           % 6
                                                       % 7
flat_length(List) ->                                   % 8
    flat_length(List, 0).                              % 9
                                                       % 10
flat_length([H|T], N) when list(H) ->                  % 11
    flat_length(H, flat_length(T, N));                 % 12
flat_length([H|T], N) ->                               % 13
    flat_length(T, N + 1);                             % 14
flat_length([], N) ->                                  % 15
    N.                                                 % 16
```

Program 2.5

Each line is commented `% 1`, etc. Comments start with the '`%`' character (which can occur anywhere in a line) and are delimited by the end of line.

Line 1 contains the *module* declaration. This must come before any other declarations or any code.

The leading '`-`' in lines 1 and 3 is called the *attribute prefix*. `module(lists2)` is an example of an *attribute*.

Lines 2, 4, etc., are blank – sequences of one or more blanks, lines, tabs, newline characters, etc., are treated as if they were a single blank.

Line 3 declares that the function `flat_length`, which has one argument, will be found in and should be *exported* from the module.

Lines 5 and 6 contain comments.

Lines 8 and 9 contain a definition of the function `flat_length/1`. This consists of a single *clause*.

The expression `flat_length(List)` is referred to as the *head* of the clause. The expressions following the '`->`' are referred to as the *body* of the clause.

Lines 11 to 16 contain the definition of the function `flat_length/2` – this function consists of three clauses; these are separated by semicolons '`;`' and the last one is terminated by a full stop '`.`'.

The first argument of `flat_length/2` in line 11 is the list `[H|T]`. `H` is referred to as the *head* of the list, `T` is referred to as the *tail* of the list. The expression `list(H)` which comes between the keyword **`when`** and the '`->`' arrow is called a *guard.* The body of the function is evaluated if the patterns in the function head match and if the guard tests succeed.

The first clause of `flat_length/2` is called a *guarded clause*; the other clauses are said to be *unguarded.*

`flat_length/2` is a *local function* – i.e. cannot be called from outside the module (this is because it did not occur in the **`export`** attribute).

The module `lists2` contains definitions of the functions `flat_length/1` *and* `flat_length/2`. These represent *two entirely different functions* – this is in contrast to languages such as C or Pascal where a function name can only occur once with a *fixed* number of arguments.

2.5.2 Clauses

Each function is built from a number of *clauses.* The clauses are separated by semicolons '`;`'. Each individual clause consists of a clause head, an optional guard and a body. These are described below.

2.5.3 Clause heads

The head of a clause consists of a function name followed by a number of arguments separated by commas. Each argument is a valid pattern.

When a function call is made, the call is sequentially matched against the set of clause heads which define the function.

2.5.4 Clause guards

Guards are conditions which have to be fulfilled before a clause is chosen.

A guard can be a simple test or a sequence of simple tests separated by commas. A simple test is an arithmetic comparison, a term comparison, or a call to a system predefined test function. Guards can be viewed as an extension of pattern matching. User-defined functions cannot be used in guards.

To evaluate a guard all the tests are evaluated. If all are true then the guard succeeds, otherwise it fails. The order of evaluation of the tests in a guard is undefined.

If the guard succeeds then the body of this clause is evaluated. If the guard test fails, the next candidate clause is tried, etc.

Once a matching head and guard of a clause have been selected the system *commits* to this clause and evaluates the body of the clause.

We can write a version of `factorial` using guarded clauses.

```
factorial(N) when N == 0 -> 1;
factorial(N) when N > 0  -> N * factorial(N - 1).
```

Note that in the above example we could have reversed the clause order, thus:

```
factorial(N) when N > 0  -> N * factorial(N - 1);
factorial(N) when N == 0 -> 1.
```

since in this case the combination of head patterns and guard tests serves to identify the correct clause uniquely.

2.5.5 Guard tests

The complete set of guard tests is as follows:

Guard	Succeeds if
`atom(X)`	`X` is an atom
`constant(X)`	`X` is not a list or tuple
`float(X)`	`X` is a float
`integer(X)`	`X` is an integer
`list(X)`	`X` is a list or `[]`
`number(X)`	`X` is an integer or float
`pid(X)`	`X` is a process identifier
`port(X)`	`X` is a port
`reference(X)`	`X` is a reference
`tuple(X)`	`X` is a tuple
`binary(X)`	`X` is a binary

In addition, certain BIFs, together with arithmetic expressions, are allowed in guards. These are as follows:

```
element/2, float/1, hd/1, length/1, round/1, self/0, size/1
trunc/1,   tl/1, abs/1, node/1, node/0, nodes/0
```

2.5.6 Term comparisons

The term comparison operators which are allowed in a guard are as follows:

Operator	Description	Type
`X > Y`	X greater than Y	coerce
`X < Y`	X less than Y	coerce
`X =< Y`	X equal to or less than Y	coerce
`X >= Y`	X greater than or equal to Y	coerce
`X == Y`	X equal to Y	coerce
`X /= Y`	X not equal to Y	coerce
`X =:= Y`	X equal to Y	exact
`X =/= Y`	X not equal to Y	exact

The comparison operators work as follows: firstly, both sides of the operator are evaluated where possible (i.e. in the case when they are arithmetic expressions, or contain guard function BIFs); then the comparison operator is performed.

For the purposes of comparison the following ordering is defined:

`number < atom < reference < port < pid < tuple < list`

Tuples are ordered first by their size then by their elements. Lists are ordered by comparing heads, then tails.

When the arguments of the comparison operator are both numbers and the type of the operator is *coerce* then if one argument is an `integer` and the other a `float` the `integer` is converted to a `float` before performing the comparison.

The *exact* comparison operators perform no such conversion.

Thus `5.0 == 1 + 4` succeeds whereas `5.0 =:= 1 + 4` fails.

Examples of guarded function clause heads:

```
foo(X, Y, Z) when integer(X), integer(Y), integer(Z), X == Y + Z ->
foo(X, Y, Z) when list(X), hd(X) == {Y, length(Z)}  ->
foo(X, Y, Z) when {X, Y, size(Z)} == {a, 12, X} ->
foo(X) when list(X), hd(X) == c1, hd(tl(X)) == c2 ->
```

Note that no new variables may be introduced in a guard.

2.5.7 Clause bodies

The body of a clause consists of a sequence of one or more expressions which are separated by commas. All the expressions in a sequence are evaluated sequentially. The value of the sequence is defined to be the value of the *last* expression in the sequence. For example, the second clause of `factorial` could be written:

```
factorial(N) when N > 0 ->
    N1 = N - 1,
    F1 = factorial(N1),
    N * F1.
```

During the evaluation of a sequence, each expression is evaluated and the result is either matched against a pattern or discarded.

There are several reasons for splitting the body of a function into a sequence of calls:

- To ensure sequential execution of code – each expression in a function body is evaluated sequentially, while functions occurring in a nested function call could be executed in any order.
- To increase clarity – it may be clearer to write the function as a sequence of expressions.
- To unpack return values from a function.
- To reuse the results of a function call.

Multiple reuse of a function value can be illustrated as follows:

```
good(X) ->
        Temp = lic(X),
        {cos(Temp), sin(Temp)}.
```

would be preferable to:

```
bad(X) ->
        {cos(lic(X)),   sin(lic(X))}.
```

which means the same thing. `lic` is some *l*ong and *i*nvolved *c*alculation, i.e. some function whose value is expensive to compute.

2.6 Primitives

ERLANG provides the primitives `case` and `if` which can be used for conditional evaluation in the body of a clause without having to use an additional function.

2.6.1 Case

The `case` expression allows choice between alternatives within the body of a clause and has the following syntax:

```
case Expr of
    Pattern1 [when Guard1]  -> Seq1;
    Pattern2 [when Guard2]  -> Seq2;
    ...
    PatternN [when GuardN] -> SeqN
end
```

Firstly, Expr is evaluated, then, the value of Expr is sequentially matched against the patterns Pattern1, ..., PatternN until a match is found. If a match is found and the (optional) guard test succeeds, then the corresponding call sequence is evaluated. Note that case guards have the same form as function guards. The value of the case primitive is then the value of the selected sequence.

At least one pattern *must* match – if none of the patterns match then a run-time error will be generated and the error handling mechanism of Chapter 7 will be activated.

For example, suppose we have some function allocate(Resource) which tries to allocate Resource. Assume this function returns either {yes, Address} or no. Such a function could be used within a case construct as follows:

```
...
case allocate(Resource) of
    {yes,Address} when Address > 0, Address =< Max ->
        Sequence 1 ... ;
     no ->
        Sequence 2 ...
end
...
```

In Sequence 1... the variable Address will be bound to the appropriate value returned by allocate/1.

To avoid the possibility of a match error we often add an additional pattern which is guaranteed to match[6] as the last branch of the case primitive:

```
case Fn of
    ...
    _ ->
        true
end
```

2.6.2 If

if expressions have the syntax:

```
if
    Guard1 ->
        Sequence1 ;
    Guard2 ->
        Sequence2 ;
    ...
end
```

[6] Sometimes called a *catchall*.

In this case the guards `Guard1,...` are evaluated sequentially. If a guard succeeds then the related sequence is evaluated. The result of this evaluation becomes the value of the `if` form. If guards have the same form as function guards. As with `case` it is an error if none of the guards succeeds. The guard test `true` can be added as a 'catchall' if necessary:

```
if
    ...
    true ->
        true
end
```

2.6.3 Examples of case and if

We can write the factorial function in a number of different ways using `case` and `if`.
Simplest:

```
factorial(0) -> 1;
factorial(N) -> N * factorial(N - 1).
```

Using function guards:

```
factorial(0) -> 1;
factorial(N) when N > 0 -> N * factorial(N - 1).
```

Using `if`:

```
factorial(N) ->
    if
        N == 0 -> 1;
        N >  0 -> N * factorial(N - 1)
    end.
```

Using `case`:

```
factorial(N) ->
    case N of
        0 -> 1;
        N when  N > 0 ->
            N * factorial(N - 1)
    end.
```

Using variables to store temporary results:

```
factorial(0) ->
    1;
factorial(N) when N > 0 ->
    N1 = N - 1,
    F1 = factorial(N1),
    N * F1.
```

All of the above definitions are correct and equivalent[7] – the choice among them is a matter of aesthetics.[8]

2.7 Arithmetic Expressions

Arithmetic expressions are formed from the following operators:

Operator	Description	Type	Operands	Prio
`+ X`	`+ X`	unary	mixed	1
`- X`	`- X`	unary	mixed	1
`X * Y`	`X * Y`	binary	mixed	2
`X / Y`	`X / Y` (floating point division)	binary	mixed	2
`X div Y`	integer division of `X` and `Y`	binary	integer	2
`X rem Y`	integer remainder of `X` divided by `Y`	binary	integer	2
`X band Y`	bitwise and of `X` and `Y`	binary	integer	2
`X + Y`	`X + Y`	binary	mixed	3
`X - Y`	`X - Y`	binary	mixed	3
`X bor Y`	bitwise or of `X` and `Y`	binary	integer	3
`X bxor Y`	arithmetic bitwise xor `X` and `Y`	binary	integer	3
`X bsl N`	arithmetic bitshift left of `X` by `N` bits	binary	integer	3
`X bsr N`	bitshift right of `X` by `N` bits	binary	integer	3

Unary operators have one argument, *binary* operators have two arguments. *Mixed* means that the argument can be either an `integer` or `float`. Unary operators return a value of the same type as their argument.

The *binary* mixed operators (i.e. `*`, `-`, `+`) return an object of type `integer` if both their arguments are integers, or `float` if at least one of their arguments is a `float`. The floating point division operator `/` returns a `float` irrespective of its arguments.

Binary integer operators (i.e. `band`, `div`, `rem`, `bor`, `bxor`, `bsl`, `bsr`) must have integer arguments and return integers.

The order of evaluation depends upon the priority of the operator: all priority 1 operators are evaluated, then priority 2, etc. Any bracketed expressions are evaluated first.

[7] Well *almost* – how about `factorial(-1)`?

[8] If in doubt, choose the most beautiful!

Operators with the same priority are evaluated left to right. For example:

```
A - B - C - D
```

is evaluated as if it had been written:

```
(((A - B) - C) - D)
```

2.8 Scope of Variables

Variables in a clause exist between the point where the variable is first bound and the last textual reference to that variable in the clause. The binding instance of a variable can only occur in a pattern matching operation; this can be thought of as *producing* the variable. All subsequent references to the variable *consume* the value of the variable. *All variables occurring in expressions must be bound.* It is illegal for the first use of a variable to occur in an expression. For example:

```
f(X) ->                   % 1
     Y = g(X),            % 2
     h(Y, X),             % 3
     p(Y).                % 4
```

In line 1, the variable `X` is defined (i.e. it becomes bound when the function is entered). In line 2, `X` is consumed, `Y` is defined (first occurrence). In line 3, `X` and `Y` are consumed and in line 4, `Y` is consumed.

2.8.1 Scope rules for if, case and receive

Variables which are introduced within the `if`, `case` or `receive` primitives are implicitly exported from the bodies of the primitives. If we write:

```
f(X) ->
     case g(X) of
          true ->  A = h(X);
          false -> A = k(X)
     end,
     ...
```

then the variable `A` is available after the `case` primitive where it was first defined.

When exporting variables from an `if`, `case` or `receive` primitive one more rule should be observed:

The set of variables introduced in the different branches of an `if`, `case` *or* `receive` *primitive must be the same for all branches in the primitive except if the missing variables are not referred to after the primitive.*

Example: `float_to_list(1.5)` ⟹ `[49,46,53,48,48,...,48]`.

`integer_to_list(I)`
Converts the integer `I` to a list of ASCII characters.
Example: `integer_to_list(1245)` ⟹ `[49,50,52,53]`.

`list_to_atom(L)`
Converts the list of ASCII characters in `L` to an atom.
Example: `list_to_atom([119,111,114,108,100])` ⟹ `world`.

`list_to_float(L)`
Converts the list of ASCII characters in `L` to a floating point number.
Example: `list_to_float([51,46,49,52,49,53,57])` ⟹ `3.14159`.

`list_to_integer(L)`
Converts the list of ASCII characters in `L` to an integer.
Example: `list_to_integer([49,50,51,52])` ⟹ `1234`.

`hd(L)`
Returns the first element in the list `L`.
Example: `hd([a,b,c,d])` ⟹ `a`.

`tl(L)`
Returns the tail of the list `L`
Example: `tl([a,b,c,d])` ⟹ `[b,c,d]`.

`length(L)`
Returns the length of the list `L`
Example: `length([a,b,c,d])` ⟹ `4`.

There are also `tuple_to_list/1` and `list_to_tuple/1`, which are dealt with in Chapter 4. Several other list processing BIFs are also provided, for example, `list_to_pid(AsciiList)`, `pid_to_list(Pid)`. These are described in Appendix B.

3.2 Some Common List Processing Functions

The following sections give some examples of simple list processing functions. All the functions described in this section are contained in the module `lists` which is contained in the standard ERLANG distribution (see Appendix C for more details).

3.2.1 member

`member(X, L)` returns `true` if `X` is an element of the list `L`, otherwise `false`.

```
member(X, [X|_]) -> true;
member(X, [_|T]) -> member(X, T);
member(X, [])    -> false.
```

The first clause in member matches the case where X is the first element of the list, in which case member returns true. If the first clause does not match, then the second clause will match if the second argument of member is a non-empty list, in which case the pattern [_|T] matches a non-empty list and binds T to the tail of the list, and then member is called with the original argument X and the tail of the input list T. The first two clauses of member say that X is a member of a list if it is the *first* element (head) of the list, or if it is contained in the remainder of the list (tail). The third clause of member states that X cannot be a member of the empty list [] and false is returned.

We illustrate the evaluation of member as follows:

```
> lists:member(a,[1,2,a,b,c]).
(0)lists:member(a,[1,2,a,b,c])
(1).lists:member(a, [2,a,b,c])
(2)..lists:member(a,[a,b,c])
(2)..true
(1).true
(0)true
true
> lists:member(a,[1,2,3,4]).
(0)lists:member(a, [1,2,3,4])
(1).lists:member(a, [2,3,4])
(2)..lists:member(a, [3,4])
(3)...lists:member(a, [4])
(4)....lists:member(a, [])
(4)....false
(3)...false
(2)..false
(1).false
(0)false
false
```

3.2.2 append

append(A,B) concatenates the two lists A and B.

```
append([H|L1], L2) -> [H|append(L1, L2)];
append([], L) -> L.
```

The second clause of append is the easiest to understand – it says that appending any list L to the empty list just results in L.

The first clause gives a rule for appending a non-empty list to some other list. So, for example:

```
append([a,b,c], [d,e,f])
```

reduces to:

```
[a | append([b,c], [d,e,f])]
```

But what is the value of `append([b,c],[d,e,f])`? It is (of course) `[b,c,d,e,f]`, so the value of `[a|append([b,c], [d,e,f])]` is `[a|[b,c,d,e,f]]` which is another way of writing `[a,b,c,d,e,f]`.

The behaviour of `append` is seen as follows:

```
> lists:append([a,b,c],[d,e,f]).
(0)lists:append([a,b,c],[d,e,f])
(1).lists:append([b,c], [d,e,f])
(2)..lists:append([c],[d,e,f])
(3)...lists:append([], [d,e,f])
(3)...[d,e,f]
(2)..[c,d,e,f]
(1).[b,c,d,e,f]
(0)[a,b,c,d,e,f]
[a,b,c,d,e,f]
```

3.2.3 reverse

`reverse(L)` reverses the order of the elements in the list `L`.

```
reverse(L) -> reverse(L, []).

reverse([H|T], Acc) ->
    reverse(T, [H|Acc]);
reverse([], Acc) ->
    Acc.
```

`reverse(L)` makes use of an *auxiliary* function `reverse/2` which accumulates the final result in its second parameter.

If a call is made to `reverse(L, Acc)` when `L` is a non-empty list, then the first element of `L` is removed from `L` and *added* to the head of the list `Acc`. Thus `reverse([x,y,z], Acc)` results in a call to `reverse([y,z], [x|Acc])`. Eventually the first argument to `reverse/2` is reduced to the empty list, in which case the second clause of `reverse/2` matches and the function terminates.

This can be illustrated as follows:

```
> lists:reverse([a,b,c,d]).
(0)lists:reverse([a,b,c,d])
(1).lists:reverse([a,b,c,d], [])
(2)..lists:reverse([b,c,d], [a])
(3)...lists:reverse([c,d], [b,a])
(4)....lists:reverse([d], [c,b,a])
(5).....lists:reverse([], [d,c,b,a])
(5).....[d,c,b,a]
(4)....[d,c,b,a]
(3)...[d,c,b,a]
(2)..[d,c,b,a]
(1).[d,c,b,a]
(0)[d,c,b,a]
[d,c,b,a]
```

3.2.4 delete_all

`delete_all(X, L)` deletes all occurrences of `X` from the list `L`.

```
delete_all(X, [X|T]) ->
    delete_all(X, T);
delete_all(X, [Y|T]) ->
    [Y | delete_all(X, T)];
delete_all(_, []) ->
    [].
```

The patterns of recursion involved in `delete_all` are similar to those involved in `member` and `append`.

The first clause of `delete_all` matches when the element to be deleted is at the head of the list being examined.

In the second clause we know that `Y` is different from `X` (otherwise the first clause would have matched). We retain the first element of the list being examined `Y`, and call `delete_all` on the tail of the list.

The third clause matches when the second parameter of `delete_all` has been reduced to the empty list.

```
> lists:delete_all(a,[1,2,a,3,a,4]).
[1,2,3,4]
```

3.3 Examples

In the following sections we give some slightly more complex examples of list processing functions.

3.3.1 sort

Program 3.1 is a variant of the well-known quicksort algorithm. `sort(X)` returns a sorted list of the elements of the list `X`.

```
-module(sort).
-export([sort/1]).

sort([]) -> [];
sort([Pivot|Rest]) ->
    {Smaller, Bigger} = split(Pivot, Rest),
    lists:append(sort(Smaller), [Pivot|sort(Bigger)]).

split(Pivot, L) ->
    split(Pivot, L, [], []).

split(Pivot, [], Smaller, Bigger) ->
    {Smaller,Bigger};
split(Pivot, [H|T], Smaller, Bigger) when H < Pivot ->
    split(Pivot, T, [H|Smaller], Bigger);
split(Pivot, [H|T], Smaller, Bigger) when H >= Pivot ->
    split(Pivot, T, Smaller, [H|Bigger]).
```

Program 3.1

The first element of the list to be sorted is used as a pivot. The original list is partitioned into two lists `Smaller` and `Bigger`: all the elements in `Smaller` are less than `Pivot` and all the elements in `Bigger` are greater than or equal to `Pivot`. The lists `Smaller` and `Bigger` are then sorted and the results combined.

The function `split(Pivot, L)` returns the tuple `{Smaller,Bigger}`, where all the elements in `Bigger` are greater than or equal to `Pivot` and all the elements in `Smaller` are less than `Pivot`. `split(Pivot, L)` works by calling the auxiliary function `split(Pivot, L, Smaller, Bigger)`. Two accumulators, `Smaller` and `Bigger`, are used to store the elements in `L` which are smaller than and greater than or equal to `Pivot`, respectively. The code in `split/4` is very similar to that in `reverse/2` except that two accumulators are used instead of one. For example:

```
 > lists:split(7,[2,1,4,23,6,8,43,9,3]).
{[3,6,4,1,2],[9,43,8,23]}
```

If we call `sort([7,2,1,4,23,6,8,43,9,3])`, the first thing which happens is that `split/2` is called with pivot 7. This results in two lists: `[3,6,4,1,2]` whose elements are less than the pivot, 7, and `[9,43,8,23]` whose elements are greater than or equal to the pivot.

Assuming that `sort` works then `sort([3,6,4,1,2])` ⟹ `[1,2,3,4,6]` and `sort([9,43,8,23])` ⟹ `[8,9,23,43]`. Finally, the sorted lists are appended with the call:

```
> append([1,2,3,4,6], [7 | [8,9,23,43]]).
[1,2,3,4,6,7,8,9,23,43]
```

With a little ingenuity the call to `append` can be removed, as in the following:

```
qsort(X) ->
        qsort(X, []).

%% qsort(A,B)
%%   Inputs:
%%      A = unsorted List
%%      B = sorted list where all elements in B
%%          are greater than any element in A
%%   Returns
%%      sort(A) appended to B

qsort([Pivot|Rest], Tail) ->
    {Smaller,Bigger} = split(Pivot, Rest),
    qsort(Smaller, [Pivot|qsort(Bigger,Tail)]);
qsort([], Tail) ->
    Tail.
```

We can compare the performance of this with the first version of sort by using the BIF `statistics/1` (see Appendix B, which provides information about the performance of the system). If we compile and run the code fragment:

```
...
statistics(reductions),
lists:sort([2,1,4,23,6,7,8,43,9,4,7]),
{_, Reductions1} = statistics(reductions),
lists:qsort([2,1,4,23,6,7,8,43,9,4,7]),
{_, Reductions2} = statistics(reductions),
...
```

We can find out how many reductions (function calls) it took to evaluate the call the `sort` and `qsort` functions. In our example `sort` took `93` reductions and `qsort` took `74`, a 20 percent improvement.

3.3.2 Sets

Program 3.2 is a simple collection of set manipulation functions. The obvious way to represent sets in ERLANG is as an unordered list of elements without duplication.

The set manipulation functions are as follows:

`new()`
: Returns an empty set.

`add_element(X, S)`
: Adds an element `X` to the set `S` and returns a new set.

`del_element(X, S)`
: Deletes the element `X` from the set `S` and returns a new set.

`is_element(X, S)`
: Returns **`true`** if the element `X` is contained in the set `S`, otherwise **`false`**.

`is_empty(S)`
: Returns **`true`** if the set `S` is empty otherwise **`false`**.

`union(S1, S2)`
: Returns the union of the sets `S1` and `S2`, i.e. the set of all elements which are contained in *either* `S1` *or* `S2`.

`intersection(S1, S2)`
: Returns the intersection of the sets `S1` and `S2`, i.e. the set of all elements which are contained in *both* `S1` *and* `S2`.

Strictly speaking, we should not say **`new`** returns an empty set but rather **`new`** returns a *representation of* an empty set. If we represent the sets as lists, then the set operations can be written as follows:

```
-module(sets).
-export([new/0, add_element/2, del_element/2,
         is_element/2, is_empty/1, union/2, intersection/2]).

new() -> [].

add_element(X, Set) ->
    case is_element(X, Set) of
        true  -> Set;
        false -> [X|Set]
    end.

del_element(X, [X|T]) -> T;
del_element(X, [Y|T]) -> [Y|del_element(X,T)];
del_element(_, [])    -> [].

is_element(H, [H|_])   -> true;
```

```
is_element(H, [_|Set]) -> is_element(H, Set);
is_element(_, [])      -> false.

is_empty([]) -> true;
is_empty(_)  -> false.

union([H|T], Set) -> union(T, add_element(H, Set));
union([], Set)    -> Set.

intersection(S1, S2) -> intersection(S1, S2, []).

intersection([], _, S) -> S;
intersection([H|T], S1, S) ->
    case is_element(H,S1) of
        true  -> intersection(T, S1, [H|S]);
        false -> intersection(T, S1, S)
    end.
```

Program 3.2

Running the code in Program 3.2:

```
> S1 = sets:new().
[]
> S2 = sets:add_element(a, S1).
[a]
> S3 = sets:add_element(b, S2).
[b,a]
> sets:is_element(a, S3).
true
> sets:is_element(1, S2).
false
> T1 = sets:new().
[]
> T2 = sets:add_element(a, T1).
[a]
> T3 = sets:add_element(x, T2).
[x,a]
> sets:intersection(S3, T3).
[a]
10> sets:union(S3,T3).
[b,x,a]
```

This implementation is not particularly efficient, but it is sufficiently simple to be (hopefully) correct. At a later stage it could be replaced by a more efficient version.

3.3.3 Prime numbers

In our final example (Program 3.3) we see how a list of prime numbers can be generated using the *sieve of Eratosthenes algorithm.*

```
-module(siv).
-compile(export_all).

range(N, N) ->
    [N];
range(Min, Max) ->
    [Min | range(Min+1, Max)].

remove_multiples(N, [H|T]) when H rem N == 0 ->
    remove_multiples(N, T);
remove_multiples(N, [H|T]) ->
    [H | remove_multiples(N, T)];
remove_multiples(_, []) ->
    [].

sieve([H|T]) ->
    [H | sieve(remove_multiples(H, T))];
sieve([]) ->
    [].

primes(Max) ->
    sieve(range(2, Max)).
```

Program 3.3

Note that in Program 3.3 we use the compiler annotation `-compile(export_all)` – this implicitly exports all functions in the module so they can be called without giving explicit export declarations.

`range(Min, Max)` returns a list of the integers between `Min` and `Max`.

`remove_multiples(N, L)` removes all multiples of `N` from the list `L`:

```
> siv:range(1,15).
[1,2,3,4,5,6,7,8,9,10,11,12,13,14,15]
> siv:remove_multiples(3,[1,2,3,4,5,6,7,8,9,10]).
[1,2,4,5,7,8,10]
```

`sieve(L)` retains the head of the list `L` and recursively removes all multiples of the head of the list from the sieved tail of the list:

```
> siv:primes(25).
[2,3,5,7,11,13,17,19,23]
```

3.4 Common Patterns of Recursion on Lists

Although a typical program may use many different functions which operate on lists, most list processing functions are variations on one of a small number of themes. Most list processing functions involve elements of:

- Searching for an element in a list and doing something when the element is found.
- Building an output list where the output list has the same shape as the input list but where something has been done to each element in the list.
- Doing something when we have encountered the *n*th item in a list.
- Scanning the list and building a new list or lists which are in some way related to the original list.

We will consider each of these in turn.

3.4.1 Searching for elements in a list

Here we have the following pattern of recursion:

```
search(X, [X|T]) ->
    ... do something ...
    ...;
search(X, [_|T]) ->
    search(X, T);
search(X, []) ->
    ... didn't find it ...
```

The first case matches when we have located the item of interest. The second case matches when the head of the list does not match the item of interest, in which case the tail of the list is processed. The final case matches when the elements in the list have been exhausted.

Comparing the above with the code for `member/2` (Section 3.2.1) we see we replace the code for ... `do something` ... by `true` and the code for ... `didn't find it` ... by false.

3.4.2 Building an isomorphic list

We may wish to build a list which has the same *shape* as the input list, but where we have performed some operation to each element on the list. This we could express as follows:

```
isomorphic([X|T]) ->
    [something(X)|isomorphic(T)];
```

```
isomorphic([]) ->
    [].
```

So, for example, if we wanted to write a function which doubled each element of a list we could write:

```
double([H|T]) ->
    [2 * H | double(T)];
double([]) ->
    [].
```

So for example:

```
> lists1:double([1,7,3,9,12]).
[2,14,6,18,24]
```

This actually only works on the *top level* of a list, so if we wanted to traverse all levels of the list, we would have to change the definition to:

```
double([H|T]) when integer(H)->
    [2 * H | double(T)];
double([H|T]) when list(H) ->
    [double(H) |double(T)];
double([]) ->
    [].
```

The latter version successfully traverses deep lists:

```
> lists1:double([1,2,[3,4],[5,[6,12],3]]).
[2,4,[6,8],[10,[12,24],6]]
```

3.4.3 Counting

We often need counters so that we can do something when we hit the *n*th element in a list:

```
count(Terminal, L) ->
        ... do something ...;
count(N, [_|L]) ->
        count(N-1, L).
```

Thus a function to extract the *n*th element of a list (assuming it exists) can be written:

```
nth(1, [H|T]) ->
    H;
nth(N, [_|T]) ->
    nth(N - 1, T).
```

The technique of counting downwards towards some terminal condition is often preferable to counting upwards. To illustrate this consider `nth1`, which also determines the *n*th element of a list but this time counting upwards:

```
nth1(N, L) ->
    nth1(1, N, L).

nth1(Max, Max, [H|_]) ->
    H;
nth1(N, Max, [_|T]) ->
    nth1(N+1, Max, T).
```

This requires the use of one additional parameter and an auxiliary function.

3.4.4 Collecting elements of a list

Here we wish to do something to elements of a list, producing a new list or lists. The pattern of interest is:

```
collect(L) ->
    collect(L, []).

collect([H|T], Accumulator) ->
    case pred(H) of
        true ->
            collect(T, [dosomething(H)|Accumulator]);
        false ->
            collect(T, Accumulator)
    end;
collect([], Accumulator) ->
    Accumulator.
```

Here we introduce an auxiliary function with an additional argument which is used to store the result which will eventually be returned to the calling program.

Using such a schema we could, for example, write a function which returns a list where every even element in the list has been squared and every odd element removed:

```
funny(L) ->
    funny(L, []).
```

Chapter 4

Programming with Tuples

Tuples are used to group together several objects to form a new complex object. The object `{E1,E2,E3,...,En}` is referred to as a *tuple* of *size n*. Tuples are used for data structures with *fixed* numbers of elements; data structures containing a *variable* number of elements should be stored in *lists*.

4.1 Tuple Processing BIFs

Several BIFs are available for manipulation of tuples:

`tuple_to_list(T)`
: Converts the tuple `T` to a list.
Example: `tuple_to_list({1,2,3,4})` ⟹ `[1,2,3,4]`.

`list_to_tuple(L)`
: Converts the list `L` to a tuple.
Example: `list_to_tuple([a,b,c])` ⟹ `{a,b,c}`.

`element(N, T)`
: Returns the `N`th element of the tuple `T`.
Example: `element(3,{a,b,c,d})` ⟹ `c`.

`setelement(N, T, Val)`
: Returns a new tuple which is a copy of of the tuple `T` where the `N`th element of the tuple has been replaced by `Val`.
Example: `setelement(3, {a,b,c,d}, xx)` ⟹ `{a,b,xx,d}`.

`size(T)`
: Returns the number of elements in the tuple `T`.
Example: `size({a,b,c})` ⟹ `3`.

4.2 Multiple Return Values

We often want to return several values from a function. This is conveniently achieved by using a tuple.

For example, the function `parse_int(List)` extracts an integer from the beginning of the list of ASCII characters `List`, if any, and returns a *tuple* containing the extracted integer and the remainder of the list, or, the atom `eoString` if the list does not contain an integer.

```
parse_int(List) ->
    parse_int(skip_to_int(List), 0).

parse_int([H|T], N) when H >= $0, H =< $9 ->
    parse_int(T, 10 * N + H - $0);
parse_int([], 0) ->
    eoString;
parse_int(L, N) ->
    {N,L}.
```

`skip_to_int(L)` returns the first sublist of `L` which starts with the ASCII code for the digit 0 to 9.

```
skip_to_int([]) ->
    [];
skip_to_int([H|T]) when H >= $0, H =< $9 ->
    [H|T];
skip_to_int([H|T]) ->
    skip_to_int(T).
```

If we choose the string `"abc123def"` (recall that `"abc123def"` is shorthand for `[97,98,99,49,50,51,100,101,102]`) to test `parse_int`:

```
> tuples:parse_int("abc123def")
{123,[100,101,102]}}
```

`parse_int` can be used as the basis of a parser to extract all integers embedded in a string.

```
parse_ints([]) ->
    [];
parse_ints(L) ->
    case parse_int(L) of
        eoString ->
            [];
        {H,Rest} ->
            [H|parse_ints(Rest)]
    end.
```

Thus:

```
> tuples:parse_ints("abc,123,def,456,xx").
[123,456]
```

4.3 Encrypting PIN Codes

Almost every day the authors are faced with the problem of having to remember a lot of different secret numbers – PIN codes for credit cards, door codes, etc. Can these be written down in such a way that the information would be useless to some nasty criminal?

Suppose we have a LISA credit card with secret PIN code of 3451. This can be encoded as follows:

```
a b c d e f g h i j k l m n o p q r s t u v w x y z
1 0 5 3 4 3 2 7 2 5 4 1 9 4 9 6 3 4 1 4 1 2 7 8 5 0   lisa
```

This can be written on a piece of paper knowing that should the paper fall into the wrong hands the secret will be safe.

How do we decode the information? The secret password is declarative – from which we can easily read off the PIN code (3451) – try it!

We easily construct a function encode(Pin,Password)[1] which performs such an encryption:

```
encode(Pin, Password) ->
    Code = {nil,nil,nil,nil,nil,nil,nil,nil,nil,
            nil,nil,nil,nil,nil,nil,nil,nil,nil,
            nil,nil,nil,nil,nil,nil,nil,nil},
    encode(Pin, Password, Code).

encode([], _, Code) ->
    Code;
encode(Pin, [], Code) ->
    io:format("Out of Letters~n",[]);
encode([H|T], [Letter|T1], Code) ->
    Arg = index(Letter) + 1,
    case element(Arg, Code) of
        nil ->
            encode(T, T1, setelement(Arg, Code, index(H)));
        _ ->
            encode([H|T], T1, Code)
    end.
```

[1]The code for encode/2 and other examples in this chapter calls functions in the module io. This module is a standard module providing the user with formatted input and output. It is further described in Chapter 13 and in Appendix C.

```
index(X) when X >= $0, X =< $9 ->
    X - $0;
index(X) when X >= $A, X =< $Z ->
    X - $A.
```

Thus for example:

```
> pin:encode("3451","DECLARATIVE").
{nil,nil,5,3,4,nil,nil,nil,nil,nil,nil,1,nil,nil,nil,
 nil,nil,nil,nil,nil,nil,nil,nil,nil,nil,nil}
```

We now fill in the unfilled slots `nil` with random digits:

```
print_code([], Seed) ->
    Seed;
print_code([nil|T], Seed) ->
    NewSeed = ran(Seed),
    Digit = NewSeed rem 10,
    io:format("~w ",[Digit]),
    print_code(T, NewSeed);
print_code([H|T],Seed) ->
    io:format("~w ",[H]),
    print_code(T, Seed).

ran(Seed) ->
    (125 * Seed + 1) rem 4096.
```

Then we need a few small functions to glue everything together:

```
test() ->
    title(),
    Password = "DECLARATIVE",
    entries([{"3451",Password,lisa},
             {"1234",Password,carwash},
             {"4321",Password,bigbank},
             {"7568",Password,doorcode1},
             {"8832",Password,doorcode2},
             {"4278",Password,cashcard},
             {"4278",Password,chequecard}]).

title() ->
    io:format("a b c d e f g h i j k l m \
               n o p q r s t u v w x y z~n",[]).
```

```
entries(List) ->
    {_,_,Seed} = time(),
    entries(List, Seed).

entries([], _) -> true;
entries([{Pin,Password,Title}|T], Seed) ->
    Code = encode(Pin, Password),
    NewSeed = print_code(tuple_to_list(Code), Seed),
    io:format("  ~w~n",[Title]),
    entries(T, NewSeed).
```

And we can run the program:

```
1> pin:test().
a b c d e f g h i j k l m n o p q r s t u v w x y z
1 0 5 3 4 3 2 7 2 5 4 1 9 4 9 6 3 4 1 4 1 2 7 8 5 0   lisa
9 0 3 1 2 5 8 3 6 7 0 4 5 2 3 4 7 6 9 4 9 2 7 4 9 2   carwash
7 2 2 4 3 1 2 1 8 3 0 1 5 4 1 0 5 6 5 4 3 0 3 8 5 8   bigbank
1 0 6 7 5 7 6 9 4 5 4 8 3 2 1 0 7 6 1 4 9 6 5 8 3 4   doorcode1
1 4 3 8 8 3 2 5 6 1 4 2 7 2 9 4 5 2 3 6 9 4 3 2 5 8   doorcode2
7 4 7 4 2 5 6 5 8 5 8 8 9 4 7 6 5 0 1 2 9 0 9 6 3 8   cashcard
7 4 7 4 2 7 8 7 4 3 8 8 9 6 3 8 5 2 1 4 1 2 1 4 3 4   chequecard
true
```

This information can then be printed in a tiny font, glued to the back of a postage stamp and hidden inside your tie.[2]

4.4 Dictionaries

We define a dictionary to be a set of `Key-Value` pairs where the keys in the dictionary are unique.[3] The values stored in the dictionary may be duplicated. There are no restrictions on the data types of either the key or the value but the dictionary may only be searched by the key.

We define the following operations on a dictionary:

`new()`
: Create and return a new empty dictionary.

`lookup(Key, Dict)`
: Search the dictionary for a `Key-Value` pair and return `{value,Value}` if found, else return `undefined`.

[2]Only one of the authors wears a tie.

[3]This is not to be confused with a *data dictionary* in database management systems.

`add(Key, Value, Dict)`
: Add a new `Key-Value` pair to the dictionary and return the new dictionary reflecting the changes made by the `add` function.

`delete(Key, Dict)`
: Remove any `Key-Value` pair from the dictionary and return the new dictionary.

Program 4.1 is an example of how such a dictionary is written keeping the `Key-Value` pairs as tuples `{Key, Value}` in a list. While this is not an especially efficient way of implementing a dictionary it will serve as an example.

```
-module(dictionary).
-export([new/0,lookup/2,add/3,delete/2]).

new() ->
    [].

lookup(Key, [{Key,Value}|Rest]) ->
    {value,Value};
lookup(Key, [Pair|Rest]) ->
    lookup(Key, Rest);
lookup(Key, []) ->
    undefined.

add(Key, Value, Dict) ->
    NewDict = delete(Key, Dict),
    [{Key,Value}|NewDict].

delete(Key, [{Key,Value}|Rest]) ->
    Rest;
delete(Key, [Pair|Rest]) ->
    [Pair|delete(Key, Rest)];
delete(Key, []) ->
    [].
```

Program 4.1

We can use `dictionary` to build and manipulate a small database containing the authors' shoe sizes:

```
D0 = dictionary:new().
[]
> D1 = dictionary:add(joe, 42, D0).
[{joe,42}]
```

```
> D2 = dictionary:add(mike, 41, D1).
[{mike,41},{joe,42}]
> D3 =  dictionary:add(robert, 43, D2).
[{robert,43},{mike,41},{joe,42}]
> dictionary:lookup(joe, D3).
{value,42}
> dictionary:lookup(helen, D3).
undefined
...
```

4.5 Unbalanced Binary Trees

Dictionaries are suitable for storing small numbers of data items, but, when the number of items grows, it may be desirable to organise the data in a tree structure which imposes an ordering relation on the keys used to access the data. Such structures can be accessed in a time which is proportion to the logarithm of the number of items in the structure – lists have linear access time.

The simplest tree organisation we will consider is the *unbalanced binary tree*. Internal nodes of the tree are represented by `{Key,Value,Smaller,Bigger}`. `Value` is the value of some object which has been stored at some node in the tree with key `Key`. `Smaller` is a subtree where all the keys at the nodes in the tree are smaller than `Key`, and `Bigger` is a subtree where all the keys at the nodes in the tree are greater than or equal to `Key`. Leaves in the tree are represented by the atom `nil`.

We start with the function `lookup(Key,Tree)` which searches `Tree` to see if an entry associated with `Key` has been stored in the tree.

```
lookup(Key, nil) ->
    not_found;
lookup(Key, {Key,Value,_,_}) ->
    {found,Value};
lookup(Key, {Key1,_,Smaller,_}) when Key < Key1 ->
    lookup(Key, Smaller);
lookup(Key, {Key1,_,_,Bigger}) when Key > Key1 ->
    lookup(Key, Bigger).
```

The function `insert(Key,Value,OldTree)` is used to insert new data into the tree. It returns a new tree.

```
insert(Key, Value, nil) ->
    {Key,Value,nil,nil};
insert(Key, Value, {Key,_,Smaller,Bigger}) ->
    {Key,Value,Smaller,Bigger};
insert(Key, Value, {Key1,V,Smaller,Bigger}) when Key < Key1 ->
    {Key1,V,insert(Key, Value, Smaller),Bigger};
insert(Key, Value, {Key1,V,Smaller,Bigger}) when Key > Key1 ->
    {Key1,V,Smaller,insert(Key, Value, Bigger)}.
```

Clause 1 handles insertion into an empty tree, clause 2 overwriting of an existing node. Clauses 3 and 4 determine the action to be taken when the value of the current key is less than, or greater than or equal to, the value of the key stored at the current node in the tree.

Having built a tree, we would like to display it in a way which reflects its structure.

```
write_tree(T) ->
    write_tree(0, T).

write_tree(D, nil) ->
    io:tab(D),
    io:format('nil', []);
write_tree(D, {Key,Value,Smaller,Bigger}) ->
    D1 = D + 4,
    write_tree(D1, Bigger),
    io:format('~n', []),
    io:tab(D),
    io:format('~w ===> ~w~n', [Key,Value]),
    write_tree(D1, Smaller).
```

We can create a test function to insert data into a tree and print it:

```
test1() ->
    S1 = nil,
    S2 = insert(4,joe,S1),
    S3 = insert(12,fred,S2),
    S4 = insert(3,jane,S3),
    S5 = insert(7,kalle,S4),
    S6 = insert(6,thomas,S5),
    S7 = insert(5,rickard,S6),
    S8 = insert(9,susan,S7),
    S9 = insert(2,tobbe,S8),
    S10 = insert(8,dan,S9),
    write_tree(S10).
```

Evaluating `tuples:test1()` results in Figure 4.1.

```
                nil
          12 ===> fred
                        nil
                    9 ===> susan
                              nil
                         8 ===> dan
                              nil
               7 ===> kalle
                        nil
                    6 ===> thomas
                              nil
                         5 ===> rickard
                              nil
     4 ===> joe
                nil
          3 ===> jane
                     nil
               2 ===> tobbe
                     nil
```

Figure 4.1 An unbalanced binary tree

Note that the tree is not very well 'balanced'. Inserting a sequence of keys in strict sequential order, for example evaluating the insertion sequence:

```
T1 = nil,
T2 = insert(1,a,T1),
T3 = insert(2,a,T2),
T4 = insert(3,a,T3),
T5 = insert(4,a,T4),
...
T9 = insert(8,a,T8).
```

gives rise to a tree which has degenerated into a list (see Figure 4.2).

The technique we have used is good when the order of the keys is random. If a sequence of insertions occurs with an ordered set of keys the tree degenerates to a list. In Section 4.6 we will show how to build balanced binary trees.

```
                                        nil
                                 8 ===> a
                                    nil
                             7 ===> a
                                nil
                         6 ===> a
                            nil
                     5 ===> a
                        nil
                 4 ===> a
                    nil
             3 ===> a
                nil
         2 ===> a
            nil
     1 ===> a
        nil
```

Figure 4.2 Degenerate case of an unbalanced binary tree

We also need to be able to delete elements from a binary tree.

```
delete(Key, nil) ->
    nil;
delete(Key, {Key,_,nil,nil}) ->
    nil;
delete(Key, {Key,_,Smaller,nil}) ->
    Smaller;
delete(Key, {Key,_,nil,Bigger}) ->
    Bigger;
delete(Key, {Key1,_,Smaller,Bigger}) when Key == Key1 ->
    {K2,V2,Smaller2} = deletesp(Smaller),
    {K2,V2,Smaller2,Bigger};
delete(Key, {Key1,V,Smaller,Bigger}) when Key < Key1 ->
    {Key1,V,delete(Key, Smaller),Bigger};
delete(Key, {Key1,V,Smaller,Bigger}) when Key > Key1 ->
    {Key1,V,Smaller,delete(Key, Bigger)}.
```

Deletion from a binary tree is simple when the node being deleted is a leaf of the tree, or if only one subtree hangs from the node (clauses 1 to 4). In clauses 6 and 7 the node has not been located and the search proceeds in the appropriate subtree.

In clause 5 the node to be deleted has been located, but this node is an `internal` node in the tree (i.e. the node has `both` a `Smaller` and `Bigger` subtree. In this case the node having the `largest` key in the `Smaller` subtree is located and the tree rebuilt from this node.

```
deletesp({Key,Value,nil,nil}) ->
    {Key,Value,nil};
deletesp({Key,Value,Smaller,nil}) ->
    {Key,Value,Smaller};
deletesp({Key,Value,Smaller,Bigger}) ->
    {K2,V2,Bigger2} = deletesp(Bigger),
    {K2,V2,{Key,Value,Smaller,Bigger2}}.
```

4.6 Balanced Binary Trees

In the previous section we saw how to create a simple binary tree. Unfortunately the behaviour of this tree can degenerate to that of a list in cases where non-random insertions and deletions to the tree are made.

A better technique is to keep the tree *balanced* at all times.

A simple criterion for *balance* is that used by Adelson-Velskii and Landis [1] (described in [29]), namely that a tree is said to be *balanced* if at every node the heights of the subtrees at the node differ by at most 1. Trees having this property are often referred to as *AVL trees.* It can be shown for such a tree that location, insertion and deletion from the tree can be performed in $O(\log N)$ time units, where N is the number of nodes in the tree.

Suppose we represent an AVL tree by `{Key,Value,Height,Smaller,Bigger}` tuples and the empty tree by `{_,_,0,_,_}`. Then location of an unknown item in the tree is easily defined:

```
lookup(Key, {nil,nil,0,nil,nil}) ->
    not_found;
lookup(Key, {Key,Value,_,_,_}) ->
    {found,Value};
lookup(Key, {Key1,_,_,Smaller,Bigger}) when Key < Key1 ->
    lookup(Key,Smaller);
lookup(Key, {Key1,_,_,Smaller,Bigger}) when Key > Key1 ->
    lookup(Key,Bigger).
```

The code for `lookup` is almost identical to that of an unbalanced binary tree. Insertion in the tree is done as follows:

```
insert(Key, Value, {nil,nil,0,nil,nil}) ->
    E = empty_tree(),
    {Key,Value,1,E,E};
```

```
insert(Key, Value, {K2,V2,H2,S2,B2}) when Key == K2 ->
    {Key,Value,H2,S2,B2};
insert(Key, Value, {K2,V2,_,S2,B2}) when Key < K2 ->
    {K4,V4,_,S4,B4} = insert(Key, Value, S2),
    combine(S4, K4, V4, B4, K2, V2, B2);
insert(Key, Value, {K2,V2,_,S2,B2}) when Key > K2 ->
    {K4,V4,_,S4,B4} = insert(Key, Value, B2),
    combine(S2, K2, V2, S4, K4, V4, B4).

empty_tree() ->
    {nil,nil,0,nil,nil}.
```

The idea is to find the place where the item has to be inserted into the tree and then rebalance the tree if the insertion has caused the tree to become unbalanced. The rebalancing of the tree is achieved with the function `combine`.[4]

```
combine({K1,V1,H1,S1,B1},AK,AV,
        {K2,V2,H2,S2,B2},BK,BV,
        {K3,V3,H3,S3,B3} ) when H2 > H1, H2 > H3 ->
            {K2,V2,H1 + 2,
             {AK,AV,H1 + 1,{K1,V1,H1,S1,B1},S2},
             {BK,BV,H3 + 1,B2,{K3,V3,H3,S3,B3}}
            };
combine({K1,V1,H1,S1,B1},AK,AV,
        {K2,V2,H2,S2,B2},BK,BV,
        {K3,V3,H3,S3,B3} ) when H1 >= H2, H1 >= H3 ->
            HB = max_add_1(H2,H3),
     HA = max_add_1(H1,HB),
     {AK,AV,HA,
             {K1,V1,H1,S1,B1},
             {BK,BV,HB,{K2,V2,H2,S2,B2},{K3,V3,H3,S3,B3}}
            };
combine({K1,V1,H1,S1,B1},AK,AV,
        {K2,V2,H2,S2,B2},BK,BV,
        {K3,V3,H3,S3,B3} ) when H3 >= H1, H3 >= H2 ->
            HA = max_add_1(H1,H2),
     HB = max_add_1(HA,H3),
     {BK,BV,HB    ,
             {AK,AV,HA,{K1,V1,H1,S1,B1},{K2,V2,H2,S2,B2}},
             {K3,V3,H3,S3,B3}
            }.
```

[4] A detailed description of the combination rules can be found in [9].

```
max_add_1(X,Y) when X =< Y ->
    Y + 1;
max_add_1(X,Y) when X > Y ->
    X + 1.
```

Displaying such a tree is easy:

```
write_tree(T) ->
    write_tree(0, T).

write_tree(D, {nil,nil,0,nil,nil}) ->
    io:tab(D),
    io:format('nil', []);
write_tree(D, {Key,Value,_,Smaller,Bigger}) ->
    D1 = D + 4,
    write_tree(D1, Bigger),
    io:format('~n', []),
    io:tab(D),
    io:format('~w ===> ~w~n', [Key,Value]),
    write_tree(D1, Smaller).
```

We are now ready to see the results of our labour. Suppose we make 16 insertions into an AVL tree with the sequence of keys `1,2,3,...,16`. This results in Figure 4.3, which is now balanced (compare with the degenerate tree of the previous section).

Finally, deletion from the AVL tree:

```
delete(Key, {nil,nil,0,nil,nil}) ->
    {nil,nil,0,nil,nil};
delete(Key, {Key,_,1,{nil,nil,0,nil,nil},{nil,nil,0,nil,nil}}) ->
    {nil,nil,0,nil,nil};
delete(Key, {Key,_,_,Smaller,{nil,nil,0,nil,nil}}) ->
    Smaller;
delete(Key, {Key,_,_,{nil,nil,0,nil,nil},Bigger}) ->
    Bigger;
delete(Key, {Key1,_,_,Smaller,{K3,V3,_,S3,B3}}) when Key == Key1 ->
    {K2,V2,Smaller2} = deletesp(Smaller),
    combine(Smaller2, K2, V2, S3, K3, V3, B3);
delete(Key, {K1,V1,_,Smaller,{K3,V3,_,S3,B3}}) when Key < K1 ->
    Smaller2 = delete(Key, Smaller),
    combine(Smaller2, K1, V1, S3, K3, V3, B3);
delete(Key, {K1,V1,_,{K3,V3,_,S3,B3},Bigger}) when Key > K1 ->
    Bigger2 = delete(Key, Bigger),
    combine( S3, K3, V3, B3, K1, V1, Bigger2).
```

```
                    nil
                16 ===> a
                    nil
            15 ===> a
                nil
        14 ===> a
                nil
            13 ===> a
                nil
    12 ===> a
                nil
            11 ===> a
                nil
        10 ===> a
                nil
            9 ===> a
                nil
8 ===> a
                nil
            7 ===> a
                nil
        6 ===> a
                nil
            5 ===> a
                nil
    4 ===> a
                nil
            3 ===> a
                nil
        2 ===> a
                nil
            1 ===> a
                nil
```

Figure 4.3 A balanced binary tree

deletesp manipulates a tree, and gives us the biggest element which also is removed from the tree.

```
deletesp({Key,Value,1,{nil,nil,0,nil,nil},{nil,nil,0,nil,nil}}) ->
        {Key,Value,{nil,nil,0,nil,nil}};
deletesp({Key,Value,_,Smaller,{nil,nil,0,nil,nil}}) ->
        {Key,Value,Smaller};
deletesp({K1,V1,2,{nil,nil,0,nil,nil},
         {K2,V2,1,{nil,nil,0,nil,nil},{nil,nil,0,nil,nil}}}) ->
            {K2,V2,
             {K1,V1,1,{nil,nil,0,nil,nil},{nil,nil,0,nil,nil}}
            };
deletesp({Key,Value,_,{K3,V3,_,S3,B3},Bigger}) ->
        {K2,V2,Bigger2} = deletesp(Bigger),
        {K2,V2,combine(S3, K3, V3, B3, Key, Value, Bigger2)}.
```

Chapter 5

Concurrent Programming

Processes and communication between processes are fundamental concepts in ERLANG and all concurrency, both the creation of processes and the communication between processes, is explicit.

5.1 Process Creation

A process is a self-contained, separate unit of computation which exists concurrently with other processes in the system. There is no inherent hierarchy among processes; the designer of an application may explicitly create such a hierarchy.

The BIF `spawn/3` creates and starts the execution of a new process. Its arguments are the same as `apply/3`:

```
Pid = spawn(Module, FunctionName, ArgumentList)
```

Instead of evaluating the function, however, and returning the result as in `apply`, `spawn/3` creates a new concurrent process to evaluate the function and returns the `Pid` (process *id*entifier) of the newly created process. `Pids` are used for all forms of communication with a process. The call to `spawn/3` returns *immediately* when the new process has been created and does *not* wait for the given function to evaluate.

In Figure 5.1(a) we have a process with identity `Pid1` which evaluates

```
Pid2 = spawn(Mod, Func, Args)
```

After `spawn` has returned the situation will be as in Figure 5.1(b) with two processes, `Pid1` and `Pid2`, executing concurrently. The process identifier of the new process, `Pid2`, is now known only to process `Pid1`. As `Pids` are necessary for all forms of communication, security in an ERLANG system is based on restricting the spread of the `Pid` of a process.

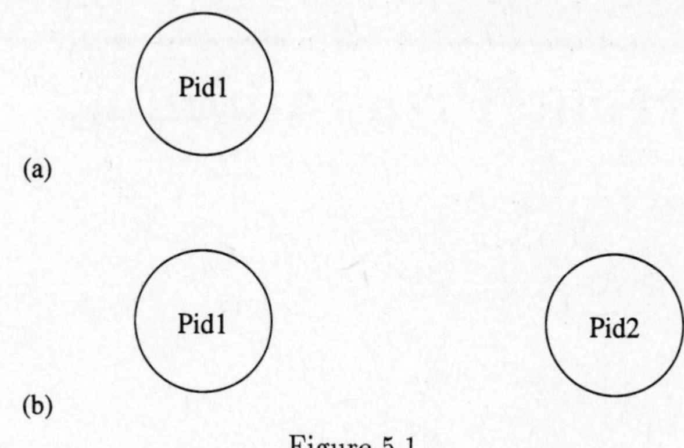

Figure 5.1

A process will automatically terminate when the evaluation of the function given in the call to `spawn` has been completed. The return value from this top-level function is lost.[1]

A process identifier is a valid data object and can be manipulated like any other object. For example, it can be stored in a list or tuple, compared to other identifiers, or sent in messages to other processes.

5.2 Inter-process Communication

In ERLANG the *only* form of communication between processes is by message passing. A message is sent to another process by the primitive '`!`' (`send`):

```
Pid ! Message
```

`Pid` is the identifier of the process to which `Message` is sent. A message can be any valid ERLANG term. `send` is a primitive which evaluates its arguments. Its return value is the message sent. So:

```
foo(12) ! bar(baz)
```

will first evaluate `foo(12)` to get the process identifier and `bar(baz)` for the message to send. As with ERLANG functions, the order of evaluation is undefined. `send` returns the message sent as its value. Sending a message is an asynchronous operation so the `send` call will *not wait* for the message either to arrive at the destination or to be received. Even if the process to which the message is being sent has already terminated the system will not notify the sender. This is in keeping with the asynchronous nature of message passing – the application must itself

[1]There is no place for the result to go.

implement all forms of checking (see below). Messages are always delivered to the recipient, and always delivered in the same order they were sent.

The primitive `receive` is used to receive messages. It has the following syntax:

```
receive
    Message1 [when Guard1] ->
        Actions1 ;
    Message2 [when Guard2] ->
        Actions2 ;
    ...
end
```

Each process has a mailbox and all messages which are sent to the process are stored in the mailbox in the same order as they arrive. In the above, `Message1` and `Message2` are *patterns* which are matched against messages that are in the process's mailbox. When a matching message is found and any corresponding guard succeeds the message is selected, removed from the mailbox and then the corresponding `ActionsN` are evaluated. `receive` returns the value of the last expression evaluated in the actions. As in other forms of pattern matching, any unbound variables in the message pattern become bound. Any messages which are in the mailbox and are not selected by `receive` will remain in the mailbox in the same order as they were stored and will be matched against in the next `receive`. The process evaluating `receive` will be suspended until a message is matched.

ERLANG has a selective receive mechanism, thus no message arriving unexpectedly at a process can block other messages to that process. However, as any messages not matched by `receive` are left in the mailbox, it is the programmer's responsibility to make sure that the system does not fill up with such messages.

5.2.1 Order of receiving messages

When `receive` tries to find a message, it will look in turn at each message in the mailbox and try to match each pattern with the message. We will show how this works with the following example.

Figure 5.2(a) shows a process mailbox containing four messages `msg_1`, `msg_2`, `msg_3` and `msg_4` in that order. Evaluating

```
receive
    msg_3 ->
        ...
end
```

results in the message `msg_3` being matched and subsequently removed from the mailbox. This leaves the mailbox in the state shown in Figure 5.2(b).

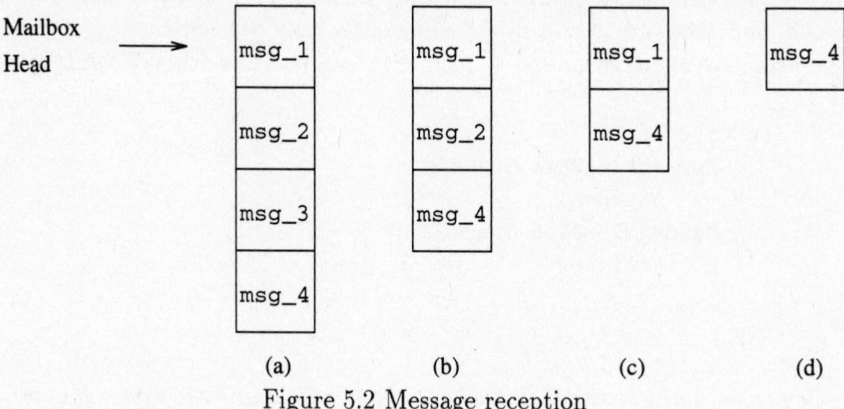

Figure 5.2 Message reception

When we evaluate

```
receive
    msg_4 ->
         ...
    msg_2 ->
         ...
end
```

receive will, for each message in the mailbox, try to match the pattern **msg_4** followed by **msg_2**. This results in **msg_2** being matched and removed from the mailbox, after which two messages will be left in the mailbox as shown in Figure 5.2(c). Finally evaluating

```
receive
    AnyMessage ->
         ...
end
```

where **AnyMessage** is an unbound variable, results in **receive** matching message **msg_1** and removing it from the mailbox resulting in Figure 5.2(d).

This means that the ordering of message patterns in a **receive** cannot directly be used as a method to implement priority messages. This can be done by using the timeout mechanism shown in Section 5.3.

5.2.2 Receiving messages from a specific process

We often want to receive messages from a specific *process*. To do this the sender must explicitly include its own process identifier in the message:

```
Pid ! {self(),abc}
```

which sends a message that explicitly contains the sender's process identifier. The BIF `self()` returns the identifier of the calling process. This could be received by:

```
receive
    {Pid,Msg} ->
        ...
end
```

If `Pid` is bound to the sender's process identifier then evaluating `receive` as above would receive messages *only* from this process.[2]

5.2.3 Some examples

Program 5.1 is a module which creates processes containing counters which can be incremented.

```
-module(counter).
-export([start/0,loop/1]).

start() ->
    spawn(counter, loop, [0]).

loop(Val) ->
    receive
        increment ->
            loop(Val + 1)
    end.
```

Program 5.1

This example demonstrates many basic concepts:

- A new counter process is started by each call to `counter:start/0`. Each process evaluates the function call `counter:loop(0)`.
- A recursive function to generate a *perpetual* process which is suspended when waiting for input. `loop` is a *tail recursive* function (see Section 9.1) which ensures that a counter process will evaluate in constant space.
- Selective message reception, in this case the message `increment`.

There are, however, many deficiencies in this example. For example:

[2]Or other processes which know the presumed sender's Pid.

- There is no way to access the value of the counter in each process as the data local to a process can only be accessed by the process itself.
- The message protocol is explicit. Other processes explicitly send `increment` messages to each counter.

```
-module(counter).
-export([start/0,loop/1,increment/1,value/1,stop/1]).

%% First the interface functions.
start() ->
    spawn(counter, loop, [0]).

increment(Counter) ->
    Counter ! increment.

value(Counter) ->
    Counter ! {self(),value},
    receive
        {Counter,Value} ->
            Value
    end.

stop(Counter) ->
    Counter ! stop.

%% The counter loop.
loop(Val) ->
    receive
        increment ->
            loop(Val + 1);
        {From,value} ->
            From ! {self(),Val},
            loop(Val);
        stop ->                        % No recursive call here
            true;
        Other ->                       % All other messages
            loop(Val)
    end.
```

Program 5.2

The next example shows how these deficiencies can be remedied. Program 5.2 is an improved module `counter` which allows us to increment counters, access their values and also stop them.

As in the previous example, a new counter process is started by evaluating `counter:start()` which returns the Pid of the new counter. To hide the message protocol we provide the interface functions `increment`, `value` and `stop` which operate on the counters.

The counter process uses the selective receive mechanism to process the incoming requests. It also presents a solution to the problem of handling unknown messages. The last clause in the `receive` has the unbound variable `Other` as its message pattern; this will match any message which is not matched by the other clauses. Here we ignore the message and continue by waiting for the next message. This is the standard technique for dealing with unknown messages: `receive` them to get them out of the mailbox.

When we access the value of a counter, we must send our Pid as part of the message to enable the counter process to send back a reply. This reply also contains the identifier of the sending process, in this case the counter, to enable the receiving process specifically to wait for the message containing the reply. It is unsafe just to wait for a message containing an unknown value, in this case a number, as any other message which happens to be sent to the process will be matched. Messages sent between processes, therefore, usually contain some way of identifying them, either by their contents, as in the request messages to the counter process, or by including some 'unique' and easily recognisable identifier, as in the reply to the value request.

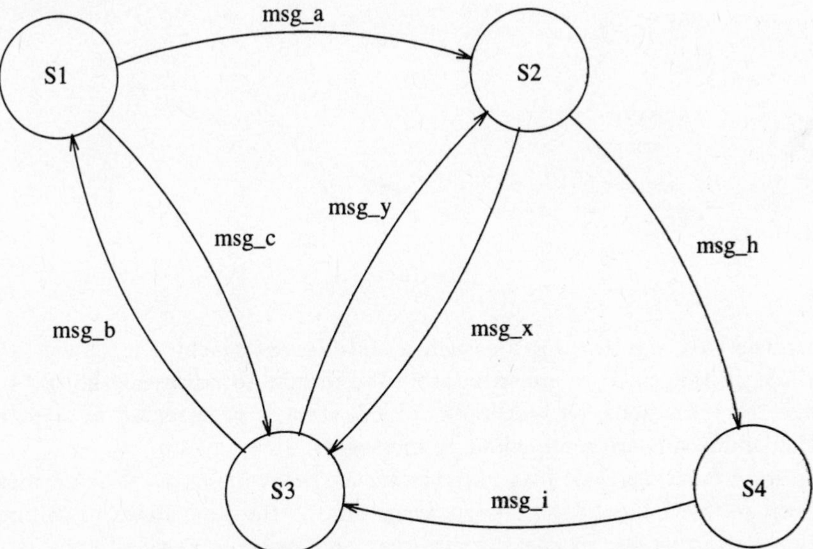

Figure 5.3 Finite state machine

We now consider modelling a finite state machine (FSM). Figure 5.3 shows a simple FSM with four states, the possible transitions and the events which cause

```
s1() ->
    receive
        msg_a ->
            s2();
        msg_c ->
            s3()
    end.

s2() ->
    receive
        msg_x ->
            s3();
        msg_h ->
            s4()
    end.

s3() ->
    receive
        msg_b ->
            s1();
        msg_y ->
            s2()
    end.

s4() ->
    receive
        msg_i ->
            s3()
    end.
```

Program 5.3

them. One easy way to program such a state×event machine is shown in Program 5.3. In this code we are only interested in how to represent the states and manage the transitions between them. Each state is represented by a separate function and events are represented by messages.

The state functions wait in a `receive` for an event message. When a message has been received the FSM makes a transition to the new state by calling the function for that state. By making sure that each call to a new state is a *last call* (see Section 9.1) the FSM process will evaluate in constant space.

State data can be handled by adding arguments to the state functions. With this model actions that are to be performed on entering a state are done before the `receive` and any actions that are to be performed on leaving the state are done in the `receive` after a message has arrived but *before* the call to the new state function.

5.3 Timeouts

The basic `receive` primitive in ERLANG can be augmented with an optional timeout. The full syntax then becomes:

```
receive
    Message1 [when Guard1] ->
        Actions1 ;
    Message2 [when Guard2] ->
        Actions2 ;
    ...
after
    TimeOutExpr ->
        ActionsT
end
```

`TimeOutExpr` is an expression which evaluates to an integer which is interpreted as a time given in *milliseconds*. The accuracy of the time will be limited by the operating system or hardware on which ERLANG is implemented – it is a local issue. If no message has been selected within this time then the timeout occurs and `ActionsT` is scheduled for evaluation. When they are actually evaluated depends, of course, on the current load of the system.

For example, consider a windowing system. Code similar to the following could occur in a process which is processing events:

```
get_event() ->
    receive
        {mouse, click} ->
            receive
                {mouse, click} ->
                    double_click
            after double_click_interval() ->
                single_click
            end
        ...
    end.
```

In this model events are represented as messages. The function `get_event` will wait for a message, and then return an atom representing the event which occurred. We want to be able to detect double mouse clicks, i.e. two mouse clicks within a short period of time. If a mouse click event is received then we evaluate another `receive` to wait for the next mouse click message. This second `receive`, however, has a timeout so if a second mouse click message does not occur within the required time (the return value of `double_click_interval`), the `receive` times out and the function `get_event` returns `single_click`. If the second mouse click message is received before the timeout then `double_click` is returned.

Two values for the argument of the timeout expression have a special meaning:

`infinity`
: The atom `infinity` specifies that the timeout will *never* occur. This can be useful if the timeout time is to be calculated at run-time. We may wish to evaluate an expression to calculate the length of the timeout: if this returns the value `infinity` then we should wait indefinitely.

`0`
: A timeout of `0` means that the timeout will occur immediately, but the system tries all messages currently in the mailbox first.

Using timeouts `receive` has more use than might at first be envisaged. The function `sleep(Time)` suspends the current process for `Time` milliseconds:

```
sleep(Time) ->
    receive
        after Time ->
            true
    end.
```

`flush_buffer()` completely empties the mailbox of the current process:

```
flush_buffer() ->
    receive
        AnyMessage ->
            flush_buffer()
        after 0 ->
            true
    end.
```

As long as there are messages in the mailbox, the first of these (the variable `AnyMessage`, which is unbound, matches any message, i.e. the first message) will be selected and `flush_buffer` called again (the timeout value of `0` ensures this), but when the mailbox is empty the function will return through the timeout clause.

Priority messages can be implemented by using the special timeout value of `0`:

```
priority_receive() ->
    receive
        interrupt ->
```

```
            interrupt
        after 0 ->
            receive
                AnyMessage ->
                    AnyMessage
            end
    end
```

The function `priority_receive` will return the first message in the mailbox *unless* the message `interrupt` has arrived, in which case `interrupt` will be returned. By first evaluating a `receive` for the message `interrupt` with a timeout of `0`, we check if that message is in the mailbox. If so we return it. Otherwise we evaluate `receive` with the pattern `AnyMessage` which will match the first message in the mailbox.

```
-module(timer).
-export([timeout/2,cancel/1,timer/3]).

timeout(Time, Alarm) ->
    spawn(timer, timer, [self(),Time,Alarm]).

cancel(Timer) ->
    Timer ! {self(),cancel}.

timer(Pid, Time, Alarm) ->
    receive
        {Pid,cancel} ->
            true
    after Time ->
        Pid ! Alarm
    end.
```

Program 5.4

Timeouts in `receive` are purely local to the `receive`. It is, however, easy to create an independent timeout. In the module `timer` in Program 5.4 the function `timer:timeout(Time,Alarm)` does this.

A call to `timer:timeout(Time, Alarm)` causes the message `Alarm` to be sent to the calling process after time `Time`. The function returns an identifier to the timer. After it has completed its task the process can wait for this message. Using the timer identifier, the calling process can cancel the timer by calling `timer:cancel(Timer)`. Note, however, that a call to `timer:cancel` does not *guarantee* that the caller will not get an alarm message – due to timing the `cancel` message may arrive after the alarm message has been sent.

5.4 Registered Processes

In order to send a message to a process, one needs to know its identifier (Pid). In some cases this is neither practical nor desirable: for example, in a large system there may be many global servers, or a process may wish to hide its identity for security reasons. To allow a process to send a message to another process without knowing its identity we provide a way to *register* processes, i.e. to give them names. The name of a registered process must be an atom.

5.4.1 Basic primitives

Four BIFs are provided for manipulating the names of registered processes:

`register(Name, Pid)`
: Associates the atom `Name` with the process `Pid`.

`unregister(Name)`
: Removes the association between the atom `Name` and a process.

`whereis(Name)`
: Returns the process identifier associated with the registered name `Name`. If no processes have been associated with this name, it returns the atom `undefined`.

`registered()`
: Returns a list of all the currently registered names.

The message sending primitive '`!`' also allows the name of a registered process as a destination. For example

```
number_analyser ! {self(), {analyse,[1,2,3,4]}}
```

means send the message `{Pid,{analyse,[1,2,3,4]}}` to the process registered as `number_analyser`. `Pid` is the processes identifier of the process evaluating `send`.

5.5 Client–Server Model

A major use of registered processes is to support programming of the *client–server model.* In this model there is a *server*, which manages some resource, and a number of *clients* which send requests to the server to access the resource, as illustrated in Figure 5.4. Three basic components are necessary to implement this model – a *server*, a *protocol* and an *access library.* We illustrate the basic principles by some examples.

In the module `counter` shown in Program 5.2 earlier each counter is a server. Clients accessing these servers use the access functions defined.

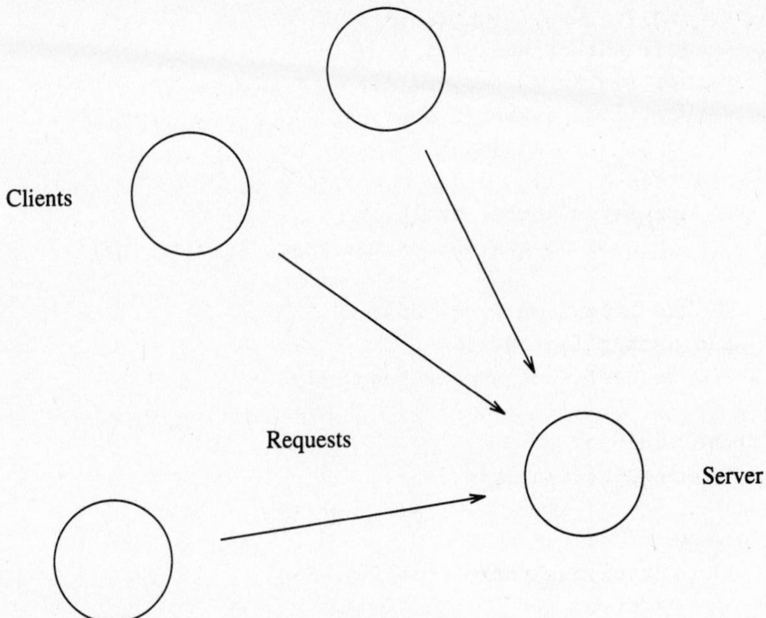

Figure 5.4 Client–server model

The example in Program 5.5 is a server which could be used in a telephone exchange to analyse telephone numbers dialled by users of the exchange. `start()` creates a number analyser server process by calling `spawn` and then registers the server process as `number_analyser`. The server process then loops in the function `server` and waits for service requests. If an `{add_number,Seq,Dest}` request is received the new number sequence is added to the lookup table along with the destination to return if this sequence is analysed. This is done by the function `insert`. The requesting process is sent the message `ack`. If the request `{analyse,Seq}` is received then number analysis is performed on the sequence `Seq` by calling `lookup`. A message containing the result of the analysis is sent to the requesting process. We do not give the definitions of the functions `insert` and `lookup` as they are not important to this discussion.

The request message sent to the server by the client contains the Pid of the client. This makes it possible to send a reply to the client. The reply message sent back to the client also contains a 'sender', the registered name of the server, allowing the client process to receive the reply message selectively. This is safer than just waiting for the first message to arrive – the client process may already have some messages in the mailbox or another process may have sent it a message *before* the server replies.

We have now written the server and defined the protocol. We have decided to implement a synchronous protocol here, in which there will always be a reply to

```
-module(number_analyser).
-export([start/0,server/1]).
-export([add_number/2,analyse/1]).

start() ->
    register(number_analyser,
             spawn(number_analyser, server, [nil])).

%% The interface functions.
add_number(Seq, Dest) ->
    request({add_number,Seq,Dest}).

analyse(Seq) ->
    request({analyse,Seq}).

request(Req) ->
    number_analyser ! {self(), Req},
    receive
        {number_analyser,Reply} ->
            Reply
    end.

%% The server.
server(AnalTable) ->
    receive
        {From, {analyse,Seq}} ->
            Result = lookup(Seq, AnalTable),
            From ! {number_analyser, Result},
            server(AnalTable);
        {From, {add_number, Seq, Dest}} ->
            From ! {number_analyser, ack},
            server(insert(Seq, Dest, AnalTable))
    end.
```

Program 5.5

each request made to the server. In the reply from the server we give the 'sender' as **number_analyser**, the registered name of the server, not wishing to disclose the Pid of the server.

We now define *interface functions* to access the server in a standard manner. The functions **add_number** and **analyse** implement the client's side of the protocol described above. They both use the local function **request** to send the request and receive the reply.

```
-module(allocator).
-export([start/1,server/2,allocate/0,free/1]).

start(Resources) ->
    Pid = spawn(allocator, server, [Resources,[]]),
    register(resource_alloc, Pid).

% The interface functions.
allocate() ->
    request(alloc).

free(Resource) ->
    request({free,Resource}).

request(Request) ->
    resource_alloc ! {self(),Request},
    receive
        {resource_alloc,Reply} ->
            Reply
    end.
```

Program 5.6

The next example, shown in Program 5.6, is a simple resource allocator. The server is started with an initial list of 'resources' which it is to manage. Other processes can send a request to allocate one of these resources, or to free a resource when it is no longer needed.

The server process keeps two lists, one with free resources and one with allocated resources. By moving a resource from one list to another the allocator server can keep track of its resources and knows which are allocated and which are free.

When a request to allocate a resource is received, the function `allocate/3` is called. It checks to see if a free resource is available. If so, the resource is sent back to the requester in a `yes` message and added to the allocated list, otherwise a `no` message is sent back. The free list is a list of the free resources and the allocated list is a list of tuples `{Resource,AllocPid}`. Before an allocated resource is freed, i.e. deleted from the allocated list and added to the free list, we first check if this is a known resource; if it is not, then `error` is returned.

5.5.1 Discussion

The purpose of the *interface functions* is to create abstractions which hide the specific details of the protocols used between the clients and the server. A *user*

```
% The server.
server(Free, Allocated) ->
    receive
        {From,alloc} ->
            allocate(Free, Allocated, From);
        {From,{free,R}} ->
            free(Free, Allocated, From, R)
    end.

allocate([R|Free], Allocated, From) ->
    From ! {resource_alloc,{yes,R}},
    server(Free, [{R,From}|Allocated]);
allocate([], Allocated, From) ->
    From ! {resource_alloc,no},
    server([], Allocated).

free(Free, Allocated, From, R) ->
    case lists:member({R,From}, Allocated) of
        true ->
            From ! {resource_alloc,ok},
            server([R|Free], lists:delete({R,From}, Allocated));
        false ->
            From ! {resource_alloc,error},
            server(Free, Allocated)
    end.
```

Program 5.6 (cont.)

of a service does not need to know the details of the protocols used to implement the service, or the internal data structures and algorithms used in the server. An *implementor* of the service is then free to change any of these *internal details* at any time while maintaining the same user interface.

Moreover, the process which replies to the server request may not be the actual server itself, but a different process to which the request has been delegated. In fact, a 'single' server may actually be a large network of communicating processes which implement a service, all of which would be hidden from the user by the interface functions. It is the set of interface functions which should be *published*, that is to say made available to users, as these functions provide the only *legal* means of accessing the services provided by a server.

The client–server model as programmed in ERLANG is extremely flexible. The facilities of *monitors* or *remote procedure calls*, etc. can be easily programmed. In special circumstances *implementors* might bypass the interface functions and interact directly with a server. As ERLANG does not *force* either the creation or the use of such interfaces it is the responsibility of the designers of a system to ensure that they are created where necessary. ERLANG provides no 'packaged solutions' for constructing remote procedures calls, etc., but rather the primitives from which solutions can be constructed.

5.6 Process Scheduling, Real-time and Priorities

We have not yet mentioned how processes are scheduled in an ERLANG system. While this is an implementation-dependent issue, there are some criteria all implementations satisfy:

- The scheduling algorithm must be *fair*, that is, any process which can be run will be run, if possible in the same order as they became runnable.
- No process will be allowed to block the machine for a long time. A process is allowed to run for a short period of time, called a *time slice*, before it is rescheduled to allow another runnable process to be run.

Typically, time slices are set to allow the currently executing process to perform about 500 reductions[3] before being rescheduled.

One of the requirements of the ERLANG language was that it should be suitable for *soft* real-time applications where response times must be in the order of milliseconds. A scheduling algorithm which meets the above criteria is good enough for such an ERLANG implementation.

The other important feature for ERLANG systems that are to be used for real-time applications is memory management. ERLANG hides all memory managment from the user. Memory is automatically allocated when needed for new data structures and deallocated at a later time when these data structures are no longer in use. Allocating and reclaiming of memory must be done in such a manner as not to block the system for any length of time, preferably for a shorter time than the time slice of a process so that the real-time nature of an implementation will not be affected.

5.6.1 Process priorities

All newly created processes run at the same priority. Sometimes, however, it is desirable to have some processes which are run more often or less often than other processes: for example, a process that is to run only occasionally to monitor the state of the system. To change the priority of a process the BIF `process_flag` is used as follows:

```
process_flag(priority, Pri)
```

[3] A reduction is equivalent to a function call.

`Pri` is the new priority of the process in which the call is evaluated and can have the value `normal` or `low`. Runnable processes with priority `low` are run less often than runnable processes with priority `normal`. The default for all processes is `normal`.

5.7 Process Groups

All ERLANG processes have a Pid associated with them called the process's group leader. Whenever a new process is created, the new process will belong to the same process group as the process that evaluated the `spawn` statement. Initially the first process of the system is the group leader for itself, hence it will be group leader of all subsequently created processes. This means that all ERLANG processes are arranged in a tree, with the first created process at the root.

The following BIFs can be used to manipulate the process groups.

`group_leader()`
: Returns the Pid of the group leader for the evaluating process.

`group_leader(Leader, Pid)`
: Sets the group leader of process `Pid` to be the process `Leader`

The concept of process groups is used by the ERLANG input/output system which will be described in Chapter 13.

Chapter 6

Distributed Programming

This chapter describes how to write distributed ERLANG applications which run on a network of ERLANG *nodes*. We describe the language primitives which support implementation of distributed systems. ERLANG processes map naturally onto a distributed system and all the concurrency primitives and error detection primitives of ERLANG described in previous chapters have the same properties in a distributed system as in a single node system.

6.1 Motivation

There are a number of reasons for writing distributed applications. Some of these are as follows:

Speed. We split our application in different parts which can be evaluated in parallel on different nodes. For example, a compiler could arrange for each function in a module to be compiled on a separate node. The compiler itself could coordinate the activities of all the nodes.
Another example could be a real-time system which consists of a pool of nodes, where jobs are allocated to different nodes in a round-robin fashion in order to decrease the response time of the system.

Reliability and fault tolerance. To increase the reliability of a system we could arrange for several nodes to co-operate in such a manner that the failure of one or more nodes does not effect the operational behavior of the system as a whole.

Accessing resources which reside on another node. Certain hardware or software may only be accessible from a specific computer.

Inherent distribution in the application. Conference systems, booking systems and many types of multi-computer real-time system are examples of such applications.

Extensibility. A system can be designed so that additional nodes can be added in order to increase the capacity of the system. Then if the system is too slow, we can improve performance by buying more processors.

6.2 Distributed mechanisms

The following BIFs are used for distributed programming:

`spawn(Node, Mod, Func, Args)`
: Spawns a process on a remote node.

`spawn_link(Node, Mod, Func, Args)`
: Spawns a process on a remote node and creates a link to the process.

`monitor_node(Node, Flag)`
: If `Flag` is `true`, this BIF makes the evaluating process monitor the node `Node`. If `Node` should fail or be nonexistent, a `{nodedown, Node}` message will be sent to the evaluating process. If `Flag` is `false`, monitoring is turned off.

`node()`
: Returns our own node name.

`nodes()`
: Returns a list of the other known node names.

`node(Item)`
: Returns the node name of the origin of `Item` where `Item` can be a Pid, reference or a port.

`disconnect_node(Nodename)`
: Disconnects us from the node `Nodename`.

The *node* is a central concept in distributed ERLANG. In a distributed ERLANG system the term *node* means an executing ERLANG system which can take part in distributed transactions. An individual ERLANG system becomes part of a distributed ERLANG system by starting a special process called the net kernel. This process evaluates the BIF `alive/2`. The net kernel is described in 9.7. Once the net kernel is started, the system is said to be *alive*.

Once the system is alive, a node name is assigned to it, this name is returned by the BIF `node()`. This name is an atom and it is guaranteed to be globally unique. The format of the name can differ between different implementations of ERLANG but it is always an atom consisting of two parts separated by an `'@'` character.

The BIF `node(Item)` where `Item` is a Pid, port or reference returns the name of the node where `Item` was created. For example, if `Pid` is a process identifier, `node(Pid)` returns the name of the node where `Pid` was started.

The BIF `nodes/0` returns a list of all other nodes in the network which we are currently connected to.

The BIF `monitor_node(Node, Flag)` can be used to monitor nodes. An ERLANG process evaluating the expression `monitor_node(Node, true)` will be notified with a `{nodedown, Node}` message if `Node` fails or if the network connection to `Node` fails. Unfortunately it is not possible to differentiate between node failures and network failures. For example, the following code suspends until the node `Node` fails:

```
.....
monitor_node(Node, true),
receive
    {nodedown, Node} ->
          .....
end,
          .....
```

If no connection exists, and `monitor_node/2` is called, the system will try to setup a connection and deliver a `nodedown` message if the connection fails. If two consecutive `monitor_node/2` calls are performed with the same node then *two* `nodedown` messages will be delivered if the node fails.

A call to `monitor_node(Node, false)` will only decrement a counter, indicating the number of `nodedown` messages that should be delivered to the calling process if `Node` fails. The reason for this behavior is that we often want to encapsulate remote calls within a matching pair of `monitor_node(Node, true)` and `monitor_node(Node, false)`.

The BIFs `spawn/3` and `spawn_link/3` create new processes on the local node. To create a new process on an arbitrary node we use the BIF `spawn/4`, so:

```
Pid = spawn(Node, Mod, Func, Args),
```

spawns a process on `Node` and `spawn_link/4` spawns a linked process on a remote node.

A Pid is returned, which can be used in the normal manner. If the node does not exist a Pid is returned but in this case the Pid is not of much use since obviously no process is running. In the case of `spawn_link/4` an `'EXIT'` signal will be sent to the originating process if the node does not exist.

Almost all operations which are normally allowed on Pids are allowed on remote Pids as well. Messages can be sent to remote processes and links can be created between local and remote processes just as if the processes were executing on a local node. Another property of remote Pids is that sending messages to a remote process is syntactically and semantically identical to sending to a local process. This means, for example, that messages to remote process are always delivered in the same order they were sent, never corrupted and never lost. This is all taken care of by the run-time system. The only error control of message reception which is possible, is by the `link` mechanism which is under the control of the programmer or by explicitly synchronizing the sender and receiver of a message.

6.3 Registered Processes

The BIF `register/2` is used to register a process by name on a local node. To send a message to a registered process on a remote node we use the notation:

```
{Name, Node} ! Mess.
```

If there is a process registered as `Name` on node `Node`, then `Mess` will be sent to that process. If the node or the registered process does not exist, the message will be lost. The registration of global names among a set of nodes is discussed in Section 11.4.

6.4 Connections

At the language level there is a concept of connections between ERLANG nodes. Initially when the system is started the system is not 'aware' of any other nodes and evaluating `nodes()` will return `[]`. Connections to other nodes are not explicitly set up by the programmer. A connection to a remote node `N`, is setup by the run-time system the first time when `N` is referred to. This is illustrated below:

```
1> nodes().
   []
2> P = spawn('klacke@super.eua.ericsson.se', M, F, A).
   <24.16.1>
3> nodes().
   ['klacke@super.eua.ericsson.se']
4> node(P).
   'klacke@super.eua.ericsson.se'
```

To setup a connection to a remote node, we only have to use the name of a node in any expression involving a remote node. The only means provided for detecting network errors is by using the link BIFs or the `monitor_node/2` BIF. To remove a connection to a node the BIF `disconnect_node(Node)` can be used.

The coupling between nodes is extremely loose. Nodes may come and go dynamically in a similar manner to processes. A system which is not so loosely coupled can be achieved with configuration files or configuration data. In a production environment it is common to have a fixed number of nodes with fixed node names.

6.5 A Banking Example

In this section we will show how to combine the `monitor_node/2` BIF together with the ability to send a message to a registered process on a remote node. We implement a very simple bank server which can process requests from remote sites, for example, automatic teller machines, to deposit and withdraw money. Program 6.1 is the code for the central bank server:

```
-module(bank_server).
-export([start/0, server/1]).
start() ->
    register(bank_server, spawn(bank_server, server, [[]])).

server(Data) ->
    receive
        {From, {deposit, Who, Amount}} ->
            From ! {bank_server, ok},
            server(deposit(Who, Amount, Data));
        {From, {ask, Who}} ->
            From ! {bank_server, lookup(Who, Data)},
            server(Data);
        {From, {withdraw, Who, Amount}} ->
            case lookup(Who, Data) of
                undefined ->
                    From ! {bank_server, no},
                    server(Data);
                Balance when Balance > Amount ->
                    From ! {bank_server, ok},
                    server(deposit(Who, -Amount, Data));
                _ ->
                    From ! {bank_server, no},
                    server(Data)
            end
    end.

lookup(Who, [{Who, Value}|_]) -> Value;
lookup(Who, [_|T]) -> lookup(Who, T);
lookup(_, _) -> undefined.

deposit(Who, X, [{Who, Balance}|T]) ->
    [{Who, Balance+X}|T];
deposit(Who, X, [H|T]) ->
    [H|deposit(Who, X, T)];
deposit(Who, X, []) ->
    [{Who, X}].
```

Program 6.1

The code in Program 6.1 runs at the head office of the bank. At the teller machines (or at the branch offices) we run the code in Program 6.2 which interacts with the head office server.

```
-module(bank_client).
-export([ask/1, deposit/2, withdraw/2]).

head_office() -> 'bank@super.eua.ericsson.se'.

ask(Who) ->                 call_bank({ask, Who}).
deposit(Who, Amount)  -> call_bank({deposit, Who, Amount}).
withdraw(Who, Amount) -> call_bank({withdraw, Who, Amount}).

call_bank(Msg) ->
    Headoffice = head_office(),
    monitor_node(Headoffice, true),
    {bank_server, Headoffice} ! {self(), Msg},
    receive
        {bank_server, Reply} ->
            monitor_node(Headoffice, false),
            Reply;
        {nodedown, Headoffice} ->
            no
    end.
```

Program 6.2

The client program defines three interface functions which can be used to access the server at the head office:

`ask(Who)`
: Returns the balance of the customer `Who`.

`deposit(Who, Amount)`
: Deposits `Amount` in the account of customer `Who`.

`withdraw(Who, Amount)`
: Tries to withdraw `Amount` from `Who`'s account.

The function `call_bank/1` implements a remote procedure call. If the head office node is non operational, this will be discovered by the `call_bank/1` function, and `no` is returned.

The name of the head office node was explicitly stated in the source code. In later chapters we will show several ways to hide this information.

Chapter 7

Error Handling

It is inevitable that even an ERLANG programmer will not write perfect programs. Syntax errors (and some semantic errors) in source code can be detected by the compiler, but programs may still contain logical errors. Logical errors resulting from an unclear or inaccurate implementation of a specification can only be detected by extensive compliancy tests. Other errors come to light as run-time errors.

Functions are evaluated in ERLANG processes. A function may fail for many reasons, for example:

- A match operation may fail.
- A BIF may be evaluated with an incorrect argument.
- We may try to evaluate an arithmetic expression in which one of the terms does not evaluate to a number.

ERLANG cannot, of course, correct such failures, but it provides programmers with several mechanisms for the detection and containment of failures. Using these mechanisms, programmers can design robust and fault-tolerant systems. ERLANG has mechanisms for:

- Monitoring the evaluation of an expression.
- Monitoring the behaviour of other processes.
- Trapping evaluation of undefined functions.

7.1 Catch and Throw

`catch` and `throw` provide a mechanism for monitoring the evaluation of an expression. They can be used for:

- Protecting sequential code from errors (`catch`).
- Non-local return from a function (`catch` combined with `throw`).

The normal effect of failure in the evaluation of an expression (a failed match, etc.) is to cause the process evaluating the expression to terminate abnormally. This default behaviour can be changed using `catch`. This is done by writing:

```
catch Expression
```

If failure does not occur in the evaluation of an expression `catch Expression` returns the value of the expression. Thus `catch atom_to_list(abc)` returns `[97,98,99]` and `catch 22` returns 22.

If failure occurs during the evaluation of an expression, `catch Expression` returns the tuple `{'EXIT', Reason}` where `Reason` is an atom which gives an indication of what went wrong (see Section 7.4). Thus `catch an_atom - 2` returns `{'EXIT',badarith}` and `catch atom_to_list(123)` returns `{'EXIT',badarg}`.

When a function has been evaluated, control is returned to the caller. `throw/1` gives a mechanism for bypassing this. If we evaluate `catch Expression` as above, and during evaluation of `Expression` we evaluate `throw/1`, then a direct return is made to the `catch`. Note that 'catches' can be nested; in this case a failure or a throw causes a direct return to the most recent `catch`. Evaluating `throw/1` when not 'within' a `catch` causes a run-time failure.

The following example describes the behaviour of `catch` and `throw`. We define the function `foo/1`:

```
foo(1) ->
    hello;
foo(2) ->
    throw({myerror, abc});
foo(3) ->
    tuple_to_list(a);
foo(4) ->
    exit({myExit, 222}).
```

Suppose a process whose identity is `Pid` evaluates this function when `catch` is not involved.

`foo(1)` – Evaluates to `hello`.

`foo(2)` – Causes `throw({myerror, abc})` to be evaluated. Since we are not evaluating this within the scope of a `catch` the process evaluating `foo(2)` terminates with an error.

`foo(3)` – The process evaluating `foo(3)` evaluates the BIF `tuple_to_list(a)`. This BIF is used to convert a tuple to a list. In this case its argument is not a tuple so the process terminates with an error.

`foo(4)` – The BIF `exit/1` is evaluated. This is not evaluated within a `catch` so the process evaluating `foo(4)` terminates. We will see how the argument `{myExit, 222}` is used later.

`foo(5)` – The process evaluating `foo(5)` terminates with an error since no head of the function `foo/1` matches `foo(5)`.

Now we see what happens when we make the same calls to `foo/1` within the scope of a `catch`:

```
demo(X) ->
    case catch foo(X) of
        {myerror, Args} ->
            {user_error, Args};
        {'EXIT', What} ->
            {caught_error, What};
        Other ->
            Other
    end.
```

`demo(1)` – Evaluates to `hello` as before. Since no failure occurs and we do not evaluate `throw`, `catch` returns the result of evaluating `foo(1)`.

`demo(2)` – Evaluates to `{user_error, abc}`. `throw({myerror, abc})` was evaluated causing the surrounding `catch` to return `{myerror, abc}` and `case` to return `{user_error, abc}`.

`demo(3)` – Evaluates to `{caught_error, badarg}`. `foo(3)` fails and `catch` evaluates to `{'EXIT', badarg}`.

`demo(4)` – Evaluates to `{caught_error, {myexit, 222}}`.

`demo(5)` – Evaluates to `{caught_error,function_clause}`.

Note that, within the scope of a catch, you can easily 'fake' a failure by writing `throw({'EXIT', Message})` - this is a *design decision.*[1]

7.1.1 Using catch and throw to guard against bad code

A simple ERLANG shell may be written as follows:

```
-module(s_shell).
-export([go/0]).

go() ->
    eval(io:parse_exprs('=> ')),      % '=>' is the prompt
    go().
```

[1] Not a bug, or undocumented feature!

```
eval({form,Exprs}) ->
    case catch eval:exprs(Exprs, []) of % Note the catch
        {'EXIT', What} ->
            io:format("Error: ~w!~n", [What]);
        {value, What, _} ->
            io:format("Result: ~w~n", [What])
    end;
eval(_) ->
    io:format("Syntax Error!~n", []).
```

The standard library function `io:parse_exprs/1` reads and parses an ERLANG expression returning `{form,Exprs}` if the expression read is correct.

If correct, the first clause `eval({form,Exprs})` matches and we call the library function `eval:exprs/2` to evaluate the expression. We do this within a `catch` since we have no way of knowing if the evaluation of the expression will cause a failure or not. For example, evaluating `1 - a` would cause an error, but evaluating `1 - a` within a `catch` catches this error.[2] With the `catch`, the `{'EXIT', What}` pattern in the `case` clause matches when we have a failure and the `{value, What, _}` matches for successful evaluation.

7.1.2 Using catch and throw for non-local return of a function

Suppose we want to write a parser to recognise a simple list of integers. This could be written as follows:

```
parse_list(['[',']'|T]) ->
    {nil, T};
parse_list(['[', X|T]) when integer(X) ->
    {Tail, T1} = parse_list_tail(T),
    {{cons, X, Tail}, T1}.

parse_list_tail([',',X|T]) when integer(X) ->
    {Tail, T1} = parse_list_tail(T),
    {{cons, X, Tail}, T1};
parse_list_tail([']'|T]) ->
    {nil, T}.
```

For example:

```
> parse_list(['[',12,',',20,']']).
{{cons,12,{cons,20,nil}},[]}
```

[2]It is possible to crash this shell. How this can be done is left as an exercise for the user!

If we try to parse an incorrect list the following happens:

```
> try:parse_list(['[',12,',',a]).
!!! Error in process <0.16.1> in function
!!!     try:parse_list_tail([',',a])
!!! reason function_clause
** exited: function_clause **
```

Suppose we now want to get out of the recursion and still maintain a knowledge of what went wrong. This could be written as follows:

```
parse_list1(['[',']'|T]) ->
    {nil, T};
parse_list1(['[', X|T]) when integer(X) ->
    {Tail, T1} = parse_list_tail1(T),
    {{cons, X, Tail}, T1};
parse_list1(X) ->
    throw({illegal_token, X}).

parse_list_tail1([',',X|T]) when integer(X) ->
    {Tail, T1} = parse_list_tail1(T),
    {{cons, X, Tail}, T1};
parse_list_tail1([']'|T]) ->
    {nil, T};
parse_list_tail1(X) ->
    throw({illegal_list_tail, X}).
```

If we now evaluate `parse_list1` within a `catch` we obtain the following:

```
> catch  parse_list1(['[',12,',',a]).
{illegal_list_tail,[',',a]}
```

We have exited directly from within a recursion without following the normal route out of the recursion.

7.2 Process Termination

A process terminates normally if it completes the evaluation of the function with which if it was spawned or it evaluates the BIF `exit(normal)` (not within a `catch`). See Program 7.1.

`test:start()` creates a process with the registered name `my_name` which evaluates `test:process()`.

```
-module(test).
-export([process/0, start/0]).

start() ->
    register(my_name, spawn(test, process, [])).

process() ->
    receive
        {stop, Method} ->
            case Method of
                return ->
                    true;
                Other ->
                    exit(normal)
            end;
        Other ->
            process()
    end.
```

Program 7.1

`my_name ! {stop, return}` causes `test:process()` to evaluate to true and the process to terminate normally.

`my_name ! {stop, hello}` also causes the process to terminate normally since it evaluates the BIF `exit(normal)`.

Any other message, such as `my_name ! any_other_message` will cause the process to evaluate `test:process()` recursively (with last call optimisation, see Section 9.1) and the process will not terminate.

A process terminates abnormally if it evaluates the BIF `exit(Reason)` where `Reason` is any valid ERLANG term *except* the atom `normal`. As we have already seen, it will not terminate if the `exit(Reason)` is evaluated within the context of a `catch`.

A process may also terminate abnormally if it evaluates code which causes a run-time failure (for example, a match which fails or a divide by zero). The various types of run-time failure are discussed later.

7.3 Linked Processes

Processes can monitor each other's behaviour. This can be described in terms of two concepts, process `links` and `EXIT` signals. During execution, processes can establish links to other processes (and ports, see Section 9.4). If a process terminates (normally or abnormally), a special `EXIT` signal is sent to all processes (and ports) which are currently linked to the terminating process. This signal has the following format:

```
{'EXIT', Exiting_Process_Id, Reason}
```

The `Exiting_Process_Id` is the process identity of the terminating process. `Reason` is any ERLANG term.

On receipt of an `EXIT` signal in which the `Reason` is not the atom `normal` the default action of the receiving process is to terminate and send `EXIT` signals to all processes to which it is currently linked. `EXIT` signals where `Reason` is the atom `normal` are, by default, ignored.

The default handling of `EXIT` signals can be overridden to allow a process to take any required action on receipt of an `EXIT` signal (see Section 7.5).

7.3.1 Creating and deleting links

Processes can be linked to other processes and ports. All process links are bidirectional, i.e. if process A is linked to process B then process B is automatically linked to process A.

A link is created by evaluating the BIF `link(Pid)`. Calling `link(Pid)` when a link already exists between the calling process and `Pid` has no effect.

All links which a process has are deleted when that process terminates. A link can also be explicitly removed by evaluating the BIF `unlink(Pid)`. As all links are bidirectional this will also remove the link *from* the other process. Calling `unlink(Pid)` when no link exists between the calling process and `Pid` has no effect.

The BIF `spawn_link/3` creates both a new process and a link to the new process. It behaves as if it had been defined as:

```
spawn_link(Module, Function, ArgumentList) ->
    link(Id = spawn(Module, Function, ArgumentList)),
    Id.
```

with the exception that `spawn` and `link` are performed atomically. This is to avoid the spawning process being killed by an `EXIT` signal before it executes the link. Linking to a process which does not exist causes the signal `{'EXIT', Pid, noproc}` to be sent to the process evaluating `link(Pid)`.

In Program 7.2 the function `start/1` sets up a number of processes in a linked chain and registers the first of these processes as a registered process with the name `start` (see Figure 7.1). The function `test/1` sends a message to this registered process. Each process prints a message indicating its position in the chain and what message it received. The message `stop` causes the last process in the

```
-module(normal).
-export([start/1, p1/1, test/1]).

start(N) ->
    register(start, spawn_link(normal, p1, [N - 1])).

p1(0) ->
    top1();
p1(N) ->
    top(spawn_link(normal, p1, [N - 1]),N).

top(Next, N) ->
    receive
        X ->
            Next ! X,
            io:format("Process ~w received ~w~n", [N,X]),
            top(Next,N)
    end.

top1() ->
    receive
        stop ->
            io:format("Last process now exiting ~n", []),
            exit(finished);
        X ->
            io:format("Last process received ~w~n", [X]),
            top1()
    end.

test(Mess) ->
    start ! Mess.
```

Program 7.2

chain to evaluate the BIF `exit(finished)` which causes the process to terminate abnormally.

We start three processes (see Figure 7.1(a))

```
> normal:start(3).
true
```

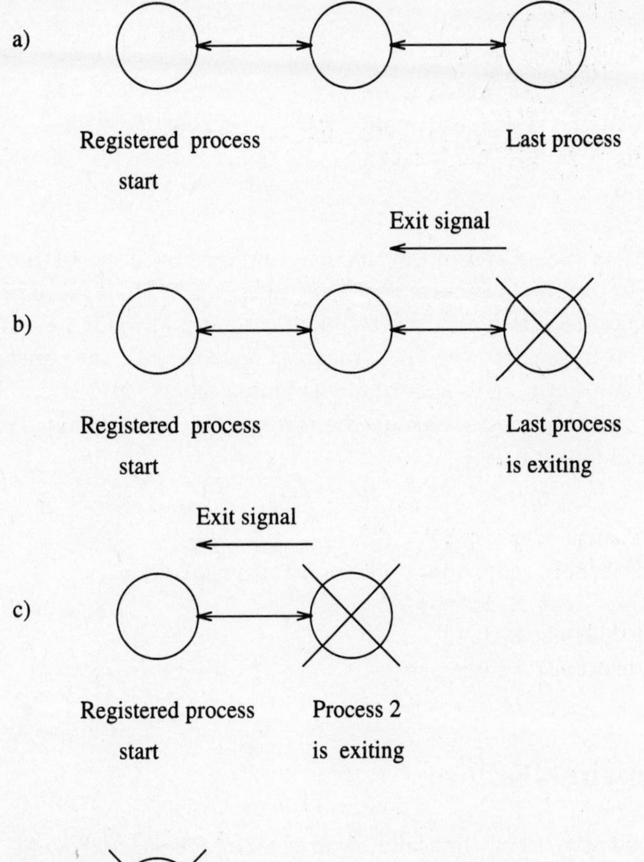

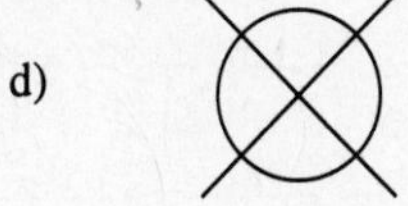

Figure 7.1 Process exit signal propagation

and send the message 123 to the first of the processes:

```
> normal:test(123).
Process 2 received 123
Process 1 received 123
Last process received 123
123
```

We send the message `stop` to the first process:

```
> normal:test(stop).
Process 2 received stop
Process 1 received stop
Last process now exiting
stop
```

This message was passed down the chain and we see how it causes the last process in the chain to terminate abnormally. This causes an `EXIT` signal to be sent to the penultimate process which also now terminates abnormally (Figure 7.1(b)), in turn sending an exit message to the first process (Figure 7.1(c)), the registered process `start` which also terminates abnormally (Figure 7.1(d)).

If we try to send a new message to the registered process, `start`, this fails since this process no longer exists:

```
> normal:test(456).
!!! Error in process <0.42.1> in function
!!!     normal:test(456)
!!! reason badarg
** exited: badarg **
```

7.4 Run-time Failure

As mentioned above, a run-time failure will cause a process to terminate abnormally if the failure is not within the scope of a `catch`. When a process terminates abnormally it sends `EXIT` signals to all the processes to which it is linked. These signals contain an `atom` which gives the reason for the failure. The most common reasons are:

`badmatch`
: A match has failed. For example, a process matching `1 = 3` terminates and the EXIT signal `{'EXIT', From, badmatch}` is sent to its linked processes.

`badarg`
: A BIF has been called with an argument of an incorrect type. For example, calling `atom_to_list(123)` causes the process evaluating the BIF to terminate and the EXIT signal `{'EXIT', From, badarg}` to be sent to its linked processes. `123` is not an atom.

`case_clause`
: No branch of a `case` expression matches. For example, a process evaluating:

```
M = 3,
case M of
    1 ->
        yes;
    2 ->
        no
end.
```

terminates and the EXIT signal `{'EXIT', From, case_clause}` is sent to its linked processes.

`if_clause`
: No branch of an `if` expression has matched. For example, a process evaluating:

```
M = 3,
if
    M == 1 ->
        yes;
    M == 2 ->
        no
end.
```

terminates and the EXIT signal `{'EXIT', From, if_clause}` is sent to its linked processes.

`function_clause`
: None of the heads of a function matches the arguments with which a function is called. For example, a process evaluating `foo(3)` when `foo/1` has been defined as:

```
foo(1) ->
    yes;
foo(2) ->
    no.
```

terminates and `{'EXIT', From, function_clause}` is sent to its linked processes.

`undef`
: A process which tries to evaluate a function which does not exist terminates and `{'EXIT', From, undef}` is sent to its linked processes (see Section 7.6).

`badarith`
: A process which evaluates a bad arithmetical expression (for example, a process evaluating `1 + foo`) terminates and `{'EXIT', Pid, badarith}` is sent to its linked processes.

`timeout_value`
: A bad timeout value is given in a `receive` expression; for example, the timeout value is not an integer or the atom `infinity`.

`nocatch`
: A `throw` is evaluated and there is no corresponding `catch`.

7.5 Changing the Default Signal Reception Action

The BIF `process_flag/2` can be used to change the default action taken by a process when it receives an `EXIT` signal. Evaluating `process_flag(trap_exit,true)` changes the default action as shown below and `process_flag(trap_exit,false)` causes the process to resume the default action.

As mentioned above, the format of `EXIT` signal is:

```
{'EXIT', Exiting_Process_Id, Reason}
```

A process which has evaluated the function `process_flag(trap_exit,true)` will *never* be *automatically* terminated when it receives any `EXIT` signal from another process. All `EXIT` signals, including those in which the `Reason` is the atom `normal`, will be converted into messages which can be received in the same way as any other messages. Program 7.3 illustrates how processes can be linked to each other and how `EXIT` signals can be received by a process which has evaluated `process_flag(trap_exit,true)`.

The example is started by:

```
> link_demo:start().
true
```

`link_demo:start()` spawns the function `demo/0` and registers the process with the name `demo`. `demo/0` turns off the default `EXIT` signal handling mechanism and calls `demo1/0` which waits for a message.

A normal exit is demonstrated by:

```
> link_demo:demonstrate_normal().
true
Demo process received normal exit from <0.13.1>
```

The process evaluating `demonstrate_normal/0` (in this case a process created by the ERLANG shell) finds the process identity of the registered process `demo` and creates a link to it. The function `demonstrate_normal/0` has no more clauses, so the process evaluating it has nothing left to do and terminates normally. This causes the signal:

```
{'EXIT', Process_Id, normal}
```

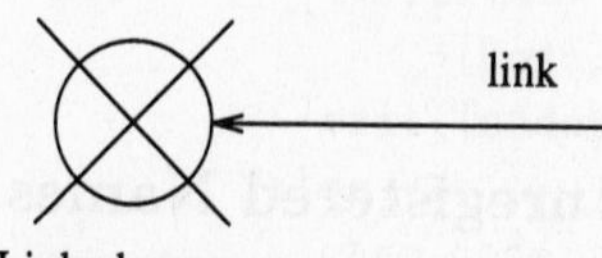

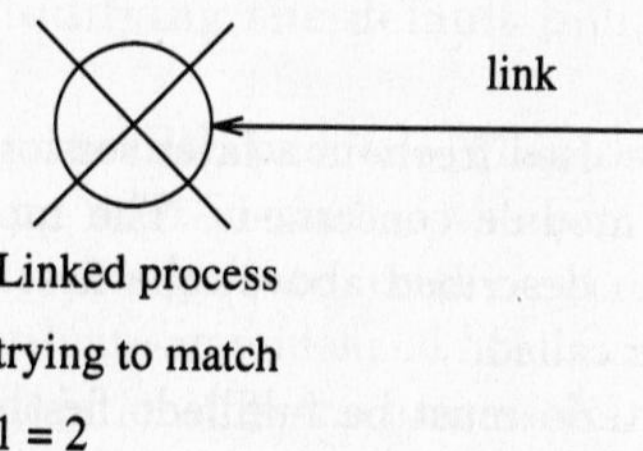

```
-module(link_demo).
-export([start/0, demo/0, demonstrate_normal/0, demonstrate_exit/1,
        demonstrate_error/0, demonstrate_message/1]).

start() ->
    register(demo, spawn(link_demo, demo, [])).

demo() ->
    process_flag(trap_exit, true),
    demo1().

demo1() ->
    receive
        {'EXIT', From, normal} ->
            io:format(
                "Demo process received normal exit from ~w~n",
                [From]),
            demo1();
        {'EXIT', From, Reason} ->
            io:format(
                "Demo process received exit signal ~w from ~w~n",
                [Reason, From]),
            demo1();
        finished_demo ->
            io:format("Demo finished ~n", []);
        Other ->
            io:format("Demo process message ~w~n", [Other]),
            demo1()
    end.

demonstrate_normal() ->
    link(whereis(demo)).

demonstrate_exit(What) ->
    link(whereis(demo)),
    exit(What).

demonstrate_message(What) ->
    demo ! What.

demonstrate_error() ->
    link(whereis(demo)),
    1 = 2.
```

Program 7.3

to be sent to the registered prc
exits, so it converts the signa
demo1/0 causing the text:

```
Demo process recei
```

to be output (see Figure 7.2). (

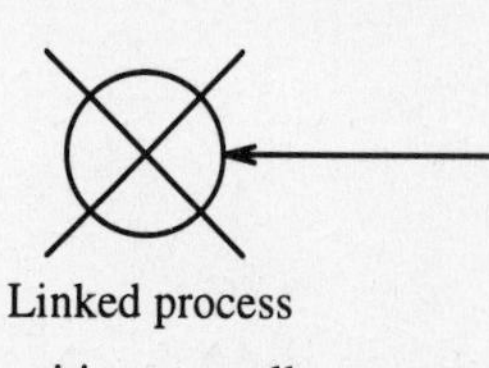

Figur

An abnormal exit is demonst

```
> link_demo:demons
Demo process recei
** exited: hello **
```

In the same way as in demons
link to the registered process dem
in this case by exit(hello).
demonstrate_exit/1 to termin

```
{'EXIT', Process_Id
```

to be sent to the registered proc
demo converts the signal to a m
causing the text:

```
Demo process receiv
```

to be output. demo1/0 now calls

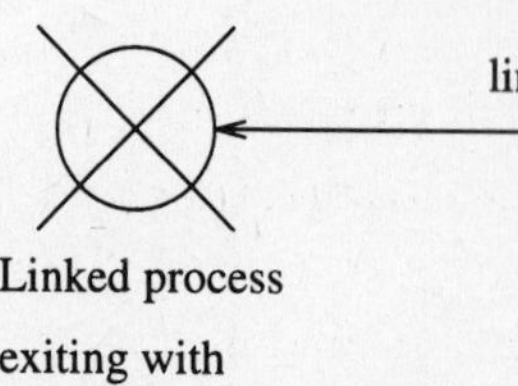

Figure 7.3

8.3 Isolating Computations

In some applications we may wish to isolate a computation completely so that it cannot influence other processes. The ERLANG shell is such a case. The simple shell in Chapter 7 is deficient. An expression evaluated in this shell can influence the process performing the evaluation in a number of ways:

- It can send the identity of the process running the shell (`self/0`) to other processes which can subsequently create links to this process or send it messages.
- It can register or unregister this process.

Program 8.1 is another way to write a shell:

```
-module(c_shell).
-export([start/0, eval/2]).

start() ->
    process_flag(trap_exit, true),
    go().

go() ->
    eval(io:parse_exprs('-> ')),
    go().

eval({form, Exprs}) ->
    Id = spawn_link(c_shell, eval, [self(), Exprs]),
    receive
        {value, Res, _} ->
            io:format("Result: ~w~n", [Res]),
            receive
                {'EXIT', Id, _ } ->
                    true
            end;
        {'EXIT', Id, Reason} ->
            io:format("Error: ~w!~n", [Reason])
    end;
eval(_) ->
    io:format("Syntax Error!~n", []).

eval(Id, Exprs) ->
    Id ! eval:exprs(Exprs, []).
```

Program 8.1

In the next case (Figure 7.4) we see that calling `link_demo:demonstrate_normal()` and `link_demo:demonstrate_exit(normal)` are equivalent:

```
> link_demo:demonstrate_exit(normal).
Demo process received normal exit from <0.13.1>
** exited: normal **
```

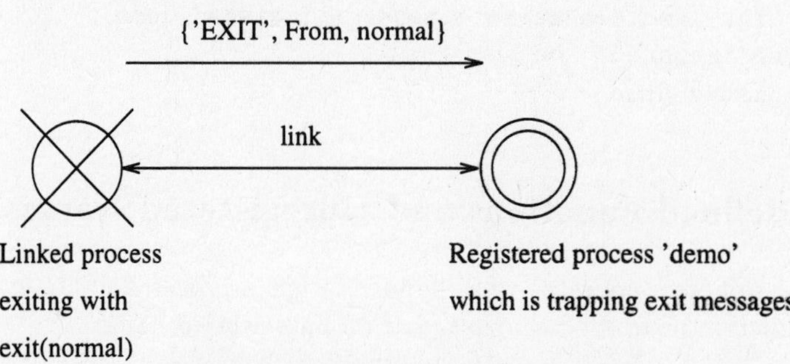

Figure 7.4 Evaluating `exit(normal)`

The next case demonstrates what happens if run-time errors occur.

```
> link_demo:demonstrate_error().
!!! Error in process <0.17.1> in function
!!!      link_demo:demonstrate_error()
!!! reason badmatch
** exited: badmatch **
Demo process received exit signal badmatch from <0.17.1>
```

`link_demo:demonstrate_error/0`, as above, creates a link to the registered process `demo`. `link_demo:demonstrate_error/0` tries to match `1 = 2`. This is incorrect and causes the process which evaluated `link_demo:demonstrate_error/0` to terminate abnormally, sending the signal `{'EXIT', Process_Id, badmatch}` to the registered process `demo` (see Figure 7.5).

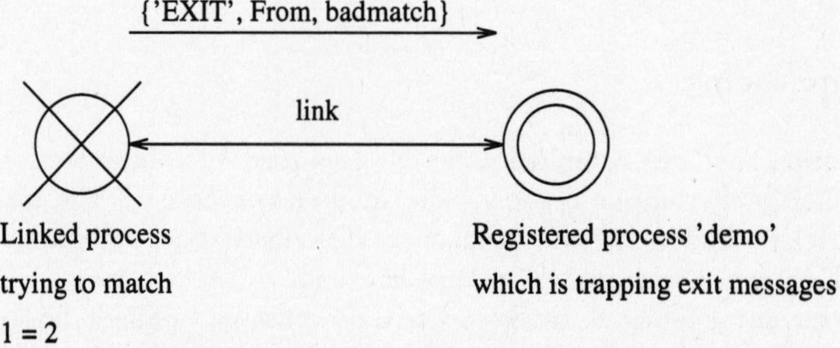

Figure 7.5 Process failing with a match error

In the next case we simply send the `hello` message to the registered process `demo` which receives this message:

```
> link_demo:demonstrate_message(hello).
Demo process message hello
hello
```

Since no link has been set up, no EXIT signals are sent or received.

The demo is finished by making the call below:

```
> link_demo:demonstrate_message(finished_demo).
Demo finished
finished_demo
```

7.6 Undefined Functions and Unregistered Names

The final class of error concerns what happens when a process tries to evaluate an undefined function or to send a message to an unregistered name.

7.6.1 Calling an undefined function

If a process tries to evaluate `Mod:Func(Arg0,...,ArgN)` and that function is undefined, then the call is converted to:

```
error_handler:undefined_function(Mod, Func, [Arg0,...,ArgN])
```

It is assumed that the module `error_handler` has been loaded (a module with name `error_handler` is predefined in the standard distribution). The module `error_handler` could be defined as in Program 7.4.

If the module was loaded then a run-time failure has occurred. If the module has not been loaded we try to load the module and, if this succeeds, we try to evaluate the function which was being called.

The module `code` knows which modules have been loaded and knows how to load code.

7.6.2 Autoloading

Once a function has been compiled it can be used freely in a later session without having explicitly to compile or 'load' the module concerned. The module will be automatically loaded (by the mechanism described above) the first time any function which *exported* from the module is called.

In order for autoloading to work two criteria must be fulfilled: firstly, the file name of the file containing the ERLANG module (minus the '.erl' extension) must be the same as the module name; and secondly, the default search paths used by the system when loading code must be such that the system can locate the unknown module.

```
-module(error_handler).
-export([undefined_function/3]).

undefined_function(Module, Func, Args) ->
    case code:is_loaded(Module) of
        {file,File} ->
           % the module is loaded but not the function
           io:format("error undefined function:~w ~w ~w",
                [Module, Func, Args]),
           exit({undefined_function,{Module,Func,Args}});
        false ->
           case code:load_file(Module) of
                {module, _} ->
                    apply(Module, Func, Args);
                {error, _} ->
                    io:format("error undefined module:~w",
                    [Module]),
                    exit({undefined_module, Module})
           end
     end.
```

Program 7.4

7.6.3 Sending a message to an unregistered name

`error_handler:unregistered_name(Name,Pid,Message)` is called if an attempt is made to send a message to a registered process and no such process exists. `Name` is the name of the non-existent registered process, `Pid` is the process identifier of the caller and `Message` is the message that should have been sent to the registered process.

7.6.4 Modifying the default behaviour

Evaluating the BIF `process_flag(error_handler, MyMod)` causes the module `MyMod` to be used instead of the default `error_handler`. This allows users to define their own (private) error handlers which are evaluated when an attempt is made to evaluate an undefined function or send a message to an unregistered name. This change is *local* to the process doing the evaluation. Caution is advised when defining a non-standard error handler: if you change the standard error handler and make a mistake, the system may not do what you think!

It is also possible to change the default behaviour by loading a new version of the module `error_handler`. As this change affects all processes except those which

have set their own local error handler it is very dangerous.

7.7 Catch Versus Trapping Exits

Evaluation within the scope of a `catch` and trapping of exits are completely different. Trapping exits affects what happens when a process receives `EXIT` signals from another process. `catch` only effects the evaluation of an expression in the process in which `catch` is used.

```
-module(tt).
-export([test/0, p/1]).

test() ->
    spawn_link(tt, p,[1]),
    receive
        X ->
            X
    end.

p(N) ->
    N = 2.
```

Program 7.5

Evaluating `tt:test()` in Program 7.5 creates a linked process which matches `N` (whose value is 1) with `2`. This fails, causing the signal `{'EXIT',Pid,badmatch}` to be sent to the process which evaluated `tt:test()` and which is now waiting for a message. If this process is not trapping exits it also terminates abnormally.

If, instead of calling `tt:test()`, we call `catch tt:test()`, exactly the same thing happens: the failing match occurs in another process outside the scope of the `catch`. Adding `process_flag(trap_exit, true)` before `spawn_link(tt,p,[1])` would cause `tt:test()` to receive the signal `{'EXIT',Pid,badmatch}` and convert it into a message.

Chapter 8

Programming Robust Applications

Chapter 7 described the mechanisms available in ERLANG for handling errors. In this chapter we see how these mechanisms can be used to build robust and fault-tolerant systems.

8.1 Guarding Against Bad Data

Consider the server for analysing telephone numbers described in Chapter 5 (Program 5.5). The main loop of the server contains the following code:

```
server(AnalTable) ->
    receive
        {From, {analyse,Seq}} ->
            Result = lookup(Seq, AnalTable),
            From ! {number_analyser, Result},
            server(AnalTable);
        {From, {add_number, Seq, Key}} ->
            From ! {number_analyser, ack},
            server(insert(Seq, Key, AnalTable))
    end.
```

In the above `Seq` is a sequence of digits comprising a telephone number, e.g. `[5,2,4,8,9]`. When writing the `lookup/2` and `insert/3` functions we could check that `Seq` was a list of items each of which is obtained by pressing a key on a telephone keypad.[1] Not doing such a check would result in a run-time failure if, for example, `Seq` was the atom `hello`. An easier way to do the same thing is to evaluate `lookup/2` and `insert/3` within the scope of a catch:

[1] That is, one of the digits 0 to 9 and * and #.

```
server(AnalTable) ->
    receive
        {From, {analyse,Seq}} ->
            case catch lookup(Seq, AnalTable) of
                {'EXIT', _} ->
                    From ! {number_analyser, error};
                Result ->
                    From ! {number_analyser, Result}
            end,
            server(AnalTable);
        {From, {add_number, Seq, Key}} ->
            From ! {number_analyser, ack},
            case catch insert(Seq, Key, AnalTable) of
                {'EXIT', _} ->
                    From ! {number_analyser, error},
                    server(AnalTable); % Table not changed
                NewTable ->
                    server(NewTable)
            end
    end.
```

Note that by using `catch` it is easy to write the number analysis function for the normal case and to let ERLANG's error handling mechanisms deal with errors such as `badmatch`, `badarg` and `function_clause`.

In general, a server should be designed so that it cannot be 'crashed' by sending it bad data. In many cases the data sent to a server comes from the access functions to the server. In the above example the process identity of the client process `From` which is sent to the number analysis server comes from the access function, for example:

```
lookup(Seq) ->
    number_analyser ! {self(), {analyse,Seq}},
    receive
        {number_analyser, Result} ->
            Result
    end.
```

and the server need not check that `From` is a process identity. We are, in this case, guarding against inadvertent programming errors. A malicious program could bypass the access routines and crash the server by sending:

```
number_analyser ! {55, [1,2,3]}
```

which would result in the number analyser trying to send a message to `55` and subsequently crashing.

8.2 Robust Server Processes

The design of a reliable server process is best described by way of an example.

Chapter 5 (Program 5.6) shows a resource allocator. In this allocator a resource which has been allocated to a process will not be returned to the allocator if the process making the allocation terminates (erroneously or normally) without freeing the resource. This can be circumvented by:

- Setting the server to trap `EXIT` signals (`process_flag(trap_exit, true)`).
- Creating links between the allocator and processes which have allocated one or more resources.
- Handling `EXIT` signals from such processes.

This is illustrated in Figure 8.1.

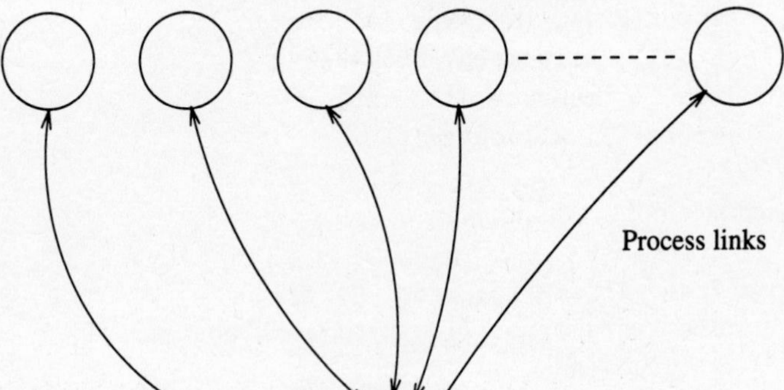

Figure 8.1 Robust allocator process with clients

The access routines to the allocator are left unchanged. Starting the modified allocator is done as follows:

```
start_server(Resources) ->
    process_flag(trap_exit, true),
    server(Resources, []).
```

The 'server' loop is modified to receive `EXIT` signals.

```
server(Free, Allocated) ->
    receive
        {From,alloc} ->
            allocate(Free, Allocated, From);
        {From,{free,R}} ->
            free(Free, Allocated, From, R);
        {'EXIT', From, _ } ->
            check(Free, Allocated, From)
    end.
```

`allocate/3` is modified so that we create a link to the process doing the allocation (if a resource is available).

```
allocate([R|Free], Allocated, From) ->
    link(From),
    From ! {resource_alloc,{yes,R}},
    server(Free, [{R,From}|Allocated]);
allocate([], Allocated, From) ->
    From ! {resource_alloc,no},
    server([], Allocated).
```

`free/4` becomes more complicated:

```
free(Free, Allocated, From, R) ->
    case lists:member({R, From}, Allocated) of
        true ->
            From ! {resource_alloc, yes},
            Allocated1 = lists:delete({R, From}, Allocated),
            case lists:keysearch(From, 2, Allocated1) of
                false ->
                    unlink(From);
                _ ->
                    true
            end,
            server([R|Free], Allocated1);
        false ->
            From ! {resource_alloc, error},
            server(Free, Allocated)
    end.
```

First we check that the resource being freed really is allocated to the process which is freeing it. `lists:member({R,From}, Allocated)` returns `true` if this is the case. We create a new list of allocated resources as before. We cannot simply unlink `From`, but must first check that `From` has not allocated other resources. If

`keysearch(From, 2, Allocated1)` (see Appendix C) returns `false`, `From` has not allocated other resources and we can unlink `From`.

If a process to which we have created a link terminates, the server will receive an `EXIT` signal and we call `check(Free, Allocated, From)`.

```
check(Free, Allocated, From) ->
    case lists:keysearch(From, 2, Allocated) of
        false ->
            server(Free, Allocated);
        {value, {R, From}} ->
            check([R|Free],
                   lists:delete({R, From}, Allocated), From)
    end.
```

If `lists:keysearch(From, 2, Allocated)` returns `false` we have no resource allocated to this process. If it returns `{value, {R, From}}` we see that resource `R` has been allocated and we must add this to the list of free resources and delete it from the list of allocated resources before continuing checking to see if any more resources have been allocated by the process. Note that in this case we do not need to unlink the process since it will already have been unlinked when it terminated.

Freeing an unallocated resource is probably a serious error. We could change `free/1` in Program 5.6 to kill the process doing the erroneous freeing:[2]

```
free(Resource) ->
    resource_alloc ! {self(),{free,Resource}},
    receive
        {resource_alloc, error} ->
            exit(bad_allocation); % exit added here
        {resource_alloc, Reply} ->
            Reply
    end.
```

A process which is killed in this way will, if it has allocated resources, be linked to the server. The server will thus receive an `EXIT` signal which will be handled as above and the allocated resources will be freed.

The above illustrates the following points:

- The interface to a server can be designed in such a way that clients use access functions (in this case `allocate/0` and `free/1`) and have no idea of what goes on 'behind the scenes'. The communication between clients and the server process is hidden from the user. In particular, clients need not know the process identity of the server and thus cannot interfere with its execution.
- A server which traps `EXIT` signals and creates links to its clients can monitor clients and take appropriate actions if the clients die.

[2] This is probably good programming practice since it will force programmers to correct such errors.

8.3 Isolating Computations

In some applications we may wish to isolate a computation completely so that it cannot influence other processes. The ERLANG shell is such a case. The simple shell in Chapter 7 is deficient. An expression evaluated in this shell can influence the process performing the evaluation in a number of ways:

- It can send the identity of the process running the shell (`self/0`) to other processes which can subsequently create links to this process or send it messages.
- It can register or unregister this process.

Program 8.1 is another way to write a shell:

```
-module(c_shell).
-export([start/0, eval/2]).

start() ->
    process_flag(trap_exit, true),
    go().

go() ->
    eval(io:parse_exprs('-> ')),
    go().

eval({form, Exprs}) ->
    Id = spawn_link(c_shell, eval, [self(), Exprs]),
    receive
        {value, Res, _} ->
            io:format("Result: ~w~n", [Res]),
            receive
                {'EXIT', Id, _ } ->
                    true
            end;
        {'EXIT', Id, Reason} ->
            io:format("Error: ~w!~n", [Reason])
    end;
eval(_) ->
    io:format("Syntax Error!~n", []).

eval(Id, Exprs) ->
    Id ! eval:exprs(Exprs, []).
```

Program 8.1

The process running the shell traps `EXIT` signals. Commands are evaluated in a separate process (`spawn_link(c_shell, eval, [self(), Exprs])`) which is linked to the shell process. Despite the fact that we give `c_shell:eval/2` the process identity of the shell, this cannot be misused since it is not given as an argument to the function doing the actual evaluation, `eval:exprs/2`.

8.4 Keeping Processes Alive

Some processes may be vital to the 'well-being' of a system. For example, in a conventional time-sharing system, each terminal line is often served by a process which is responsible for input and output to the terminal. If such a process dies the terminal becomes unusable. Program 8.2 is a server which keeps processes alive by re-creating any which terminate.

The server process which is registered as `keep_alive` maintains a list of tuples `{Id, Mod, Func, Args}`, containing the process identity, the module, function and arguments of the processes which it is keeping alive. It starts these processes using the BIF `spawn_link/3` so it is also linked to each such process. Since the server traps `EXIT`s, it receives an `EXIT` signal if any of the processes it is keeping alive terminates. By searching the list of tuples it can re-create such a process.

Program 8.2, of course, needs improvement. As it stands it is impossible to remove a process from the list of processes to keep alive. Also, if we try starting a process for which the `module:function/arity` does not exist, the server will go into an infinite loop. Creating a correct program without these deficiencies is left as an exercise for the reader.

8.5 Discussion

The default action of a process which receives a signal in which the 'reason' is not `normal`, is to terminate and propagate the signal to its links (see Section 7.3). It is easy to create a layered operating system by using links and trapping `EXIT` signals. Processes at the top layer of such a system (the application processes) do not trap `EXIT`s. Processes in the same transaction are linked to each other. Lower layer processes (operating system processes) trap `EXIT`s and have links to application processes which they need to monitor (see Figure 8.2). Examples of this type of operating system structure are the relations between the switch server and telephony application processes in Chapter 15 and the file system in Chapter 13.

An application process which terminates abnormally causes `EXIT` signals to be sent to all the processes in its transaction and thus kill the entire transaction. The operating system processes which are linked to application processes in the failing transaction also receive `EXIT` signals and can clean up undesired side-effects and maybe restart the transaction.

```
-module(keep_alive).
-export([start/0, start1/0, new_process/3]).

start() ->
    register(keep_alive, spawn(keep_alive, start1, [])).

start1() ->
    process_flag(trap_exit, true),
    loop([]).

loop(Processes) ->
    receive
        {From, {new_proc, Mod, Func, Args}} ->
            Id = spawn_link(Mod, Func, Args),
            From ! {keep_alive, started},
            loop([{Id, Mod, Func, Args}|Processes]);

        {'EXIT', Id, _} ->
            case lists:keysearch(Id, 1, Processes) of
                false ->
                    loop(Processes);
                {value, {Id, Mod, Func, Args}} ->
                    P = lists:delete({Id,Mod,Func,Args},
                                     Processes),
                    Id1 = spawn_link(Mod, Func, Args),
                    loop([{Id1, Mod, Func, Args} | P])
            end
    end.

new_process(Mod, Func, Args) ->
    keep_alive ! {self(), {new_proc, Mod, Func, Args}},
    receive
        {keep_alive, started} ->
            true
    end.
```

Program 8.2

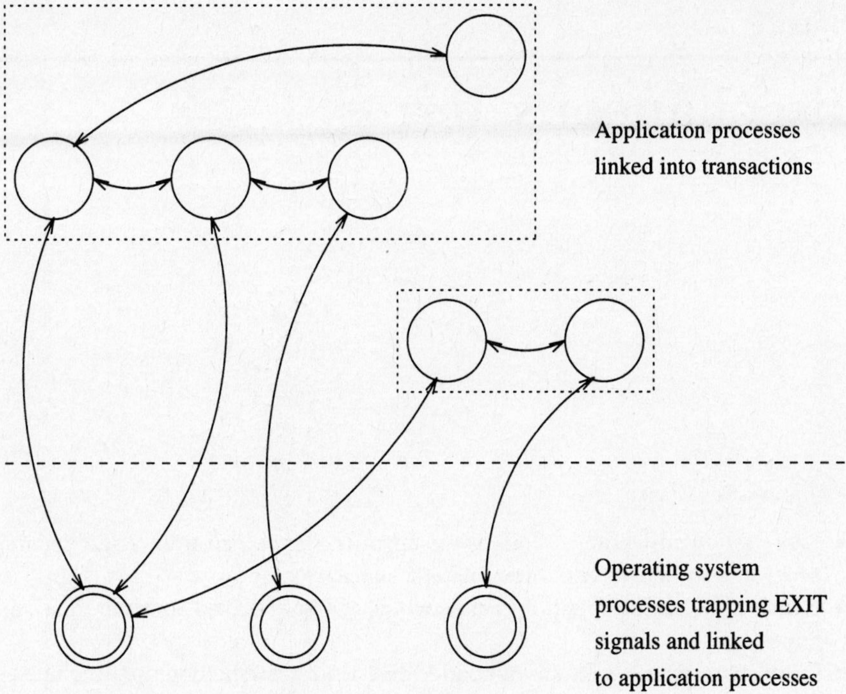

Figure 8.2 Operating system and application processes

Chapter 9

Miscellaneous Items

This chapter deals with:

- Last call optimisation – This is an optimisation which allows tail recursive programs to be evaluated in constant space.
- References – These provide names which are guaranteed to be unique on all nodes.
- Code replacement – In an embedded real-time system code updates must be made *on the fly*, that is, without stopping the system.
- Ports – These provide a mechanism for communicating with the external world.
- Binaries – A built-in data type which can be used to store and manipulate an area of untyped memory.
- Process dictionaries – These can be used in a process to store and retrieve global data destructively.
- The net kernel – The net kernel is responsible for coordinating all network operations in a distributed ERLANG system.
- Hashing – This is a method of mapping a term onto a unique integer which can be used to implement highly efficient table lookup methods.
- Efficiency – We discuss how to write efficient ERLANG programs.

9.1 Last Call Optimisation

ERLANG provides *last call optimisation*, which allows functions to be evaluated in constant space. The principal technique used to store persistent data is to store it in structures which are manipulated in a server process (a typical example of this was shown in Section 5.5). In order for such a technique to work correctly the server must make use of the last call optimisation.

If this is not done then the server will eventually run out of space and the system will not function correctly.

9.1.1 Tail recursion

We introduce the idea of *tail recursion* by showing how the same function can be written in two different styles, one of which is tail recursive. Consider the function `length` defined as follows:

```
length([_ | T]) ->
    1 + length(T);
length([]) ->
    0.
```

Suppose we evaluate `length([a, b, c])`. The first clause defining `length` reduces the problem to evaluating `1 + length([b,c])`. Unfortunately, the `+` operation cannot be performed *immediately* but must be *delayed* until the value of `length([b, c])` is available. The system must *remember* that it has to perform a `+` operation and at a later stage (when the value of `length([b,c])` is known) *retrieve* the fact that it has to do a `+` operation and then actually perform the operation.

The *pending* operations are stored in a local data area. The size of this area is at least `K * N` storage locations (where `K` is some constant representing the overhead incurred in each new evaluation of `length` and `N` is the number of pending operations).

We now write an equivalent function to compute the length of a list which makes use of an accumulator (see Section 3.4.4) and which evaluates in constant space (we call this `length1` to avoid confusion):

```
length1(L) ->
    length1(L, 0).

length1([_|T], N) ->
    length1(T, 1 + N);
length1([], N) ->
    N.
```

To evaluate `length1([a, b, c])` we first evaluate `length1([a, b, c], 0)`. This reduces to the evaluation of `length1([b, c], 1 + 0)`. The `+` operation can now be performed *immediately* (because *both* its arguments are known). Successive function evaluations in the calculation of `length1([a, b, c])` are thus:

```
length1([a, b, c])
length1([a, b, c], 0)
length1([b, c], 1 + 0)
length1([b, c], 1)
length1([c], 1 + 1)
length1([c], 2)
```

```
length1([], 1 + 2)
length1([], 3)
3
```

A *tail recursive function* is one which does not accumulate any pending operations before recursing. A clause is tail recursive if the last expression in the body of the clause is a call to the function itself or a constant. A function is tail recursive if all its clauses are tail recursive.

For example:

```
rev(X) -> rev(X, []).

rev([], X) -> X;
rev([H|T], X) -> rev(T, [H|X]).
```

is tail recursive, but:

```
append([], X) -> X;
append([H|T], X) -> [H | append(T, X)].
```

is not tail recursive since the last expression evaluated in the body of the second clause (the `|` operation in `[H|append(T,X)]`) is neither a call to `append` nor a constant.

9.1.2 Last call optimisation

Tail recursion is a special case of the more general *last call optimisation* (LCO). The last call optimisation applies whenever the last expression occurring in the body of a clause is a function evaluation.

For example:

```
g(X) ->
    ...
    h(X).

h(X) ->
    ...
    i(X).

i(X) ->
    ...
    g(X).
```

defines a set of three mutually recursive functions. The LCO allows the evaluation of `g(X)` to take place in constant space.

A careful examination of the server examples given in this book will reveal that all are written so as to execute in constant[1] space.

9.2 References

References are unique objects. The BIF `make_ref()` returns a globally unique object guaranteed to be different from every other object in the system and all other (possibly) running ERLANG nodes. The only thing that can be done with references is to compare them for equality.

For example, we could use the following interface function in the client–server model.

```
request(Server, Req) ->
    Server ! {R = make_ref(), self(), Req},
        receive
            {Server, R, Reply} ->
                Reply
        end.
```

`request(Server, Req)` sends a request `Req` to the server with name `Server`; the request contains a unique reference `R`. The reply from the server is checked to ensure the presence of the unique reference `R`. This method of communication with the server provides 'end-to-end' confirmation that the request has been processed.

9.3 Code Replacement

In an embedded real-time system we may wish to make code updates without stopping the system. We may, for example, want to correct a software error in a large telephone exchange without interrupting the service being offered.

Code replacement during operation is a common requirement in large 'soft' real-time control systems which have a long operational life and a large volume of software. It is not usually a requirement in dedicated 'hard' real-time software which is often assigned to specific processors or burnt into ROM.

9.3.1 Example of code replacement

Consider Program 9.1.

We begin by compiling and loading the code for `code_replace`. Then we start the program and send the messages `hello`, `global` and `process` to the process

[1]Excepting, of course, for the space required for the local data structures of the server.

```
-module(code_replace).
-export([test/0, loop/1]).

test() ->
    register(global, spawn(code_replace, loop, [0])).

loop(N) ->
     receive
         X ->
              io:format('N = ~w Vsn A received ~w~n',[N, X])
    end,
    code_replace:loop(N+1).
```

Program 9.1

which is created. Finally we edit the program, changing the version number from A to B, recompile and load the program and send the process the message **hello**.

The following dialogue results:

```
%%% start by compiling and loading the code
%%%   (this is done by c:c)
>  c:c(code_replace).
...
> code_replace:test().
true
> global ! hello.
N = 0 Vsn A received hello
hello
> global ! global.
N = 1 Vsn A received global
global
> global ! process.
N = 2 Vsn A received process
%%% edit the file code_replace.erl
%%% recompile and load
> c:c(code_replace).
....
> global ! hello.
N = 3 Vsn B received hello
```

Here we see that the local variable N which is used as an argument to `loop/1` is preserved despite the fact we have recompiled and loaded the code in `loop/1` while it is being executed.

Observe that the server loop was written as follows:

```
-module(xyz).

loop(Arg1, ..., ArgN) ->
    receive
        ...
    end,
    xyz:loop(NewArg1, ..., NewArgN).
```

This has a subtly different meaning from the code:

```
-module(xyz).

loop(Arg1, ..., ArgN) ->
    receive
        ...
    end,
    loop(NewArg1, ..., NewArgN).
```

In the first case the call `xyz:loop(...)` means call the *latest* version of `loop` in the module `xyz`. In the second case (without the explicit module name) it means call the version of `loop` in the *currently executing module.*

Use of an explicitly qualified module name (`module:func`) causes `module:func` to be *dynamically* linked into the run-time code. *Every time* a call is made using a fully qualified module name the system will evaluate the function using the latest available version of the code. Addresses of local functions within a module are resolved at compile-time – they are *static* and cannot be changed at run-time.

In the example dialogue `c:c(File)` compiles and loads the code in `File`. This is discussed in more detail in Section 13.3.

9.4 Ports

Ports provide the basic mechanism for communication with the external world. Application programs written in ERLANG may wish to interact with objects which exist outside the ERLANG system. When building complex systems it may be desirable to interface ERLANG programs to existing software packages, for example windowing or database systems, or programs written in foreign languages, for example, C or Modula2.

From the programmer's point of view, it is desirable to view all activities occurring outside ERLANG as if they were programmed in ERLANG. To create this illusion we must arrange that objects outside ERLANG behave as if they were normal ERLANG processes. To achieve this, an abstraction called a `Port` provides a byte-oriented communication channel between ERLANG and the external world.

Evaluating the expression `open_port(PortName, PortSettings)` creates a new port which behaves in a similar manner to a process. The process which evaluates `open_port` is called the *connected* process for the port. The purpose of the connected process is to provide a destination for all incoming messages to the port. An external object sends a message to ERLANG by writing a sequence of bytes to the port associated with that object. The port then sends a message containing this sequence of bytes to the connected process.

Any process in the system can be linked to a port, and `EXIT` signals between ports and ERLANG processes behave exactly as if the port were an ERLANG process. Only *three* messages are understood by a port:

```
Port ! {PidC, {command, Data}}
Port ! {PidC, {connect, Pid1}}
Port ! {PidC, close}
```

`PidC` *must* be the `Pid` of the connected process. The meanings of these messages are as follows:

`{command, Data}`
: Send the bytes described by `Data` to the external object. `Data` is a possibly non-flat[2] list whose individual elements are integers in the range `0.255` or a single binary object. No reply.

`close`
: Close the port. The port will reply by sending a `{Port, closed}` message to the connected process.

`{connect, Pid1}`
: Change the connected process of the port to `Pid1`. The port will reply by sending a `{Port, connected}` message to the previously connected process.

In addition, the connected process can receive data messages with:

```
receive
    {Port, {data, Data}} ->
        ... an external object has sent data to Erlang ...
    ...
end
```

In this section we will describe two programs which make use of a port: the first is an ERLANG process executing *inside* the ERLANG workspace; the second is a C program executing *outside* ERLANG.

9.4.1 Opening ports

Ports can be opened with a number of different settings. To open a port the BIF `open_port(PortName, PortSettings)` is used. `PortName` is one of:

[2] A flat list is a list containing no sub-lists.

`{spawn, Command}`
: Start an *external* program or start a driver with the name of `Command` if there is one. ERLANG drivers are described in Appendix E. `Command` is the name of the external program which will be run. `Command` runs outside the ERLANG workspace if no driver with the name `Command` can be found.

`Atom`
: `Atom` is assumed to be the name of an external resource. A transparent connection between ERLANG and the resource named by the atom is established. The behaviour of connection depends upon the type of the resource. If `Atom` represents a file then a single message is sent to the ERLANG process containing the entire contents of the file. Sending messages to the port causes data to be written to the file.

`{fd, In, Out}`
: Allow an ERLANG process to access any currently opened file descriptors used by ERLANG. The file descriptor `In` can be used for standard input and `Out` for standard output. Very few processes need to use this: only various servers in the ERLANG operating system (`shell` and `user`). Note this is very UNIX-specific.

`PortSettings` is a list of settings for the port. Valid values are:

`{packet, N}`
: Messages are preceded by their length, which is sent in `N` bytes with the most significant byte first. Valid values for `N` are `1, 2` or `4`.

`stream`
: Output messages are sent without packet lengths – a private protocol must be used between the ERLANG process and the external object.

`use_stdio`
: Only valid for `{spawn, Command}`. Make spawned (UNIX) process use standard input and output (i.e. file descriptors 0 and 1) for communicating with ERLANG.

`nouse_stdio`
: The opposite of above. Use file descriptors 3 and 4 for communicating with ERLANG.

`in`
: The port can be used for input only.

`out`
: The port can be used for output only.

`binary`
: The port is a binary port (described later).

`eof`
: The port will not be closed on end of file and produce an `'EXIT'` signal, rather it will remain open and send an `{Port,eof}` to the process that is connected to the port, hence output can still be sent to the port.

The default is `stream` for *all* types of port and `use_stdio` for spawned ports.

9.4.2 The port as seen by an Erlang process

Program 9.2 defines a simple ERLANG process which opens a port and sends it a sequence of messages. The external object connected to the port processes and replies to these messages. After a short delay the ERLANG process closes the port.

```
-module(demo_server).
-export([start/0]).

start() ->
    Port = open_port({spawn, demo_server}, [{packet, 2}]),
    Port ! {self(), {command, [1,2,3,4,5]}},
    Port ! {self(), {command, [10,1,2,3,4,5]}},
    Port ! {self(), {command, "echo"}},
    Port ! {self(), {command, "abc"}},
    read_replies(Port).

read_replies(Port) ->
    receive
        {Port, Any} ->
            io:format('erlang received from port:~w~n', [Any]),
            read_replies(Port)
    after 2000 ->
            Port ! {self(), close},
            receive
                {Port, closed} ->
                    true
            end
    end.
```

Program 9.2

In Program 9.2 `open_port(PortName, PortSettings)` starts an *external* program. `demo_server` is the name of the external program which will be run.

The expression `Port ! {self(), {command, [1,2,3,4,5]}}` sends five bytes (with values 1,2,3,4,5) to the external program.

To make things interesting the external program associated with the port in this example has the following functionality:

- If the program is sent the string `"echo"` it sends the reply `"ohce"` to ERLANG.

- If the server is sent a data block whose first byte is 10 it replies with a block where all the elements in the block except the first have been doubled.
- Otherwise the data is ignored.

Running the program we obtain the following:

```
> demo_server:start().
erlang received from port:{data,[10,2,4,6,8,10]}
erlang received from port:{data,[111,104,99,101]}
true
```

9.4.3 The port as seen by an external process

The external program which executes outside the ERLANG system (as started by `open_port({spawn, demo_server}, [{packet,2}]))` can be written in any programming language supported by the host operating system. Our examples assume that we are running on a UNIX system and that the external program is a UNIX process which is programmed in C.

The C program which communicates with the ERLANG process shown in Section 9.4.2 is given in Program 9.3. This should be compiled and made into an executable file called `demo_server`.

```
/* demo_server.c */
#include <stdio.h>
#include <string.h>

/* Message data are all unsigned bytes */
typedef unsigned char byte;

main(argc, argv)
int argc;
char **argv;
{

    int len;
    int i;
    char *progname;
    byte buf[1000];

    progname = argv[0];          /* Save start name of program */

    fprintf(stderr, "demo_server in C Starting \n");
```

```
    while ((len = read_cmd(buf)) > 0){
        if(strncmp(buf, "echo", 4) == 0)
          write_cmd("ohce", 4);
        else if(buf[0] == 10){
            for(i=1; i < len ; i++)
              buf[i] = 2 * buf[i];
            write_cmd(buf, len);
        }
    }
}

/* Read the 2 length bytes (MSB first), then the data. */
read_cmd(buf)
byte *buf;
{
    int len;

    if (read_exact(buf, 2) != 2)
        return(-1);
    len = (buf[0] << 8) | buf[1];
    return read_exact(buf, len);
}

/* Pack the 2  bytes length (MSB first) and send it */
write_cmd(buf, len)
byte *buf;
int len;
{
    byte str[2];

    put_int16(len, str);
    if (write_exact(str, 2) != 2)
        return(-1);
    return write_exact(buf, len);
}

/*  [read|write]_exact are used since they may return
 *  BEFORE all bytes have been transmitted
 */
read_exact(buf, len)
byte *buf;
int  len;
{
    int i, got = 0;
```

```
    do {
        if ((i = read(0, buf+got, len-got)) <= 0)
          return (i);
        got += i;
    } while (got < len);
    return (len);
}

write_exact(buf, len)
byte *buf;
int  len;
{
    int i, wrote = 0;

    do {
        if ((i = write(1, buf+wrote, len-wrote)) <= 0)
          return (i);
        wrote += i;
    } while (wrote < len);
    return (len);
}

put_int16(i, s)
byte *s;
{
    *s = (i >> 8) & 0xff;
    s[1] = i & 0xff;
}
```

Program 9.3

Program 9.3 reads the byte sequence which was sent to the ERLANG port with the expression `len = read_cmd(buf)` and sends data back to ERLANG with `write_cmd(buf, len)`.

File descriptor 0 is used to read data from ERLANG and file descriptor 1 is used to write data to ERLANG. The C routines do the following:

`read_cmd(buf)`
: Reads a single command from ERLANG.

`write_cmd(buf, len)`
: Writes a buffer of length `len` to ERLANG.

`read_exact(buf, len)`
: Reads exactly `len` bytes.

`write_exact(buf, len)`
Writes `len` bytes.
`put_int16(i, s)`
Packs a 16-bit integer into two bytes.

The routines `read_cmd` and `write_cmd` assumes that the protocol between the external server and ERLANG consists of a two-byte header, giving the length of the data packet to be exchanged, followed by the data itself. This is illustrated in Figure 9.1.

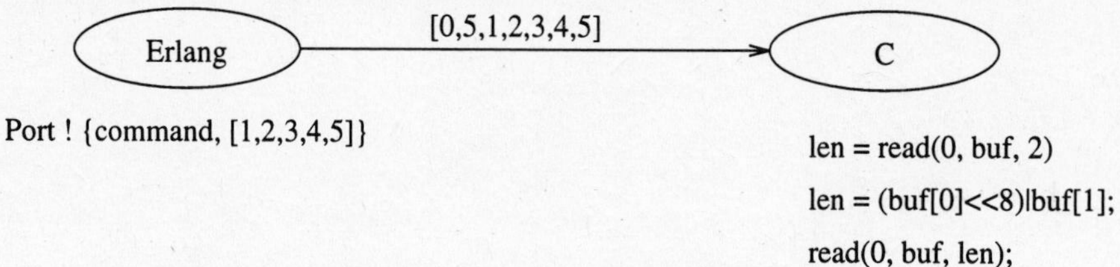

Figure 9.1 Communication with a port

This particular protocol (two-byte header plus data) was used since the port was opened by evaluating:

```
open_port({spawn, demo_server}, [{packet, 2}])
```

9.5 Binaries

A binary is a data type which is used to store an area of untyped memory. A port is a binary port if the atom `binary` appears in the `Settings` list, given as the last argument to `open_port/2`. All messages which come from a binary port are binaries.

To illustrate the difference between a binary and normal port assume that we wish to send the string `"hello"` from an external process to the ERLANG system and that the 'two-byte header plus data' convention is used. The external program outputs the following byte sequence:

```
0 5 104 101 108 108 111
```

If the ERLANG process which is connected to the port is a normal port, then the message `{Port, {data, [104,101,108,108,111]}}` will be sent to the process. If the port had been a binary port then the message would have been `{Port, {data, Bin}}`, where `Bin` is a binary data object of size 5, storing the bytes of the message. Note that in both cases there is no change to the external process which sends data to the port.

The advantage of having the port sending binary data objects instead of lists is that if the lists are long, it is considerably faster to build and send a binary data object than a list.

The following BIFs are used to manipulate binaries:

`term_to_binary(T)`
Converts the term `T` to a binary. The resulting binary data object is a representation of the term in the *external term format.*

`binary_to_term(Bin)`
Is the inverse of `term_to_binary/1`.

`binary_to_list(Bin)`
Converts the binary `Bin` to a list of integers.

`binary_to_list(Bin, Start, Stop)`
Converts a portion of the binary `Bin` into a list of characters, starting at position `Start`, and stopping at position `Stop`. The first position of the binary has position 1.

`list_to_binary(Charlist)`
Converts `Charlist` into a binary data object. This is not the same as `term_to_binary(Charlist)`. This BIF builds a binary object containing the bytes in `Charlist` as opposed to `term_to_binary(Charlist)` which builds a binary object containing the bytes of the external term format of the *term* `Charlist`.

`split_binary(Bin, Pos)`
Builds two new binaries, as if `Bin` had been split at `Pos`. Returns a tuple consisting of the two new binaries. For example:

```
1> B = list_to_binary("0123456789").
#Bin
2> size(B).
10
3> {B1,B2} = split_binary(B,3).
{#Bin,#Bin}
4> size(B1).
3
5> size(B2).
7
```

`concat_binary(ListOfBinaries)`
Returns a new binary which is formed by the concatenation of the binaries in `ListOfBinaries`.

In addition the guard test `binary(X)` succeeds if `X` is a binary data object. Binaries are primarily used for code loading in a network, but can also be used by applications that shuffle large amounts of raw data such as audio or video data. It is possible to efficiently input very large amounts of binary data through a port, work with the data , and then at a later stage, output it to another or the same port.

9.6 Process Dictionary

Each process has an associated dictionary. This dictionary can be manipulated with the following BIFs:

`put(Key, Value).`
: Adds a new `Value` to the process dictionary and associates it with `Key`. If a value is already associated with `Key` this value is deleted and replaced with the new `Value`. Returns any value previously associated with `Key`, otherwise `undefined` if no value was associated with `Key`. `Key` and `Value` can be any ERLANG terms.

`get(Key).`
: Returns the value associated with `Key` in the process dictionary. Returns `undefined` if no value is associated with `Key`.

`get().`
: Returns the entire process dictionary as a list of `{Key, Value}` tuples.

`get_keys(Value).`
: Returns a list of keys which correspond to `Value` in the process dictionary.

`erase(Key).`
: Returns the value associated with `Key` and deletes it from the process dictionary. Returns `undefined` if no value is associated with `Key`.

`erase().`
: Returns the entire process dictionary and deletes it.

The process dictionary is *local* to each process. When a process is spawned the dictionary is empty. Any function can add a `{Key, Value}` association to the dictionary by evaluating `put(Key, Value)`, the value can be retrieved later by evaluating `get(Key)`. Values stored when `put` is evaluated within the scope of a `catch` will not be 'retracted' if a `throw` is evaluated or an error occurs.

The entire dictionary can be retrieved with `get()` or erased with `erase()`. Individual items can be erased with `erase(Key)`.

We sometimes wish to access the same global data in many different functions and it can be somewhat inconvenient to pass this data as arguments to all functions in a process. This can be avoided by careful use of `put` and `get`.

The use of `get` and `put` introduces destructive operations into the language and allows the programmer to write functions with side-effects. The result of evaluating such functions may depend upon the order in which they are evaluated. The process dictionary should be used with *extreme care*. `get` and `put` are analogous to *goto*s in conventional imperative languages; they are useful in certain restricted circumstances but their use leads to unclear programs and should be avoided wherever possible. None of the programs in this book makes use of the process dictionary since we do not wish to encourage its use – it is included here and in the appendices for completeness.

```
spawn(N,M,F,A) when N /= node() ->
    monitor_node(N, true),
    {net_kernel, N} ! {self(), spawn, M, F, A, group_leader()},
    receive
        {nodedown, N} ->
             R = spawn(erlang, crasher, [N,M,F,A,noconnection]);
        {spawn_reply, Pid} ->
             R = Pid
    end,
    monitor_node(N, false),
    R;
spawn(N,M,F,A) ->
    spawn(M,F,A).

crasher(Node,Mod,Fun,Args,Reason) ->
    exit(Reason).
```

This code will result in a message to the `net_kernel` at the remote node. The remote `net_kernel` is responsible for creating a new process, and replying to the client with the Pid of the new process.

9.7.1 Authentication

The ERLANG system has built-in support for authentication which uses the idea of 'magic cookies'. A magic cookie is a secret atom assigned to each node. When started, each node is automatically assigned a random cookie. In order for node `N1` to communicate with node `N2`, it must know which magic cookie `N2` has. How `N1` finds out what `N2`'s cookie is, is not discussed here. For `N1` to communicate with `N2` it must evaluate `erlang:set_cookie(N2, N2Cookie)` where `N2Cookie` is the value of `N2`'s cookie. In addition, for `N1` to be able to receive a response from `N2`, `N2` must evaluate `erlang:set_cookie(N1, N1Cookie)` where `N1Cookie` is the value of `N1`'s cookie.

The ERLANG run-time system will insert the cookie in all messages it sends to all remote nodes. If a message arrives at a node with the wrong cookie, the run-time system will transform that message into a message of the form:

```
{From,badcookie,To,Message}
```

Where `To` is the Pid or the registered name of the intended recepient of the message and `From` is the Pid of the sender. All unauthorised attempts either to send a message or to spawn a process will be transformed into `badcookie` messages and sent to the `net_kernel`. The `net_kernel` can choose to do whatever it likes with these `badcookie` messages.

Two BIFs are used to manipulate cookies:

9.7 The Net Kernel

The `net_kernel` is a process which is used used to coordinate operations in distributed ERLANG system. The run-time system automatically sends certa messages to the `net_kernel`. The code executing in this process decides whi action to take when different system messages arrive.

An ERLANG system can be run in one of two modes. It can either run as a clos system which cannot communicate with other ERLANG systems, or it can run a system which can communicate with other systems, in which case it is said be *alive*. A system is made alive by evaluating the BIF `alive/2`. This is normal done by the ERLANG operating system and not by the user directly. The call:

```
erlang:alive(Name, Port)
```

informs a network name server that an ERLANG system has been started and available to cooperate in distributed computations.

`Name` is a atom containing the local name by which the ERLANG system w be known. The external name of this ERLANG system will be `Name@MachineNar` where `MachineName` is the name of the machine where the node resides and the cha acter `'@'` is used to separate the local name and the machine name. For exampl evaluating `erlang:alive(foo,Port)` on a host called `super.eua.ericsson.s` will start an ERLANG system with the name `foo@super.eua.ericsson.se` whic is globally unique. Several different ERLANG systems can run on the same machir provided they all have different local names.

`Port` is an ERLANG port. The external port program must comply with th internal ERLANG distribution protocol. This program is responsible for all ne working operations, such as establishing communication channels to remote node and reading or writing buffers of bytes to these nodes. Different versions of th port program allows ERLANG nodes to communicate using different networkin technologies.

Evaluating `alive/2` causes the node evaluating the expression to be added to pool of ERLANG nodes which can engage in distributed computations. The proces evaluating `alive/2` must be registered with the name `net_kernel`. If this is no the case, the BIF will fail. To disconnect a node from the network, the distributio port can be closed.

To check whether an ERLANG system is alive or not, the BIF `is_alive()` car be used. This BIF returns either `true` or `false`.

Whenever a new node becomes known a `{nodeup, Node}` message is sent to the `net_kernel`, and whenever a node fails a `{nodedown, Node}` message is sent to the `net_kernel`. All requests to create new processes with `spawn/4` or `spawn_link/4` as well as all requests to send a message to a remotely registered process with the construction `{Name, Node} ! Message`, go through the `net_kernel` process. This enables user defined `net_kernel` code for different purposes. For example, the BIF `spawn/4` is implemented in ERLANG itself. The client code to create a process at a remote node is:

`erlang:get_cookie()`
: Returns our own magic cookie.

`erlang:set_cookie(Node,Cookie)`
: Sets the magic cookie of `Node` to be `Cookie`. This can be used once the cookie of `Node` has been obtained. It will cause all messages to `Node` to contain `Cookie`. If `Cookie` really is the magic cookie of `Node` the messages will go directly to the recipient at `Node`. If it is the wrong cookie, the message will be transformed into a `badcookie` message at the receiving end, and then sent to the `net_kernel` there.

By default all nodes assume that the atom `nocookie` is the cookie of all other nodes, thus initially all remote messages will contain the cookie `nocookie`.

If the value of `Node` in the call `erlang:set_cookie(Node, Cookie)` is the name of the local node then the magic cookie of the local node is set to `Cookie`, in addition, all other nodes having cookies with the value `nocookie` have their cookie changed to `Cookie`. If all nodes start by evaluating:

```
erlang:set_cookie(node(), SecretCookie),
```

then they will all automatically be authenticated to cooperate with each other. How the application obtains the `SecretCookie` is a local issue. The secret cookie could be stored in a read-by-user, or read-by-group only file.

In a UNIX environment the default behaviour when starting a node is to read a file in the user's HOME directory called `.erlang.cookie`. A check is done to ensure that the file is properly protected, and `erlang:set_cookie(node(), Cookie)` is then evaluated, where `Cookie` is the contents of the cookie file as an atom. Hence the same user will be able to communicate safely with all other ERLANG nodes which are running with the same user id (assuming that the nodes reside on the same file system). If the nodes reside on different file systems, the user must only ensure that the cookie file on all involved file systems are identical.

9.7.2 The net_kernel messages

The following is a list of the messages which can be sent to the `net_kernel`:

- `{From,registered_send,To,Mess}` A request to send the message `Mess` to the registered process `To`.
- `{From,spawn,M,F,A,Gleader}` A request to create a new process. `Gleader` is the group leader of the requesting process.
- `{From,spawn_link,M,F,A,Gleader}` A request to create a new process and set up a link to the new process.
- `{nodeup,Node}` Whenever the system gets connected to a new node, this message is sent to the `net_kernel`. This can either be the result of a remote node contacting us, or that a process running at this node tried (successfully) to do a remote operation for the first time.

- `{nodedown,Node}` Whenever an existing node fails or a local attempt to contact a remote node fails, this message is sent to the `net_kernel`.
- `{From,badcookie,To,Mess}` Whenever a non-authenticated attempt to communicate with this node is done, a message indicating the nature of the attempt is sent to the `net_kernel`. For example, an attempt to create a new process from an un-authenticated node, will result in a

  `{From,badcookie, net_kernel, {From,spawn,M,F,A,Gleader}}`

  message being sent to the `net_kernel`.

Since the `net_kernel` runs as a user-defined process, it is possible to modify it to employ different user-defined authentication schemas. For example, if we want to have a node that disallows all remote interactions except messages sent to a special safe process called `safe`, we merely have to let our `net_kernel` ignore all attempts to create new processes and all attempts to send a message to any other process but the one called `safe`.

9.8 Hashing

ERLANG has a BIF which produces an integer hash value from an arbitrary term:

`hash(Term, MaxInt)`
: Returns an integer in the range `1..MaxInt`.

We can use the `hash` BIF to write a highly efficient dictionary lookup program. The interface to this program is almost identical to the binary tree implementation of a dictionary given in Section 4.4

```
-module(tupleStore).
-export([new/0,new/1,lookup/2,add/3,delete/2]).

new() ->
    new(256).

new(NoOfBuckets) ->
    make_tuple(NoOfBuckets, []).

lookup(Key, Tuple) ->
    lookup_in_list(Key, element(hash(Key, size(Tuple)), Tuple)).

add(Key, Value, Tuple) ->
    Index = hash(Key, size(Tuple)),
    Old   = element(Index, Tuple),
    New   = replace(Key, Value, Old, []),
    setelement(Index, Tuple, New).
```

```
delete(Key, Tuple) ->
    Index = hash(Key, size(Tuple)),
    Old   = element(Index, Tuple),
    New   = delete(Key, Old, []),
    setelement(Index, Tuple, New).

make_tuple(Length, Default) ->
    make_tuple(Length, Default, []).

make_tuple(0, _, Acc) ->
    list_to_tuple(Acc);
make_tuple(N, Default, Acc) ->
    make_tuple(N-1, Default, [Default|Acc]).

delete(Key, [{Key,_}|T], Acc) ->
    lists:append(T, Acc);
delete(Key, [H|T], Acc) ->
    delete(Key, T, [H|Acc]);
delete(Key, [], Acc) ->
    Acc.

replace(Key, Value, [], Acc) ->
    [{Key,Value}|Acc];
replace(Key, Value, [{Key,_}|T], Acc) ->
    [{Key,Value}|lists:append(T, Acc)];
replace(Key, Value, [H|T], Acc) ->
    replace(Key, Value, T, [H|Acc]).

lookup_in_list(Key, []) ->
    undefined;
lookup_in_list(Key, [{Key, Value}|_]) ->
    {value, Value};
lookup_in_list(Key, [_|T]) ->
    lookup_in_list(Key, T).
```

Program 9.4

The only difference between this and Program 4.4 is in the function **new/1**, where we need to supply the size of the hash table.

Program 9.4 is a simple implementation of a conventional hash lookup program. The hash table, `T`, is represented as a fixed size tuple. To lookup the value of the term `Key` a hash index, `I`, is computed in the range `1..size(T)`. `element(I, T)` contains a list of all `{Key, Value}` pairs which hash to the same index. This list is searched for the desired `{Key, Value}` pair.

To insert in the hash table `Key` is hashed to an integer index `I`, and a new `{Key, Value}` pair is inserted into the list found in `element(I, T)` of the hash table. Any old association with `Key` is lost.

The module `tupleStore` provides a highly efficient dictionary. For efficient access the size of the hash table should be larger than the number of elements to be inserted in the table. While lookup in such a structure is highly efficient, insertion is less so. This is because in most implementations of ERLANG the `setelement(Index, Val, T)` BIF creates an entirely new copy of the tuple `T` each time it is called.

9.9 Efficiency

The topic of efficiency comes last in our discussion of miscellaneous items. This is not because we consider the topic unimportant but because we believe that premature concern for efficiency often leads to poor program design. The primary concern must always be one of correctness, and to this aim we encourage the development of small and beautiful algorithms which are 'obviously' correct.

As an example we show how an inefficient program can be turned into an efficient program.

As an exercise we start with a file of tuples with information about employees at a fictitious company, the file has entries such as:

```
{202191,'Micky','Finn','MNO','OM',2431}.
{102347,'Harvey','Wallbanger','HAR','GHE',2420}.
... 2860 lines omitted ...
{165435,'John','Doe','NKO','GYI', 2564}.
{457634,'John', 'Bull','HMR','KIO', 5436}.
```

We want to write a program which inputs this data, builds each item into a dictionary accesses each item once, and writes the data back to a file. We want to run this program on a routine basis so we should make it as efficient as possible.

We will treat the input/output and access parts of the problem separately.

9.9.1 File access

The simplest approach we could use to input the file of tuples described above would be to use `file:consult(File)` to read the file (see Appendix C) – this takes rather a long time since each line has to be read and then parsed. A better approach is to change the format of the input file from a text to a binary file. This can be done as with the following function:

```
reformat(FileOfTerms, BinaryFile) ->
    {ok, Terms} = file:consult(FileOfTerms),
    file:write_file(BinaryFile, term_to_binary(Terms)).
```

To read the binary file and recover the original data we evaluate:

```
read_terms(BinaryFile) ->
    {ok, Binary} = file:read(BinaryFile),
    binary_to_term(Binary).
```

Reading a binary file and converting the result to a term is a lot faster than reading and parsing a list of terms, as can be seen from the following table:

Text Size bytes	Binary Size bytes	`file:consult` ms	`read_terms` ms	Ratio of times
128041	118123	42733	783	54.6
4541	4190	1433	16	89.6

For a 4.5 Kbyte file reading was 90 times faster and for a 128 Kbyte file 55 times faster; note also that the resulting binary file is somewhat smaller than the text file.

9.9.2 Dictionary access

We used three different methods to build and update a dictionary of employees. These methods were:

`lists`
: All employees records are kept in a list. Initial insertion is done by adding to the head of the list and updating by a linear scan through the list.

`avl`
: The AVL tree insertion algorithms of Section 4.6.

`hash`
: The hashing algorithm of Program 9.4.

To see the effect of these different methods we did a single insertion and single lookup of each tuple in our employee data, this yielded the following timings:

#entries	AVL insert	AVL lookup	list insert	list lookup	hash insert	hash lookup
25	5.32	0.00	0.00	0.64	1.32	0.00
50	1.32	0.32	0.00	1.00	0.32	0.00
100	2.00	0.50	0.00	1.50	0.33	0.16
200	9.91	0.50	0.00	3.00	2.08	0.17
400	28.29	0.46	0.04	5.96	4.25	0.09
800	301.38	0.54	0.02	11.98	1.77	0.15
1600	1060.44	0.61	0.02	24.20	4.05	0.14

In the above table the units are milliseconds per insertion or milliseconds per lookup. We see that for tables of size greater that 800 hash lookup is always the fastest lookup method.

From the above we can see that a program which used binary file input together with a hash algorithm for lookup would be approximately six thousand times faster than a program using `file:consult` togther with a simple list lookup method. As with conventional imperative languages, the most important factor determining program efficiency is good algorithm design.

Part II

Applications

Chapter 10

Databases

In this chapter we show how databases can be programmed in ERLANG. We also implement transaction-based systems with features such as locking, roll-back and fault tolerance. All the examples in this chapter store data in *dictionaries*. See Section 4.4 for a description of a dictionary and its interface. The same interface is used in this chapter.

10.1 The Access Functions

The different databases presented in this chapter use the same access interface defined in module `dbaccess` as follows:

`read(Dbase, Key)`
: Read the value associated with `Key` in the database `Dbase`. `{value,Value}` is returned if the key was defined, otherwise the atom `undefined`.

`write(Dbase, Key, Value)`
: Associate `Value` with `Key` in the database `Dbase` and delete any previous value associated with that key. Return `ok` when done.

`delete(Dbase, Key)`
: Delete any association that `Key` may have in the database `Dbase`. Return `ok` when done.

Program 10.1 gives an example of such an interface. The structure of the database programs follows that of the client–server model as described in Section 5.5. A synchronous protocol is used here, but no assumptions are made as to which process actually replies to the request; this feature will be used later. These interface functions isolate the user from details of the protocol used.

```
-module(dbaccess).
-export([read/2,write/3,delete/2]).

read(Key, Dbase) ->
    request(Dbase, {read,Key}).

write(Key, Value, Dbase) ->
    request(Dbase, {write,Key,Value}).

delete(Key, Dbase) ->
    request(Dbase, {delete,Key}).

request(To, Request) ->
    To ! {self(),Request},
    receive
        {db_reply,Reply} ->
            Reply
    end.
```

Program 10.1

10.2 Simple Database

The first database is a simple server process which provides an interface to the dictionary functions. In Program 10.2 a new dictionary is created in a process spawned by the function `start/0`. This process evaluates the function `server/1` which waits for, and processes, requests. We use an `import` declaration so we need not qualify every call to the dictionary functions with the module name `dictionary`.

Sending of messages is shown in Figure 10.1 where the server process sends the replies back to the client processes.

We have been careful to write `server` in a *tail recursive* manner so that the last call optimisation will ensure that it evaluates in constant space.[1] This is critical for processes that are perpetual, or at least live a long time.

[1]Except, of course, for the space required for the dictionary.

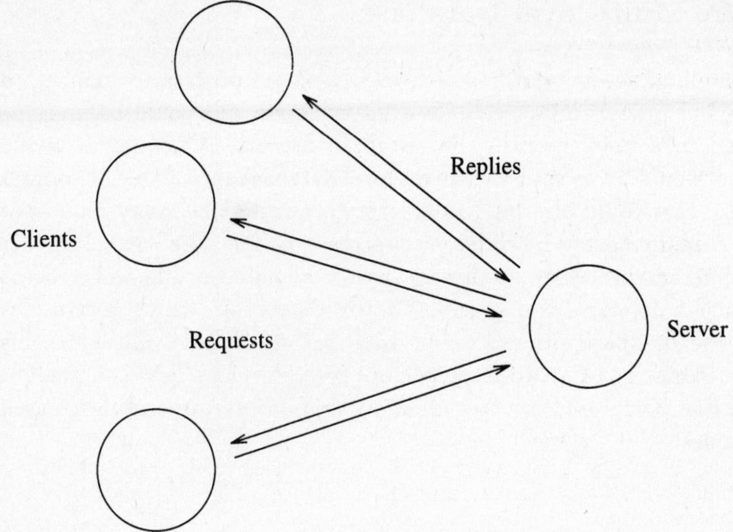

Figure 10.1

```
-module(db1).
-export([start/0,server/1]).
-import(dictionary, [new/0,lookup/2,add/3,delete/2]).

start() -> spawn(db1, server, [new()]).

server(Dict) ->
    receive
        {From,{read,Key}} ->
            From ! {db_reply,lookup(Key, Dict)},
            server(Dict);
        {From,{write,Key,Value}} ->
            NewDict = add(Key, Value, Dict),
            From ! {db_reply,ok},              %Reply after access
            server(NewDict);
        {From,{delete,Key}} ->
            NewDict = delete(Key, Dict),
            From ! {db_reply,ok},              %Reply after access
            server(NewDict)
    end.
```

Program 10.2

10.3 A Multi-level Database

The example in the previous section used a single process to manage the whole database and process all queries. In a large system this could be undesirable and could lead to a bottleneck in the database process. One way to avoid such a bottleneck would be to split the single-level database into a tree of communicating processes. This could also lead to greater throughput as many requests could be handled simultaneously by different processes in the database. In a distributed system different processes in the database could be on different processors. To access such a database the *key* must have a structure which determines how to traverse the database process tree. In Program 10.3 we illustrate this with a database consisting of a two-level tree of processes. The 'key' is actually a pair of keys, the first being used to determine to which process to send the remaining part of the request.

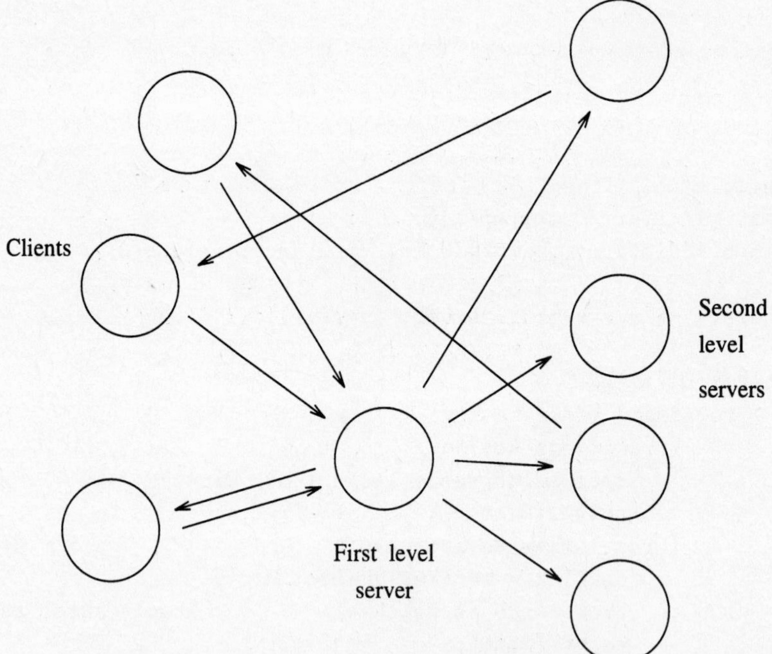

Figure 10.2 Two-level database communication

The first level of the server uses a dictionary to store the association between the first key and the second level server process which handles *all* the data associated with that key. When the database is first started only the first level server is created. When a request is received the server first determines if there is a second level which handles the key. If so, the request is forwarded to the second level in

```
-module(db2).
-export([start/0,server/1]).
-import(dictionary, [new/0,lookup/2,add/3,delete/2]).

start() ->
    spawn(db2, server, [new()]).

server(Dict) ->
    receive
        {From,{read,{Key1,Key2}}} ->
            case lookup(Key1, Dict) of
                {value,S2} ->
                    S2 ! {From,{read,Key2}};
                undefined ->
                    From ! {db_reply,undefined}
            end,
            server(Dict);
        {From,{write,{Key1,Key2},Value}} ->
            case lookup(Key1, Dict) of
                {value,S2} ->
                    S2 ! {From,{write,Key2,Value}},
                    server(Dict);
                undefined ->
                    S2 = spawn(db1, server, [new()]),
                    S2 ! {From,{write,Key2,Value}},
                    server(add(Key1, S2, Dict))
            end;
        {From,{delete,{Key1,Key2}}} ->
            case lookup(Key1, Dict) of
                {value,S2} ->
                    S2 ! {From,{delete,Key2}};
                undefined ->
                    From ! {db_reply,ok}
            end,
            server(Dict)
    end.
```

Program 10.3

exactly the same format as it was received, otherwise the first level server replies. If the request is to associate a value with a *new* first key then a *new* second level server is created. For simplicity, we use the simple database defined in the previous section as the second level server. As there is no protocol between the two levels, we cannot completely remove a second level server if all the data in that server has been deleted.

As shown in Figure 10.2, sometimes the first level server replies to the original request, and sometimes a second level server.

10.4 Transaction Management

The databases shown previously can give inconsistent results if two or more programs which are accessing them run simultaneously (*concurrently*). In this section we will show how concurrent operations can be allowed while still preserving the integrity of the database by introducing the notion of a transaction. The whole discussion will be at a fairly simple level; for a detailed discussion of the problem see [27].

A *transaction* is a single execution of a program which can contain a single query or a sequence of queries embedded in a program. Managing transactions consists mainly of trying to make these complex operations appear to be *atomic* – that is, to make it appear as if either all the queries in a transaction succeed, or none of the queries occurred. If they do succeed it must appear as if nothing else went on during that time.

An *item* is the unit of data to which access is controlled. The most common way to control access to items is by locks. A *lock* is an access privilege to an item. There are many types of lock but in our examples we use only one type which allows complete access to an item. To ensure that the (concurrent) programs accessing the database are 'well behaved' and the database remains consistent a locking protocol is required. The simplest and most popular is the *two-phase protocol* which requires that all locks precede all unlocks. We will use a simplified, very *conservative*, version of this protocol where all locks are requested at the beginning of the transaction and released at the end.

10.4.1 Atomicity

To add atomic transactions to our database we add two new functions to our access module:

`lock(Dbase, ListOfItems)`
: Request locks on all items in `ListOfItems`. Return `ok` when all the locks have been granted.

`unlock(Dbase)`
: Release all locks held by the current process and tell the database to accept all the operations done on the database since we locked it. Return `ok` when done.

These two access functions have the same synchronous protocol as those defined previously but send the messages `{lock,Items}` and `unlock`, respectively.

In this model all locks on a database will be associated with the process to which they were initially granted. This means that a process can only perform one transaction at a time on each database.

```
-module(db_lock).
-export([start/0,server/1]).
-import(dictionary, [new/0,lookup/2,add/3,delete/2]).

start() ->
    spawn(db_lock, server, [new()]).

server(Dict) ->
    receive
        {From,{lock,Items}} ->
            From ! {db_reply,ok},
            locked_server(Dict, From)          %Lock the database
    end.

locked_server(Dict, Locker) ->
    receive
        {Locker,{read,Key}} ->
            Locker ! {db_reply,lookup(Key, Dict)},
            locked_server(Dict, Locker);
        {Locker,{write,Key,Value}} ->
            NewDict = add(Key, Value, Dict),
            Locker ! {db_reply,ok},
            locked_server(NewDict, Locker);
        {Locker,{delete,Key}} ->
            NewDict = delete(Key, Dict),
            Locker ! {db_reply,ok},
            locked_server(NewDict, Locker);
        {Locker,unlock} ->
            Locker ! {db_reply,ok},
            server(Dict)                       %Unlock the database
    end.
```

Program 10.4

In Program 10.4 we define a transaction-based database in which another process can request a lock, perform the operations in the transaction and then release the lock. To simplify the problem we will assume that requesting *any* lock on the database will lock the entire database. Note that we ignore the variable `Items` in

database. The actual implementation of these is very dependent on the actual database being accessed and is not important here.

The functions in the interface are the same as in the previous database examples with one addition:

`open(DataBaseName)`
: Open the external database called `DataBaseName` and return a reference to be used with the other functions.

10.5.2 A simple external database

We assume that the external database can only be used for storing the data and keeping the `Key-Value` associations. It has no facilities for doing transaction processing, which means that we have to implement these features in ERLANG. This could be done in two different ways:

- We could make all modifications to the external database as we receive requests and keep a log of all the changes. Then if we need to abort the transaction we could retract the transaction using this log. The database, however, could then present an inconsistent view to another user (not this ERLANG system) while a transaction was in progress. Also, if the database server process were to crash in the middle of a transaction then any changes made will already have been written to the database with little chance of recovery. This could be managed by keeping an external log.
- We could keep an internal cache of all changes made to the database in our server and not write anything to the database until we (locally) unlocked it. This is much safer and will be the method we choose. Note, however, that the database still has to manage simultaneous updates.

We lock the whole external database in the same way as was done with our implementation which used the local dictionary. This locking mechanism in the external database is simple compared to one which would be necessary to allow multiple access. The external interface will, as before, still have a list of items which we wish to lock. The external database must be locked so as to appear consistent to *other* users – we provide the roll-back mechanism and fault-tolerance.

Program 10.8 is a fault-tolerant, transaction-based interface with roll-back to an external database without these features. The code is very similar to that for an internal database with the same features. The accesses, however, are markedly different. A `write` or `delete` request will *not* result in any changes being made to the external database; it will be cached in a list of modify operations requested during this transaction. The list is kept in reverse order so that when searching it for a specific key the last operation for that key will be found first. A `read` request will *first look in the cache* for any operations made on that key; if none is found then it will access the database. The function `cache_lookup` implements this.

```
-module(db_extern).
-export([start/1,server/1]).
-import(ext_dict,[open/1,lock/2,unlock/1,
                  lookup/2,add/3,delete/2]).

start(ExternName) ->
    spawn(db_extern, server, [open(ExternName)]).

server(ExtDb) ->
    process_flag(trap_exit, true),
    unlocked_server(ExtDb).

%% Cache utility functions.
cache_lookup(Key, [{write,Key,Value}|Cache], ExtDb) ->
    {value,Value};
cache_lookup(Key, [{delete,Key}|Cache], ExtDb) ->
    undefined;
cache_lookup(Key, [Entry|Cache], ExtDb) ->
    cache_lookup(Key, Cache, ExtDb);
cache_lookup(Key, [], ExtDb) ->
    lookup(Key, ExtDb).

cache_write([{write,Key,Value}|Cache], ExtDb) ->
    add(Key, Value, ExtDb),
    cache_write(cache_strip(Key, Cache), ExtDb);
cache_write([{delete,Key}|Cache], ExtDb) ->
    delete(Key, ExtDb),
    cache_write(cache_strip(Key, Cache), ExtDb);
cache_write([], ExtDb) ->
    ok.

cache_strip(Key, [{write,Key,Value}|Cache]) ->
    cache_strip(Key, Cache);
cache_strip(Key, [{delete,Key}|Cache]) ->
    cache_strip(Key, Cache);
cache_strip(Key, [Entry|Cache]) ->
    [Entry|cache_strip(Key, Cache)];
cache_strip(Key, []) ->
    [].
```

Program 10.8

```
unlocked_server(ExtDb) ->
    receive
         {From,{lock,Items}} ->
            link(From),
            lock(Items, ExtDb),
            From ! {db_reply,ok},
            locked_server(ExtDb, From)          %Lock the database
    end.

locked_server(ExtDb, Locker) ->
    locked_server(ExtDb, Locker, []).

locked_server(ExtDb, Locker, Cache) ->
    receive
        {Locker,{read,Key}} ->
            Locker ! {db_reply,cache_lookup(Key, Cache, ExtDb)},
            locked_server(ExtDb, Locker, Cache);
        {Locker,{write,Key,Value}} ->
            Locker ! {db_reply,ok},
            locked_server(ExtDb, Locker,
                          [{write,Key,Value}|Cache]);
        {Locker,{delete,Key}} ->
            Locker ! {db_reply,ok},
            locked_server(ExtDb, Locker, [{delete,Key}|Cache]);
        {Locker,unlock} ->                      %Commit and unlock
            cache_write(Cache, ExtDb),
            unlock(ExtDb),
            Locker ! {db_reply,ok},
            unlocked_server(ExtDb);
        {Locker,abort} ->                       %Abort and unlock
            unlock(ExtDb),
            Locker ! {db_reply,ok},
            unlink(Locker),
            unlocked_server(ExtDb);
        {'EXIT',Locker,Reason} ->               %Abort and unlock
            unlock(ExtDb),
            unlocked_server(ExtDb)
    end.
```

Program 10.8(cont)

When the transaction is completed successfully all the cached operations will be written to the external database. The function `cache_write` does this. Only the first operation encountered in this list must be written, since this operation overrides all the previous ones. In `cache_write` we call the function `cache_strip` for each operation encountered to remove other operations on this key in the cache. This could have been done instead each time an entry was added to the cache.

Chapter 11

Distributed Programming Techniques

The type of distributed systems which we consider here is one where several computers cooperate by sending messages over a communications network.

There are a number of major difficulties that have to be solved when designing a distributed system which is to be run on a set of cooperating computers. These include heterogeneity of the computer systems themselves, network delays, network errors, lack of a common clock and lack of a common address space.

Another important problem that has to be solved is naming. In ERLANG a Pid can be used from any node in the system. The Pid can refer to a process on the local node or on a remote node. Most operations involving Pids work in the same manner irrespective of whether the Pid refers to a local or a remote process. In particular, we can send messages to a Pid without knowing if the Pid refers to a local or remote process.

It is also necessary to be able to design services which are *location transparent*. This means that we must be able to write network clients which are unaware of the location of certain services.

This and the following chapter provide ERLANG solutions to these problems. We start by introducing several well-known techniques for programming distributed systems. These are:

- Remote procedure call, the ability to evaluate a function transparently on a remote node. This technique was originally described in [6].
- Broadcasting, the ability to send a message to a registered process on all nodes in the network.
- Promises, an asynchronous variant of remote procedure call, originally introduced in [21].
- Global name servers, the equivalent of the BIF `register/2`, for a number of nodes.
- Distributed named process groups.
- Load distribution, the ability to find out the best node to allocate to the 'next' job.

- Parallel evaluation.

These techniques (and others) are the basic building blocks for the construction of truly distributed systems. Note that many operating systems provide complex mechanisms such as RPC, global name servers, etc. as components of their systems. ERLANG, however, provides simpler primitives from which such mechanisms can be constructed. The remainder of this chapter shows how this can be done.

11.1 Remote Procedure Calls (RPC)

One of the best known programming techniques used in programming distributed systems is the RPC. This is a technique for evaluating a function transparently on a remote node. RPCs work like the client–server model in Section 5.5 except that the client and server may reside on different nodes and that the server is a simple loop which just evaluates functions on behalf of the client.

For example, the functions which provide an interface to a file system can be implemented as client functions to an RPC-server which manages the file system. The programmer need not be concerned with the details of directly talking to the node that manages the files. The programmer can manipulate the files as if they were located on the local host.

An RPC typically involves the following steps, often referred to as marshalling and unmarshalling:

- On the local node we take the name of a function and its arguments. Pack these into a network package and send the package to the node that is to execute the Procedure Call.

- On the remote node we unpack the network package and call the appropriate function.

- On the remote node we pack the result of the function call in a network message and send the result back to the originator.

- On the local node we unpack the result from the network and send it to the caller.

In ERLANG these steps are invisible to the programmer since sending a local message is performed in the same manner as sending a message to a process residing on a remote node.

To implement this in ERLANG we ensure that there is a server with the registered name `rpc` running on all nodes which receives requests to evaluate functions. This is shown in Program 11.1.

```
-module(rpc)
-export([start/0,loop/0,reply/4,call/4]).

start() ->
    register(rpc, spawn(rpc, loop, [])).

loop() ->
    receive
        {Client, {apply, Mod, Fun, Args}}  ->
            spawn(rpc, reply, [Client, Mod, Fun, Args]),
            loop()
    end.

reply(Client, Mod, Fun, Args) ->
    Client ! {rpc, node(), catch apply(Mod, Fun, Args)}.


call(Node, Mod, Fun, Args) ->
    monitor_node(Node, true),
    {rpc, Node} ! {self(), {apply, Mod, Fun, Args}},
    receive
        {rpc, Node, {'EXIT', Reason}} ->
            monitor_node(Node, false),
            {badrpc, Reason};
        {rpc, Node, What} ->
            monitor_node(Node, false),
            What;
        {nodedown, Node} ->
            {badrpc, {nodedown, Node}}
    end.
```

Program 11.1

This can be used as follows:

```
Eshell V4.1
1> L1 = [a,ee,rr,tt].
[a,ee,rr,tt]
2> L2 = [5,6,7].
[5,6,7]
3> Node = 'foobar@gin.eua.ericsson.se'.
'foobar@gin.eua.ericsson.se'
4> rpc:call(Node,lists,append,[L1,L2]).
[a,ee,rr,tt,5,6,7]
```

which appends two lists at a remote node. As another example we may wish to find the Pid of the registered process `init` on some node:

```
5> Pid = rpc:call(Node,erlang,whereis,[init])
<18.0.1>
```

Since all BIFs are defined in the module `erlang`, this method can be used to call a BIF as an RPC. Note that the `rpc` server spawns a new process for each request. This means that the same `rpc` server can concurrently execute several RPCs. This type of server is often referred to as a concurrent server, as opposed to an iterative server which processes requests one at a time in the order in which they arrive. One major advantage of the concurrent server is that if an individual request hangs, the server continues to service new requests.

Note the use of `monitor_node/2`. The client call is encapsulated within a matching pair of `monitor_node/2`s. This guarantees that a call to `rpc:call/4` always returns.

The reason we let the `rpc` server respond with the tuple `{rpc, node(), Value}` instead of the simpler `{rpc, Value}`, is that later on we will use the `rpc` server for more than just simple RPCs.

The observant reader may wonder why the RPC was not implemented as:

```
call(N,M,F,A) ->
    Id = spawn_link(N,rpc,call_and_respond, [self(),M,F,A]),
    receive
        {Id, Answer} ->
            Answer;
        {'EXIT', Id, Reason} ->
            exit(Reason)
    end.

call_and_respond(To, M, F, A) ->
    To ! {self(), catch apply(M, F, A)}.
```

This version actually involves three network messages:

- The request to `spawn_link/4` the function.
- The Pid of the spawned process.
- The response.

This is slower. On the other hand it does not need an `rpc` server to run on all nodes, which is definitely an advantage.[1] This is not yet a true RPC, since the caller must state on which node the call is to be evaluated. It is a simple matter to hide this and in Section 11.4 we show one technique to do this.

Compared to other implementations of a remote procedure call facility there is *no special interface language*. Consequently, this RPC is more general since we do not have to decide at compile-time which functions are to be called remotely.

[1] There is no free lunch.

We now show some code which uses the RPC facility. The BIF `process_info/1` returns some information about a local process, but does not work on remote processes. A version which works on remote Pids as well as local Pids is as follows:

```
my_process_info(Pid) when node(Pid) == node() ->
    process_info(Pid);
my_process_info(Pid) ->
    rpc:call(node(Pid),erlang,process_info,[Pid]).
```

Furthermore, the BIF `processes/0` only returns the Pids of the processes that are running on the local node. The following function returns the Pids of all the running processes in the network:

```
all_processes() ->
    lists:flatten(all_processes([node()|nodes()])).

all_processes([]) -> [];
all_processes([Node|Tail]) ->
    [rpc:call(Node,erlang,processes,[]) |
    all_processes(Tail)].
```

Note that our own node identity is not part of the list of nodes returned by the `nodes/0` BIF, so it has to be added to the head of the list to get the local processes as well.

The RPC shown here is both efficient and general but we had to state explicitly in the source code which node we wanted to execute the function on. Later on we will show how to hide this in a name server.

11.2 Multicalls

The RPC calls a function on a remote node and returns the answer. The reason for calling a function on a remote node instead of on the local node could be either that the function performs some desirable side-effect on that node or that we want to collect some information that is only available on that node. Examples of side-effects could be to load some new code or manipulate some hardware that is connected to the remote node.

If we want to perform some operation on a list of nodes we could of course sequentially do an RPC on all the nodes in the list. For example:

```
multicall(M,F,A) ->
    multi_call([node()|nodes()], M, F, A).
```

```
multicall([], _, _, _) ->
    [];
multicall([Node|Tail], M, F, A) ->
    [rpc:call(Node, M, F, A)|multicall(Tail, M, F, A)].
```

It is, however, much more efficient to first send out all the requests to call the function, and then collect all the answers. This is done as follows:

```
multicall(M, F, A) ->
    multicall([node()|nodes()], M, F, A).
multicall(Nodes, M, F, A) ->
    send(Nodes, M, F, A),
    receive_nodes(Nodes, [], []).

send([], _, _, _) ->
    ok;
send([N|Tail], M, F, A) ->
    monitor_node(N, true),
    {rpc, N} ! {self(), {apply, M, F, A}},
    send(Tail, M, F, A).

receive_nodes([], Replies, Bad) ->
    {Replies, Bad};
receive_nodes([Node|Tail], Replies, Bad) ->
    receive
        {rpc, Node, {'EXIT', Reason}} ->
            monitor_node(Node, false),
            receive_nodes(Tail, Replies, [{Node, Reason}|Bad]);
        {rpc, Node, What} ->
            monitor_node(Node, false),
            receive_nodes(Tail, [What|Replies], Bad);
        {nodedown, Node} ->
            receive_nodes(Tail, Replies, [{Node, nodedown}|Bad])
    end.
```

This second version is much more efficient than the first version. It returns a tuple `{Replies, Bad}` where `Replies` is an unordered list of the replies and `Bad` is a list of `{Node, Reason}` tuples for the calls that failed.

Note that both versions of `multicall` come in two versions, one with a specific list of nodes, and one with all nodes we are connected to.

11.3 Broadcasting

Sometimes we want to perform a specific task on all nodes in the network and do not wish to wait for the responses. In this case we just dispatch the requests and then continue to execute without waiting for any of the replies. For example, in a programmer's interactive shell, when we want to load some new re-compiled code on all nodes in the network, we can do this by merely broadcasting a request to load the new code.

The following function sends the message `Message` to the registered process `Name` on all connected nodes or to a specified list of nodes.

```
-module(bc0).
-export([broadcast/2]).

broadcast(Name, Message) ->
    broadcast([node()|nodes()], Name, Message).

broadcast([], _, _) ->
    done;
broadcast([Node|Tail], Name, Message) ->
    {Name, Node} ! Message,
    broadcast(Tail, Name, Message).
```

If all nodes are connected to each other this will have an effect on all nodes in the network. However, if they are not, the message will only be sent to the nodes we are connected to. This is a property of distributed ERLANG that can be avoided in a number of ways. If the application is configured with a predefined set of nodes the problem does not occur.

Another way to avoid the problem is to ensure that the network of ERLANG nodes is always *fully connected*, that is, all nodes are always connected to all the other nodes. As we mentioned in Section 9.7 the `net_kernel` always gets a `{nodeup, Node}` message whenever a new node gets connected. If the `net_kernel` then evaluates the following function, the network will always be fully connected:

```
connect_all(Node) ->
    N = rpc:call(Node, erlang, nodes, []),
    connect_all2(N).

connect_all2({badrpc, _} ->
    ok;
connect_all2([N|Tail]) ->
    ping(N),
    connect_all2(Tail);
connect_all2([]) ->
    ok.
```

```
ping(N) ->
    rpc:call(N, erlang, whereis, [net_kernel]).
```

Here we use the function ping/1 which has the side-effect of setting up a connection to a node if one does not exist.

The term *broadcasting* usually means an asynchronous send operation to an unknown number of recipients. If we have a network of ERLANG nodes that is not fully connected we can use the bc module. This broadcast is synchronous, the function broadcast/2 will only return when the requested operation has been performed on all nodes in the system, even on nodes to which we are not directly connected.

Broadcasting is implemented in Program 11.2.

```
-module(bc).
-export([start/0,broadcast/2, spawn_everywhere/3,bc_loop0/0]).

%% Interface functions
start() -> register(bc, spawn(bc, bc_loop0, [])).

broadcast(Name, Mess) -> do_bc({send, Name, Mess}).

spawn_everywhere(Mod, Fun, Args) ->  do_bc({spawn, Mod, Fun, Args}).

do_bc(Op) ->
    bc ! {self(), local, Op},
    receive
        {bc, Nodes} -> Nodes
    end.

bc_loop0() ->
    process_flag(trap_exit, true),
    bc_loop().

bc_loop() ->
    receive
        {From, operation ,Op} ->
            perform(Op),
            From ! {bc, node(), lists:delete(node(From), nodes())};
        {From, local, Op} ->
            perform(Op),
            Nodes = propagate(Op, nodes(), nodes()),
            From ! {bc, [node()|Nodes]}
    end,
    bc_loop().
```

```
perform({send, Name, Mess}) ->
    catch Name ! Mess;    %% catch in case Name doesn't exist
perform({spawn, Mod, Fun,Args}) ->
    catch spawn(Mod, Fun, Args).

propagate(_, [], Ack) -> Ack;
propagate(Op, Visit, Ack0) ->
    New = send_nodes(Op, Visit, Visit),
    NotVisited = subtract(New, Ack0),
    propagate(Op, NotVisited, union(NotVisited, Ack0)).

send_nodes(Op, [Node|Nodes], Orig) ->
    node_monitor(Node, true),
    {bc, Node} ! {self(), operation, Op},
    send_nodes(Op, Nodes, Orig);
send_nodes(Op, [], Orig) ->
    receive_nodes(Orig).

receive_nodes([]) ->
    [];
receive_nodes(Set0) ->
    receive
        {nodedown, Node} ->   %% oops
            receive_nodes(lists:delete(Node, Set0));
        {bc, Node, Nodes} ->
            node_monitor(Node, false),
            union(Nodes, receive_nodes(lists:delete(Node, Set0)))
    end.

subtract(S, []) ->
    S;
subtract(S, [H|T]) ->
    subtract(lists:delete(H, S), T).

union([], Set)    ->
    Set;
union([H|T], Set) ->
    case lists:member(H, Set) of
        true  -> union(T, Set);
        false -> union(T, [H|Set])
    end.
```

Program 11.2

The algorithm in Program 11.2 works as follows: the originating node `O` sends a message to all nodes it is connected to; it also remembers which these nodes were in the parameter `AckO`. These nodes reply to `O` with all nodes they are connected to, `O` forms the union of all the new nodes, and then subtracts the accumulated nodes `AckO` from the newly acquired nodes in order to form a list of nodes which have *not* been visited. The algorithm continues with this new list until there are no more new nodes.

This algorithm works for all kinds of topologies, is synchronous and reliable.

When the algorithm has been executed once, the topology will be changed. This is due to the fact that the originating node now has communicated with all nodes in the entire system and this node will be *connected* to all nodes. Hence, the second time the algorithm is executed, it will not recurse at all. If we want to restore the network topology to the state it had before the call to `bc:broadcast/2` we can use the following function:

```
broadcast2(Name, Mess) ->
    N = nodes(),
    broadcast(Name, Mess),
    New = subtract(nodes(), N),
    lists:map({erlang, disconnect_node}, [], New).
```

In the remainder of this chapter and the next chapter we will use the `broadcast/2` function given above.

11.4 Global Registration

The RPC in Section 11.1 had the disadvantage that the clients need to know on which node to perform the RPC. It is sometimes desirable to hide the location of a server. This is known as *location transparency*. For example, the physical location of a file server should not be found explicitly in the code. When we write non-distributed programs we use the BIF `register/2` in order to provide a service by name. To be able to write distributed applications in a similar way, we must always access our servers through a special name server. The name server runs on all nodes and maintains a dictionary of `{Name, Pid}` pairs. Whenever the name server receives a request to locate a server by name, it first looks for the name in its local dictionary. If the requested name is not found, the name server creates a new process which uses the multicast function to query all other name servers in the system if they have a server with the requested name in their dictionaries. If a `{Name, Pid}` pair is received from one of the other name servers the pair is cached locally.

The algorithm is highly dynamic and copes with the case where new nodes are started after the server has been registered. It is also efficient since a remote lookup is only made the first time the server is accessed; the second time, the `{Name, Pid}` pair is cached locally. The following code implements a global name service in ERLANG:

```
-module(global).
-export([start/0, whereis_name/1, unregister_name/1,
         register_name/2, send/2]).

%% Internal exports
-export([lookup/2, i_unreg/1, i_whereis/1, send/3,loop/0]).

start() -> register(global, spawn(global, loop, [])).

whereis_name(Name)          ->  req({whereis, Name}).
register_name(Name, Pid) ->  req({register, Name, Pid}).
send(Name, Mess)            ->  req({send,Name, Mess}).
unregister_name(Name)       ->  rpc:multicall(global, i_unreg, [Name]).

%% Local functions
i_unreg(Name) ->     req({unregister, Name}).
i_whereis(Name) ->  req({i_whereis, Name}).


lookup(From, Name) ->
    {L,_} = rpc:multicall(nodes(), global, i_whereis,[Name]),
    reply(From, L).

req(R) ->
    global ! {self(), R},
    receive
        {global, Reply} -> Reply
    end.

send(From, Name, Mess) ->
    case lookup(From, Name) of
        undefined -> ignore;
        Pid -> Pid ! Mess
    end.
```

```
reply(From, []) ->
    From ! {global, undefined},
    undefined;
reply(From, [{value, {Name, Pid}} |_]) ->
    global:register_name(Name, Pid),
    From ! {global, Pid},
    Pid;
reply(From, [_|Tail]) ->
    reply(From, Tail).

loop() ->
    process_flag(trap_exit, true),
    loop([]).

loop(Globs) ->
    receive
        {From, {whereis, Name}}  ->
            case lists:keysearch(Name, 1, Globs) of
                {value, {Name, Pid}} ->
                    From ! {global, Pid};
                false ->
                    spawn(global, lookup, [From, Name])
            end,
            loop(Globs);
        {From, {i_whereis, Name}} ->
            From ! {global, lists:keysearch(Name, 1, Globs)},
            loop(Globs);
        {From, {i_unreg, Name}} ->
            loop(delete(1, Name, Globs));
        {From, {register,Name, Pid}} ->
            link(Pid),
            From ! {global, ok},
            loop([{Name, Pid}, Globs]);
        {From, {send, Name, Mess}} ->
            case lists:keysearch(Name, 1, Globs) of
                {value, {Name, Pid}} ->
                    catch Pid ! Mess;
                false ->
                    spawn(global, send, [From, Name, Mess])
            end,
            loop(Globs);
        {'EXIT', Pid, _} ->
            loop(delete(2, Pid, Globs))
    end.
```

```
delete(_, _, []) -> [];
delete(Pos, Item, [H|Tail]) when element(Pos, H) == Item ->
    do_unlink(H),
    delete(Pos, Item, Tail);
delete(Pos, Item, [X |Tail]) -> [X | delete(Pos, Item, Tail)].

do_unlink({Name, Pid}) -> unlink(Pid).
```

Program 11.3

Note how the server links to the registered Pid in order to provide automatic un-registration. We also allow several Pids to be registered with the same name. It could be argued that we should not allow this but we will ignore this for now.

Also note how the server starts a new process to evaluate the call to `multicall/3`. This is necessary since we could otherwise get into the situation where two `global` servers were deadlocked, both waiting for the other to reply to a multicall. This is avoided by creating a new process to perform the multicall.

An obvious optimisation that could be made is to store the `{Name,Pid}` pairs in a data structure which provides faster lookup than a sequential list. This could, for example, be the hash dictionary discussed in Section 9.8. It is essential that `send/2` is efficient.

Some servers need to be locally registered, for example, the servers associated with getting input from a terminal. If, however, we wish a server to be globally registered we can use the code in module `global` to register the server. A globally registered server works both in the single node case and also when multiple nodes are involved. An example of when it is appropriate to use a globally registered name is the following: assume that we are writing some experimental software to control some hardware via an RS-232 serial connection to some hardware. The RS-232 cable can only be connected to one node. This node runs code to control all IO on the RS-232 connection. For example:

```
start() ->
    Rs232 = open_tty(),
    global:register_name(rs232, self()),
    control_loop(Rs232).

control_loop(Rs232) ->
    receive
        {From, {put_char, Ch}} ->
            do_put_char(Rs232, Ch),
            From ! {rs232, ok};
        .......
            .......
```

One client function could be a function to write a single character to the RS-232 connection:

```
put_char(Char) ->
    global:send(rs232, {self(), {put_char, Char}}),
    receive
        {rs232, Reply} -> Reply
    end.
```

The client function does not know the location of the rs232 service, it simply uses the *service by name.* This service is location transparent. In practice this means that the RS-232 cable can be plugged into any host and that the application can run at different sites without being recompiled.

11.5 Promises

Promises are an asynchronous variant of remote procedure calls. The main disadvantage of RPCs is that we have to do an *idle wait* for the answer, although we may have something better to do than to wait. The use of promises has been suggested in [21]. A promise is a place holder for a future return value from an RPC. This overcomes the disadvantages that stem from the synchronous nature of the RPC. The caller can perform the RPC, do something else and, at a later time, try to claim the computed value, which may or may not be ready. This could be implemented as follows:

```
-module(promise).
-export([call/4, yield/1, nb_yield/1, do_call/5]).

call(Node,Mod,Fun,Args) ->
    spawn(promise, do_call, [self(), Node, Mod, Fun, Args]).

yield(Key) ->
    receive
        {Key, {promise_reply, R}} ->
            R
    end.

do_call(ReplyTo, N, M, F, A) ->
    R = rpc:call(N, M, F, A),
    ReplyTo ! {self(), {promise_reply, R}}. %% self() is key
```

Each call is handled by a local process which performs the RPC. The process identifier of this process is returned as a key which can be used in a subsequent blocking yield operation. This example nicely demonstrates the power of the selective receive in ERLANG.

A non-blocking version of `yield/1` can be written as:

```
nb_yield(Key) ->
    receive
        {Key, {promise_reply, R}} ->
            {value, R};
    after 0 ->
        timed_out
    end.
```

Program 11.4

11.6 Multicasting to Process Groups

The concept of a distributed group of processes with a well-known name is very powerful. A process group can be empty or contain one or more processes that can reside on one or many nodes. The idea is to have a group of processes which are known under a single system-wide name. To send a message to the group we send the message to the name of the group and this message will be 'multicasted' to all members of the process group. When new members join the group, all old members are informed. When old members die, the remaining members are informed. The concept of a multicast message to a process group becomes considerably more useful if the following two properties hold for all messages:

- Messages which are sent to the group are all delivered in the same order to all members of the group. This property is usually referred to as 'serialisability'.
- Messages which are sent to the group are either delivered to all members of the group or none. This is called 'atomicity'.

To implement process groups in ERLANG we globally register the name of each process group with the aid of the global name server from Section 11.4. The process that stores the name is called the master of the group and all requests to join the group, leave the group or send a message to the group are handled by the group master.

This means that the master will be a bottleneck for communication to the group, but it also carries with it the very desirable property of serialisability. Since all messages to the group master arrive in sequence, it is easy to arrange that these are sent in the same order to all members of the group. We shall later show how to utilise this property, when we manage global data structures.

Program 11.5 implements serialised multicasts to named process groups:

```
-module(pg).
-export([create/1,join/2,send/2,master/1,members/1]).

create(PgName) ->
    spawn(pg, master, [PgName]).

join(PgName,Pid)    ->
    global:send(PgName, {join, Pid}).

send(PgName,Mess) ->
    global:send(PgName, {send,self(), Mess}).


members(PgName) ->
    global:send(PgName, {self(), members}),
    receive
        {PgName, {members, Members}} ->
            Members
    end.

master(PgName) ->
    process_flag(trap_exit, true),
    global:register_name(PgName, self()),
    master_loop(PgName, []).

master_loop(PgName, Members) ->
    receive
        {send, From, Message} ->
            send_all(Members,{PgName,{pg_message,From,Message}}),
            master_loop(PgName, Members);
        {join, Pid} ->
            link(Pid),
            send_all(Members, {PgName, {new_member, Pid}}),
            master_loop(PgName, [Pid|Members]);
        {From, members} ->
            From ! {PgName, {members, Members}},
            master_loop(PgName, Members);
        {'EXIT' ,From, _} ->
            Nm = lists:delete(From, Members),
            send_all(Nm,{PgName, {member_failure, From}}),
            master_loop(PgName, Nm);
    end.
```

```
send_all([], _) -> done;
send_all([P|Tail], M) ->
    P ! M,
    send_all(Tail, M).
```

Program 11.5

We make use of the global registration facility from Section 11.4. Each group has a master which globally registers itself with the name of the group. The group can thus be reached by its name.

11.6.1 Atomicity and fault-tolerance

The implementation of process groups in Program 11.5 has some problems. The group is vulnerable to the failure of the master and it does not have the 'atomicity' property. If the node where the master resides fails while the master is forwarding a message to the group members, the message may be delivered to some of the members only, and the group disappears together with the group master.

To remedy this we need to do two things. Firstly we must have a standby process running on a node where the master is not running. This standby process monitors the master, and if the node where the master runs fails, this process re-registers the name of the process group with itself as group master. Secondly we need to tag all messages from the group master with a continuously increasing integer tag. When a member receives a message with the tag out of order, the process knows that a master crash has occurred and that it has missed some messages to the group. The member must then query the (new) master for the missing messages.

The standby process is started by the original master, so the original master knows the Pid of this process. Every message the master sends to the group is first sent to this standby process and all messages are tagged with the sequence number. The standby process maintains a log with (say) the six last received messages. If the master dies, the standby process spawns a new standby process and becomes the new master itself. This new master remembers the six last multicast messages to the group. If a member has missed a message it can now query the master for one of these messages.

To implement this we modify the code from Program 11.5 as follows:

```
master(PgName) ->
    master(PgName, mk_log()).

master(PgName, Log) ->
    process_flag(trap_exit, true),
    global:register_name(PgName, self()),
    Standby = spawn_link(hd(nodes()), pg, standby, [PgName, Log]),
    master_loop(PgName, [], Standby, 0, Log).
```

```
master_loop(PgName,Members, Standby, Num, Log) ->
    receive
        {send, From, Message} ->
            Mess = {{PgName, Num}, {From, pg_message, Message}},
            Standby ! Mess,
            send_all(Members, Mess),
            master_loop(PgName, Members, Standby, Num+1, Log);
        {join, Pid} ->
            link(Pid),
            Mess = {{PgName, Num},{new_member, Pid}},
            Standby ! Mess,
            send_all(Members, Mess),
            master_loop(PgName,[Pid|Members],Standby,Num+1,Log);
        {From, members} ->
            From ! {PgName, {members, Members}},
            master_loop(PgName, Members, Standby, Num, Log);
        {'EXIT', Standby, _} ->
            P2 = spawn_link(hd(nodes()),pg,standby,[PgName,Log]),
            master_loop(PgName, Members, P2, Num, Log);
        {'EXIT', From, _} ->
            Nm = lists:delete(From, Members),
            Mess = {{PgName, Num}, {member_failure, From}},
            Standby ! Mess,
            send_all(Nm, Mess),
            master_loop(PgName, Nm, Standby, Num+1, Log);
        {From, get_lost_message, Number} ->
            From ! {PgName, {lost_message, lookup_num(Log)}},
            master_loop(PgName, Members, Standby, Num, Log)
    end.
```

And the standby process which is created by the master when the group is started runs the following code:

```
standby(Groupname, Log) ->
    process_flag(trap_exit, true),
    link(Master = global:whereis_name(Groupname)),
    standby_loop(Groupname, Master,Log).

standby_loop(Name, Master, Log) ->
    receive
        {'EXIT', Master, _} -> %% I am new master :-)
            global:unregister_name(Name), %% To sync
```

```
                master(Name, Log);
        Mess ->
                standby_loop(Name,Master,add_to_log(Mess,Log))
    end.

%% Log is implemented as a tuple of size 6
mk_log() ->
    {1, {1,2,3,4,5,6}}.
add_to_log(Mess, {Pos, Contents}) ->
    {incr(Pos), setelement(Pos, Contents, Mess)}.

incr(6) -> 1;
incr(I) -> I+1.

lookup_num(Num, {_, Log}) ->
    lookup_num(Num, Log, 1).

lookup_num(_, _, 7) ->
    notfound;
lookup_num(Num, Log, Pos) ->
    case element(Pos, Log) of
        {{Name, Num}, Mess} -> {{Name, Num}, Mess};
        _ -> lookup_num(Num, Log, Pos+1)
    end.
```

The master has a Log variable as well as the standby process. If the standby process becomes master, the six last logged messages will appear in the new master's Log variable. If some member in the group is overloaded or chooses not to receive any messages just when the master crash appears, we need to keep exactly those messages that were sent at the time of the master failure; hence the master does not update the log, this is only done by the standby process.

All messages to the group are of the form `{{Name, Num}, Mess}` where `Name` is the name of the process group and `Num` is the sequence number of the message `Mess`. The members can make a choice of managing the sequence numbers themselves or have the following function, which uses the local process dictionary, do the job:

```
receive_from_group(Name) ->
    Num = group_get(),
    receive
        {{Name, Num}, Mess} ->
            group_put(Num+1),
            {ok, Mess};
        {{Name, Num2}, Mess} when Num < Num2 ->
            get_missing_mess(Name,{{Name,Num2},Mess},Num)
    end.
```

```
%% Local dictionary funcs
group_get() ->
    case get(sequence_num) of
        undefined -> 0;
        N -> N
    end.
group_put(I) ->
    put(sequence_num, I).

get_missing_mess(Name, WrongMess, Number) ->
    global:send(Name, {self(), get_lost_message, Number}),
    receive
        {lost_message, notfound} ->
            {error, {lost_message, Number}};
        {lost_message, {{Name, Number}, Mess}} ->
            self() ! WrongMess, %% !!!!
            group_put(Number + 1),
            {ok, Mess}
    end.
```

The wrong message is re-sent to ourselves. This may or may not be the next message, but in either case, the message will be saved for future processing.

As an aside we can note that the disadvantage of doing receive in a function is that the selective receive mechanisms of ERLANG cannot be used, hence we cannot receive messages from anybody else but the process group. This is a design issue, where the advantages of exporting a clean function interface have to be weighed against the flexibility and increased complexity that comes with exporting a message interface.

With this new improved multicast service we can be guaranteed that all messages sent to the group are serialised. There is, however, still a faint possibility of a message only being delivered to a subset of the group members. This can happen in the case with several subsequent master failures. The normal fail-case when the master fails and a new master takes over is handled well. Note also that there is a small time interval when there is no master at all. After the standby process has un-registered the name and before the new master has registered the name, there is no master present at all. This, however, does not affect the atomicity of the multicast service. Messages sent to the group in this small time interval will not be delivered to any members of the group. The remedy to this would be to introduce the concept of standby processes in the global name server from Section 11.4.

11.7 Negotiation Techniques

Program 11.5 has a master–slave relationship. All programs that have a single coordinating process, a master, are vulnerable to the failure of the master. Programs that do not have a master–slave organisation, that are organised as a set of cooperating peers, are generally less sensitive to the failure of any of the members. The global name registration facility is an example of this type of program.

One technique that could be used to improve the fault-tolerance in master–slave organised programs is to let all the slaves monitor the well-being of the master. If the master crashes, the remaining members can enter a negotiation phase to appoint a new master.

This negotiation could be performed in many different ways as long as all members use the same negotiation algorithm.

The algorithm we use in the following code is to utilise the fact that all node names are unique *and* ordered:

```
slave_loop(Master, Slaves) ->
    receive
        {'EXIT', Master, Reason} ->
            L = lists:sort(lists:map({erlang, node},[],
                                     [self()|Slaves])),
            Newmaster = hd(L),
            case node() of
                Newmaster ->
                    %% We are master ...
                    global:register_name(master, self())
                    send_all(Slaves, {self(), new_master}),
                    master_loop(Slaves);
                _ ->
                    receive
                        {From, new_master} ->
                            slave_loop(From,lists:delete(From,Slaves))
                    end,
            end;

        ......
        .....
```

If all slaves execute the above code, the application can recover from the failure of the master.

It is generally easier to write a master–slave application than truly distributed applications that consist of a set of cooperating peers. The master–slave applications are, however, more sensitive to failures.

The above code fragment shows one way to improve the robustness of master–slave applications.[2]

11.8 Adaptive Load Distribution

A common and useful model of a distributed computing system is that of a pool of computational nodes and one or several master nodes which utilise the computing power of the pool. When a new job is to be assigned to the pool it is the job of the load distribution algorithm[3] to choose a node on which to execute the job. Several strategies for this are available. The most simple, called *static load distribution*, makes the decision as to where to place the job according to some hard-wired information. This could, for example, be a simple cyclic splitting where each node assigns its *i'th* job to node *i mod N* where *N* is the number of nodes in the system.

A more advanced scheme would be to have a **pool_master** start a load statistics collector process on all nodes that are to be part of the pool. This statistics collector then reports the current load of the node at regular intervals to the **pool_master**. The following function does this:

```
statistic_collector() ->
    M = global:whereis_name(pool_master),
    statistics_loop(M,undefined).

%% Do not tell the master about our
%% load if it has not  changed

statistics_loop(M, Old) ->
    sleep(1000),
    Load = statistics(run_queue),
    if
        Load == Old  ->
            statistics_loop(M, Old);
        true ->
            M ! {self(), load, Load},
            statistics_loop(M, Load)
    end.
```

The pool master then collects the statistics from the pool nodes and maintains an ordered list of the nodes with the nodes with the least load at the head of the list.

[2]Note that we cannot sort the process identifiers themselves, since they will be differently ordered on different nodes!

[3]The term load balancing is used when a run-time system migrates processes to lightly loaded nodes in run-time. This is not described here.

The statistics collector uses the BIF `statistics(run_queue)` which returns the length of the run queue at the node evaluating the BIF. The length of the run queue is the same as the number of processes which are ready to run. This has been shown in [30] to be an effective method of predicting the future load.

The major advantage of this algorithm is that it is adaptive. As the load on the system shifts due to very CPU intensive jobs being allocated to certain nodes, the algorithm notices this and will not allocate more jobs on those nodes.

The function `pool_spawn/3` can be used as an interface to the load distribution algorithm. It will spawn a process on the node with least load:

```
pool_spawn(M,F,A) ->
    Node = pool:get_node(),
    spawn(Node,M,F,A).
```

The function `pool:get_node/0` asks the `pool_master` process for the node name at the head of its list of nodes.

We could also have chosen to use the process groups from Section 11.6 to implement this. Each member of the group would run on a different node and execute the statistics collector. Instead of reporting to a `pool_master`, each statistics collector multicasts the information about the load to the group. This algorithm has the advantage that it is more tolerant to failures since there is no master process coordinating the activities.[4] It is also faster to query for a lightly loaded node since no remote calls have to be done. The query can be made directly to the local statistics collector.

11.9 Relay Techniques

The solution to several distributed programming problems is to fake the local availability of a resource. For example, a node running on a computer without a windowing system or a file system could start a server which registers itself with the name of the service, find some process which provides this service, and relay all messages to this process.

This could, for example, be the case when we run a node on an embedded target computer dedicated to controlling proprietary hardware such as a telephony switch. Assuming that a file system is running on `Masternode`, the following code fakes the availability of a file server:

```
start(Masternode) ->
    Id = spawn(pseudo, relay, [Masternode]),
    register(file_server, Id).
```

[4] Assuming that the process groups uses the standby technique described in Section 11.6.1.

```
relay(Masternode) ->
    Realfiler = rpc:call(Masternode, erlang, whereis,
                         [file_server]),
    loop(Realfiler).

loop(RealFiler) ->
    receive
        Anything ->
            Realfiler ! Anything
    end,
    loop(RealFiler).
```

The pseudo file server relays all messages to the real file server which resides on `Masternode`. This allows the server to execute on a remote node without the clients being aware of this. The advantage of this is that code which is written for a single node system can be used to access the server whether it is running remotely or locally. Hence, if there is no file system attached to the embedded target computer, this code brings a file system to the target.

11.10 Parallel Evaluation for Speed

In this section we show how to use remote processors for parallel evaluation. We use the promise mechanism described in Section 11.5.

The following function evaluates a list of `{Module,Fun,Args}` tuples in parallel on all the computation nodes:

```
parallel_eval(ArgL) ->
    Nodes = nodes(),
    Keys  = map_nodes(ArgL, Nodes, Nodes),
    lists:map({promise, yield}, [], Keys).

map_nodes([], _, _) ->
    [];
map_nodes(ArgL, [] , Orig) ->
    map_nodes(ArgL, Orig, Orig);
map_nodes([{M, F, A}|Tail], [Node|MoreNodes], Orig) ->
    [promise:call(Node, M, F, A) |
     map_nodes(Tail, MoreNodes, Orig)].
```

We use the asynchronous variant of RPC from module `promise`, and generate a list of promises, each acting as a place holder for the desired value, and then traverse the list yielding all the values with the `lists:map/3` function which is described in Appendix C. The second clause of `map_nodes/3` is entered when we have run out of nodes, that is, when there are more goals than available pool nodes.

It is interesting to note the behaviour of the list `Keys` here. Once we have the list we try to `yield` the elements one by one. If one of the calls to `yield` suspends this does not affect the evaluation of the remaining elements of the list. They all continue to evaluate and their results will be collected when the last suspended call to `yield/1` returns. It is also interesting to note that the calls to `yield/1` do not need to be made in any particular order.

The algorithm here places the jobs on different nodes in a predefined order. This algorithm does not take account of different functions being more expensive than others. Some nodes may get a lot of work and other nodes get less. This is an example of the previously mentioned *static load distribution*.

The function `lists:map(Fun, As, List)` will apply the function `Fun` to each of the elements in the expression `[Element|As]` where `Element` is each element in the list `List`. `Fun` is an arity 2 tuple `{Module,Function}`. For example:

```
1 > L = ["123", "1234", "12345"],
lists:map({erlang,length}, [], L).
[3,4,5].
```

A parallel version of the `map` function which evaluates each element in the list `List` in parallel can be implemented as follows:

```
pmap({M,F}, As, List) ->
    check(parallel_eval(build_args(M, F, As, List, [])), []).

build_args(M, F, As, [Arg|Tail], Ack) ->
    build_args(M, F, As, Tail, [{M, F, [Arg|As]}|Ack]);
build_args(_, _, _, [], Ack) ->
    Ack.

check([{badrpc, R}|Tail], _) -> exit({badrpc, R});
check([X|T], Ack) -> check(T, [X|Ack]);
check([], Ack) -> Ack.
```

If a single RPC fails, the whole computation is terminated.

11.11 Discussion

Deciding whether to spawn a process on a remote node or not is difficult. It takes longer elapsed time to spawn a process on a remote node than on the local node. The CPU time a node uses to spawn a process or send a message to a remote node is also significantly larger than the time a node uses to spawn a process or send a message on the local node. In the case of spawning processes, the process which spawns a remote process is suspended for the time it takes for the spawn request to traverse the network and the time for the new process identifier to travel back. This time can be significant and depends on the speed, quality and load of the network.

When a number of nodes are attached to an ordinary local area network it is typically 10 times more expensive and takes 100 times longer to create a remote process than a local process. The same goes for local versus remote server calls.

It is important to bear this in mind when designing distributed applications, since one of the goals with distributed computing is to make the application not only more reliable but also faster.

If we examine the RPC facility from Section 11.1 it is worth noting that we did not have to specify the interface to the RPC server. In traditional RPC systems, there is usually an interface description language involved. Examples of such languages are Sun Microsystems RPC language [23] and ASN.1 [12]. These languages do not primarily exist because one wishes to have the interface to the RPC server in a separate document from the code, but because one has to use the interface to generate stub routines which perform the marshalling procedure for a predefined set of data types.

Every data object in the ERLANG system carries information that indicates the type of that data. Since all data structures are self-identifying there is no need to have an interface description language to generate stub routines.

In traditional languages there are usually no means of distinguishing a pointer to an integer from a pointer to a character. In ERLANG we can from the data itself generate an unambiguous, machine-independent stream of bytes which uniquely represents the data object. This leads to very dynamic systems, where interfaces to services available on remote nodes can be changed in a running system. This is particularly important in many applications where we may wish to reconfigure the interfaces to an application without stopping the application itself.

An ERLANG programmer can concentrate on specifying the important logical interfaces in the system without having to be concerned with the physical interfaces or lower level protocols between computers.

It is also worth noting how small the semantic gap between a local function call and a transparent remote procedure call is. Since there are no pointer valued parameters and call-by-reference parameters in ERLANG[5] the only semantic difference is that the remote call might fail for reasons other than the local call.

Since all messages between ERLANG nodes are transformed to this unambiguous byte stream, heterogeneous systems can easily be built from many ERLANG nodes running on different types of computers and operating systems.

---

[5]Heaven forbid.

Chapter 12

Distributed Data

Many applications may wish to have some common data structures available for access and modification by several processes on several nodes. This chapter describes various techniques for sharing data between physically separated nodes.

Throughout the chapter we will assume the availability of a module called `db` which exports the following functions:[1]

`db:new(set)`
: Return a new empty dictionary with 'set' semantics, meaning one object per key.

`db:new(bag)`
: Return a new empty dictionary with 'bag' semantics, meaning multiple objects per key.

`db:insert(Dict, Key, Value)`
: Destructively update the dictionary `Dict` with a new object.

`db:lookup(Dict, Key)`
: If the dictionary is a 'set', a lookup for an object with the key `Key` returns `undefined` if no value is associated with `Key`, otherwise the associated object is returned. If the dictionary is a 'bag', a list of objects associated with the key `Key` is returned.

`db:delete(Dict, Key)`
: Destructively delete all objects in `Dict` with key `Key`.

`db:to_list(Dict)`
: Return the dictionary as a list of `{Key, Value}` tuples.

[1]Some implementations of ERLANG have BIFs to support these operations, making them highly efficient.

12.1 Shared Data

The simplest approach to the problem of sharing data between nodes is to have a central server that maintains all the data and is registered with a global name. The code to do this would use the module `global` from Section 11.4 to register itself and the module `db` to read and write the data items. This simple approach has some advantages over more advanced methods since it is:

- Easy to implement.
- Easy to verify that all data is always consistent.

The major disadvantages are:

- If the node where the central database resides fails, the entire database is lost.
- All clients must perform a network operation to access the database, thus making access to the database slower.[2]
- The central database server is a bottleneck.

In many applications it is sometimes of utmost importance that read access to the database is *very* fast, but it is acceptable to have some delays when writing or deleting in the database. One solution to distributed data in this situation is to have all data replicated on all nodes. Read accesses can then go directly to the local database and no remote network operations are necessary. Write and delete accesses to one local database will be multicasted to all the other replicas in the network. The full replication scheme is useful provided the ratio of the time required to perform read and write operations is high. An application which frequently updates shared data structures may run faster if no replication is performed.[3]

12.1.1 Process groups

If full replication is desired, we can utilise the process group technique described in Section 11.6.

Firstly, we need a server which is locally registered with the name `pgdb` on all nodes or on the nodes that need it. We assume that a process group called `global_db` has been created with `pg:create(global_db)` described in Section 11.6. The local `pgdb` joins the process group.

Program 12.1 implements a fully replicated database where the entire database is replicated on all nodes running the program.

---

[2]Assuming the network is slow, this may not always be the case.

[3]But it will not be as reliable.

```
-module(pgdb).
-export([start/0,pgdb/1,read/1,write/2])

start() ->
    Id = spawn(pgdb, pgdb, [db:new(set)]),
    register(pgdb, Id),
    pg:join(global_db, Id).

pgdb(Store) ->
    receive
        {From, {read, Key}} ->
            From ! {pgdb, db:lookup(Store, Key)},
            pgdb(Store);
        {From,{global_db, {pg_message, {write, Key, Value}}}} ->
            db:insert(Store, Key, Value),
            pgdb(Store)
    end.

%% Client interface

read(Key) ->
    request(pgdb, {read, Key}).

write(Key, Val) ->
    pg:send(global_db, {write, Key, Val}).

request(To, Req) ->
    To ! {self(), Req},
    receive
        {To, Reply} -> Reply
    end.
```

Program 12.1

Since the process group mechanism guarantees that all messages are sent in the same order to all members of the group, all local processes running the database code will never end up in different states whatever mixture of reads and writes we perform on the database. This provides a globally consistent database.

Note that if we had chosen merely to send our update requests directly to all nodes instead of using the process group to update an object, the database could easily get into an inconsistent state. If two processes simultaneously decide to update the object with key `K`, and they simply send this update request to all servers, the requests will most probably arrive in a different order at the different nodes.

All servers will store the last value that arrives, thus storing *different* values with the same key.

The major problem is the fact that there is no global ordering of events in a distributed system. Events have an order within each process but the only ordering that can be relied upon in a distributed system is when two or more processes explicitly synchronise with each other by sending and receiving messages.

If we execute a statement S and then execute another statement R on a single CPU, we *know* that S executes before R. This might seem trivial, but this is not the case in a distributed environment. In a distributed environment processes have to *explicitly* synchronise with each other to be able to ensure an execution order. To synchronise with each other means that the processes must interact with each other in such a way that the execution order is deterministic.

12.1.2 Time stamps and clocks

A different and efficient technique for maintaining replicated data servers on a set of nodes is to associate a time stamp with every item in the store. The time stamp is generated when a write request is initiated and all servers always ignore write requests for an item where the time stamp associated with the write request is smaller than the time stamp associated with the actual data. We could use the expression `{date(), time()}` to create the time stamps but there is a BIF called `now()` which provides better granularity. The BIF reads the clock of the host operating system and is guaranteed to return continuously increasing integer values.

Assume that the following server runs on all nodes and that it is registered with the name `tsdb`.

```
loop(Store) ->
    receive
        {From, {read, Key}} ->
            From ! {tsdb, value(db:lookup(Store, Key))};
        {From, {write, Key, Val, Tstamp}} ->
            %% This is an asynchronous write
            case db:lookup(Store, Key) of
                undefined ->
                    db:insert(Store, Key, {Val, Tstamp});
                {Val2, Tsold} when Tstamp > Tsold ->
                    db:insert(Store, Key, {Val, Tstamp});
                _ ->
                    ignore
            end
    end,
    loop(Store).
```

```
value({Val, _}) ->
    Val;
value(undefined) ->
    undefined.
```

And the client functions:

```
read(Key) ->
    request(tsdb, {read, Key}).

write(Key,Val) ->
    bc:broadcast(tsdb, {write, Key, Val, ts()}).
```

where the `ts()` function is:

```
ts() ->
    now().
```

One problem with the above code can occur when two different write requests are initiated with equal time stamps. This can fixed by changing the `ts()` function to:

```
ts() -> {now(), node()}.
```

Another more serious problem with using the built-in clock is that there are no guarantees that the clocks on the different nodes are always synchronised. There are always minor differences in the clocks on different computers and different clocks can sometimes get seriously skewed after a host has rebooted. Furthermore, since ERLANG can run in heterogeneous environments, the clock synchronisation between the different local host operating systems involved might not work properly, or might even be non-existent.

This can be solved by using virtual clocks. We let all servers maintain a counter that is incremented for each local write request. Each server compares all incoming counters with the local counter, and if the incoming counter is bigger than the local counter, then the local counter is adjusted accordingly. We get the following code using a virtual clock:

```
loop(Store, Vclock) ->
    receive
        {From, {read, K}} ->
            From ! {tsdb, db:lookup(Store, K)},
            loop(Store, Vclock);
        {From, {write, Key, Val}} ->
            Ts = {Vclock+1, node()},
            db:insert(Store, K, {Val, Ts}),
            bc:broadcast(nodes(), tsdb, {write, Key, Val, Ts}),
```

```
            From ! {tsdb, ok},
            loop(Store, Vclock+1);
        {write, K, V, Tstamp} ->
            case db:lookup(Store, K) of
                undefined ->
                    db:insert(Store, K, {Val, Tstamp});
                {Val2, Tsold} when Tstamp > Tsold ->
                    db:insert(Store, K, {Val, Tstamp});
                _ ->
                    ignore
            end,
            Vclock2 = element(1, Tstamp),
            loop(Store, 1 + max(Vclock, Vclock2))
    end.
```

And the client functions:

```
read(Key) ->       request(tsdb, {read, Key}).
write(Key,Val) -> request(tsdb, {write, Key, Value}).
```

This distributed fully replicated data dictionary not only performs well, it is also very simple and easy to understand. The technique for ordering events in a distributed system using virtual clocks was originally described in [20].

12.2 Partial Replication

If the database is very large, replication of the entire database on all nodes is wasteful of memory. The best utilisation of total memory is achieved when the only complete copy of the database exists on one master node. This, however comes with the price of unreliability, and the master node becoming a bottleneck

The problem of maintaining database consistency becomes more difficult if the data is partially replicated on several nodes. Depending on the application, replication of all data may be worth the trouble.

If we want our database to employ partial replication on its data, the first issue that has to be decided is the granularity of replication, and this depends on the organisation of the database itself. If, for example, the database is organised as a set of tables, each table may be the item of replication. If the database is a simple `{Key,Value}` database then the item of replication may be every `{Key,Value}` pair.

We sketch a solution for partial replication of data using a central server globally registered as `master`. Initially all data is present only in the globally registered `master` server.

Access to data is always done through a cache residing on the local node. The cache lookup can either return the object itself, in which case it is obviously resident in the cache and we return this object to the client, or it can return a tuple `{central, I}` where the `I` indicates how many read operations we have performed on this object. The `I` counter is incremented for each read attempt. Once the counter reaches a threshold value, say five, the cache decides to get a personal replica of the object.

The idea is that a node which performs mostly read operations on a `Key` will always have that particular `{Key,Value}` replicated in its cache, whereas a node which performs mostly write operations on a particular `Key` will not have the data replicated. This will lead to a situation where data which is written frequently is stored centrally at the master, thus speeding up the write requests and data which is read frequently is cached locally on all nodes which read the data, thus speeding up read requests.

```
-module(repl_db).
-export([cache/0, cache/1, read/1, write/2]).
-export([start/0, master_loop/2]).
-import(global, [send/2]).

%% This code runs locally on all participating nodes.
cache() ->
    Id = spawn(repl_db,cache,[db:new(set)]),
    register(cache,Id).

cache(Data) ->
    receive
        {From,{read,Key}} ->
            case db:lookup(Data, Key) of
                undefined ->
                    db:insert(Data, Key, {central, 1}),
                    send(master, {From, {read, Key}});
                {central, I} when I < 5 ->
                    db:insert(Data, Key, {central, I+1}),
                    send(master, {From, {read, Key}});
                {central, 5} -> %% Time to replicate
                    send(master, {self(), {replicate, Key}}),
                    receive
                        {master, {Key, Replica}} ->
                            db:insert(Data, Key, Replica)
                    end,
                    From ! {repl_db, Replica};
                Value ->   %% We got it here
                    From ! {repl_db, Value}
            end;
```

```
        {From, {write, Key, Value}} ->
            db:delete(Data, Key),
            send(master, {From, self(),{write, Key, Value}});
        {master, {invalidate, Key}} ->
            db:delete(Data, Key);
    end,
    cache(Data).
```

If a write request is made to the cache, it first deletes any replicas that it has stored, then it sends the write request to the master. The master will then send an `invalidate` message to all caches holding a copy of the object. The client functions are synchronous, and the code is written in such a way that sometimes the cache will respond directly to the client and in some cases the cache will forward the request to the master and leave it up to the master to respond to the client.

The code for the client `write/2` is:

```
write(Key, Value) ->
    cache ! {self(), {write, Key, Value}},
    receive
        {master, {Key, written}} ->
            ok
    end.
```

And the code for the client `read/1` function is:

```
read(Key) ->
    cache ! {self(), {read, Key}},
    receive
        {repl_db, Val} -> Val
    end.
```

The master maintains a list of replica holders for each key. When a request to write an item arrives at the master, it tells all the holders of replicas, except the cache who issued the request, to invalidate their replicas. This is done with the `invalidate/3` function. When the `invalidate` messages arrive at the caches the data associated with the key is removed. Thus, once an item has become written, it takes a while before the caches start to require replicas.

Once the invalidation is done, the `master` responds to the client which originally issued the write request. The master only runs on one node in the system. It uses the global register facility from Section 11.4 to register itself and it is implemented as follows:

```
start() ->
    P = spawn(repl_db, loop, []),
    global:register_name(master, P).

loop() ->
    Db = init_db(),          % code for init_db not given here
    Copies = db:new(bag),    % ... maybe reads from disc ...
    loop(Db,Copies).

loop(Db,Copies) ->
    receive
        {From, {replicate, Key}} ->
            V = db:lookup(Db, Key),
            db:insert(Copies, Key, From),
            From ! {master, {Key, V}};
        {From, {read, Key}} ->
            From ! {repl_db, db:lookup(Db, Key);
        {From, Cache, {write, Key, Value}} ->
            invalidate(Key, Cache, db:lookup(Copies, Key)),
            db:insert(Db, Key, Value),
            db:delete(Copies, Key),
            From ! {master, {Key, written}} %% to the client
    end,
    loop(Db,Copies).

invalidate(Key, _, []) ->
    done;
invalidate(Key, Cache, [Cache|Tail]) ->
    invalidate(Key, Cache, Tail);
invalidate(Key, Cache, [CopyHolder|Tail]) ->
    CopyHolder ! {master, {invalidate, Key}},
    invalidate(Key, Cache, Tail).
```

Program 12.2

Depending on the application, this database performs better than the central database. If the clients using this database mostly issue read requests, this database performs better than the central database with no replication. It has also better memory utilisation than the full replication database from Section 12.1. However, if the clients issue mostly write requests, this database has slightly worse performance than the central database.

This database also has the disadvantage of having a central server which may fail. If the `master` fails, the entire database is lost. We could of course let the master use the standby technique from Section 11.6 in order to make the system immune to the failure of the master.

Several other algorithms describing the protocols for the implementation of partially replicated objects can be found in [5]. One problem with the above code (as well as the code from Section 12.1) is the following scenario. Assume that processes `P1` and `P2` simultaneously want to increment the item associated with `Key`. Both processes execute the following code fragment:

```
X = read(Key),
write(Key, X + 1),
```

If both processes read the value simultaneously and it is, say, 17, and then `P1` increments by 1 and writes the value 18, and then just after that, `P2` also increments the value by 1 and writes the value 18. `P2` overwrites the value of `P1`. The value now written in the database is 18, when it really should have been 19.

This problem is known as the *lost update problem.* The solution to this problem is to encapsulate the read operation *and* the write operation into a single atomic *transaction* where the entire transaction either fails or succeeds.

12.3 Transactions

Transactions are a powerful tool which can be used as the basic building block in the construction of highly reliable distributed systems. A wide variety of different transaction mechanisms exists and the interested reader is referred to [14] or [7].

The goal of managing concurrent access to a database through a transaction is to ensure that each transaction executes atomically, meaning that:

- Each transaction concurrently accesses shared data without interfering with other transactions, and
- If a transaction terminates normally, then all of its effects are made permanent; otherwise it has no effect at all.

The transaction mechanism in Section 10.4 locks the entire database for the duration of the transaction. This severely restricts concurrent access to the data. A more realistic model would be to lock smaller objects than the whole database. The technique used in Section 10.4 is called *pessimistic.* It is pessimistic in the sense that it assumes that different clients of the data will interfere with each other and it always guards itself against that possibility.

Probably the most common method of implementing a transaction system is to use a technique called two-phase locking. Whenever a transaction wants to read an object it tries to set a read-lock on one copy of the object and then read it. If the read-lock cannot be granted, the request is queued for later processing. An attempt to set a read-lock is not granted if there exists a write-lock on the object. Whenever a transaction wants to write an object, a write-lock must first be obtained on all copies of the object. A write-lock is granted if there are no other locks on the object whatsoever. If the write-lock cannot be granted, the request is queued. Whenever a transaction terminates, all locks held by the transaction must be released, and all pending transactions waiting for any of the released locks must be scheduled to run again. The algorithm is called two-phase locking because each transaction has two phases: one phase where it is acquiring locks, and one where it is releasing locks.[4]

The two-phase lock algorithm is subject to deadlocks and a transaction system using two-phase locking to implement non-conflicting access to shared data must address the issue of deadlocking transactions.

A different technique is called *optimistic* which means that each transaction executes hoping that there are no interferences with other transactions. At the end of the transaction a check is made to ensure that the data the transaction wishes to write does not interfere with any other transactions. If it does, the transaction is aborted and must be restarted. If interferences are common, this leads to poor performance since many transactions are aborted and subsequently restarted. Situations can occur when a transaction is cyclically restarted and never gets a chance to terminate properly. This is called *livelock.*

Yet another technique uses time stamps in a manner similar to that described in Section 12.1.2. First each transaction is assigned a new time stamp when the transaction is started, then each object is stored together with two time stamps. The first is the time stamp of the last transactions which read the objects, and the second is the time stamp of the transactions that was the last to write the object.

Whenever a transaction T tries to read an item X, it succeeds only if the write time stamp associated with X is smaller than or equal to the time stamp of T. Hence a transaction can only read objects written by other transactions that are older than itself.

When T tries to write an object, it only succeeds if the write and the read time stamps associated with the object are smaller than or equal to the time stamp of T. Thus a transaction cannot write an object that has been accessed by any other transactions that are younger than itself. This technique is called *time stamp ordering.*

The rules for accessing data according to the time stamps ensures that no transactions conflict with each other. We also need to ensure the atomicity property. A transaction executes a series of read and write operations and then performs one of the following actions:

- Decides to commit, that is, requests that its operations are made permanent.
- Decides to abort, that is, requests that its operations should be ignored.
- Is made to abort, due to a programming error in the code executing the transaction, or due to a request being rejected by the transaction manager.

If data written by a transaction is directly written into the data storage we must be able to undo this, which can be a complicated business. Generally we want to

[4]This is not to be confused with two-phase commit which we will introduce later in this chapter.

avoid this so an alternative to writing directly in the data store is to write in a small cache and then, when the transaction requests to commit, the objects in the cache are written into the data store. If the transaction aborts, the cache is simply discarded.

12.3.1 A distributed transaction manager

In this section we present an optimistic fault-tolerant distributed transaction manager based on time stamps.[5] We shall assume that the database is logically arranged as a set of tables where each table may contain any number of objects. A logical table has a name and a list of associated nodes. This is a list of all nodes where a replica of the table is stored.

The table information must be replicated (and identical) on all nodes in the system. Physically the data is not stored as a set of tables. Data is stored in a single large storage area where the key leading to an object is of the form `{Tab, Key}` if the table `Tab` contains an object with key `Key`. Objects in our database always have the structure `{{Tab, Key}, Value}`.

Assume the following code runs on all nodes:

```
start() ->
    register(trans, spawn(trans, loop0, [])).

loop0() ->
    Dbnodes = db_config:db_nodes(),
    lists:map({erlang, monitor_node}, [true], Dbnodes),
    Tabinfo = db_config:init_tabs(db:new(set)),
    db:insert(Tabinfo, nodes, Dbnodes),
    Data = db_config:init_data(db:new(set)),
    loop(Tabinfo, Data, db:new(set), db:new(set)).
```

We assume the existence of functions `db_nodes/0` to let us know the names of all nodes where the database is supposed to run, `init_tabs/1` to initialise the table information and `init_data/1` to initialise the the data storage from disc. The `loop0/0` function also ensures that we monitor all database nodes using the BIF `monitor_node/2`.

The following are some of the client functions that interact with the local transaction manager.

```
t_begin() ->
    {db:new(set), timestamp()}.
```

[5]The casual reader might want to skip this section!

```
timestamp() -> {now(), node()}.

write({Store, Ts}, K, V) ->
    db:insert(Store, K, V).

abort({Store, Ts}) ->
    exit({abort, abort}).
```

The `t_begin/0` function which initiates a transaction returns a data structure that must be passed in any subsequent `read` or `write` calls. The data structure contains a local cache, which is used for any subsequent writes performed by the transaction, as well as the time stamp of the transaction. We do not use the technique of virtual clocks here in an attempt to keep our program small.

Any data that the transaction chooses to write with the `write/3` function is stored in this data structure. If and when the transaction chooses to commit, the objects stored in this structure are inserted into the real database. This is usually referred to as *deferred write*.

Now we come to the transaction manager itself. The following is the loop that runs on all nodes. The loop has four variables and they are all storage structures that can be destructively updated by module `db`:

- `Tabinfo`, stores the location information for the logical tables.
- `S`, is the actual data store.
- `Tstamps`, stores the time stamps.
- `Commitlist`, contains information about committed (and aborted) transactions.

The structure of the server loop is:

```
loop(Tabinfo, S, Tstamps, Commitlist) ->
    receive
        {From, {read, K, Ts}} ->
            .....
        {nodedown, N} ->
            .....
        {From, {get_nodes, Tab}} ->
            .....
        {From, {ask_commit, Objs, Nodes, Ts}} ->
            .....
        {From, {what_happened, Pid}} ->
            .....
    end,
    loop(Tabinfo, S, Tstamps, Commitlist).
```

We will split the server code in different portions with auxiliary functions and comments in between to make the text more readable. The part of the server loop which handles read requests is:

```
{From, {read, K, Ts}} ->
    {Tab, Key} = K,
    Nodes = db:lookup(Tabinfo, Tab),
    case catch lists:member(node(), Nodes) of
        true ->
            case db:lookup(Tstamps, K) of
                undefined ->
                    db:insert(Tstamps, K, {Ts, Ts}),
                    reply(From, db:lookup(S, K));
                {Tsr, Tsw} when Tsw =< Ts ->
                    db:insert(Tstamps, K, {Ts, Tsw}),
                    reply(From, db:lookup(S, K));
                {Tsr, Tsw} ->
                    reject(From, conflict)
            end;
        false when Nodes == [] ->
            reject(From, no_table);
        false ->
            reply(From, {elsewhere, hd(Nodes)});
        _ ->
            reject(From, bad_table)
        end;
```

Using auxiliary functions:

```
reply(From, R) ->
    From ! {trans, node(), {reply, R}}.

reject(From, Reason) ->
    From ! {trans, node(), {reject, Reason}}.
```

This code first checks if the logical table for the object is stored locally. If this is the case the read proceeds according to the rules for time stamp ordering. The read only succeeds if there are no younger transactions that have written the object. If the manager itself does not hold a copy of the object, it replies with the name of a node that does.

The client function to read an object is:

```
read({Store, Ts}, K) ->
    case db:lookup(Store, K) of
        undefined ->
            trans ! {self(), {read, K, Ts}},
            rec_read(K, Ts, node());
        V ->
            V
    end.

rec_read(K, Ts, N) ->
    receive
        {trans, N, {elsewhere, Node}} ->
            monitor_node(Node, true),
            {trans, Node} ! {self(), {read, K, Ts}},
            rec_read(K, Ts, Node);
        {trans, N, {reply, V}} ->
            monitor_node(N, false),
            V;
        {trans, N, {reject, Reason}} ->
            exit({abort, Reason});
        {nodedown, N} ->
            exit({abort, {noconnection, N}})
    end.
```

The read function first tries to read the object in the local server. If the local server replies with an `{elsewhere, Node}` message, the read function tries to read the object at the remote site.

A read request can be rejected for a number of reasons. It could be that a time-order conflict occurred, or that the node where the object resides failed.

A check is also made to ensure that there is at least one manager holding a copy; if this is not the case, the transaction will be rejected.

Whenever the transaction manager receives a `nodedown` message the table information must be updated accordingly. Any active transactions that have, for example, any pending read requests at the remote node, will discover this by themselves, and abort.

```
{nodedown, N} ->
    reconfigure(Tabinfo, N);

reconfigure(Tabinfo, N) ->
    reconfigure(Tabinfo, db:to_list(Tabinfo), N).
```

```
reconfigure(Ti, [], _) -> ok;
reconfigure(Ti, [{Table, Nodelist}|Tail], N) ->
    case lists:member(N, Nodelist) of
        true ->
            db:insert(Ti, Table, lists:delete(N, Nodelist));
        false ->
            ok
    end,
    reconfigure(Ti, Tail, N).
```

The table information update is done by the `reconfigure/2` function, which searches the `Tabinfo` structure and removes any references to the failed node. Since our logical tables can be replicated on several nodes, a node failure need not necessarily affect the operational behaviour of the system as a whole. This was one of our primary reasons for designing a distributed system as opposed to a single node system.

Finally we come to the case where a transaction decides to commit.

The two-phase commit protocol is a protocol where the process executing the transaction, henceforth called the coordinator, asks all participating transaction managers if they are ready to commit this particular transaction. If all the participating managers reply with an `accept` message, the coordinator sends `do_commit` to all the participants. If one or more of the participants fails or replies with a `reject` message, the coordinator decides to abort the whole transactions by sending a `do_abort` message to all the participants.

Even this algorithm has a weak spot, when a participant has sent its `accept` message, it must wait for the coordinator to tell it whether to abort or commit. If no such message arrives, the coordinator has most probably failed and the participant does not know whether to commit or abort. It must then ask the remaining nodes what to do before it can proceed.

Remember that one of the goals with transactions was to allow not only non-conflicting but also concurrent access to the database. Therefore it is of utmost importance that the managers themselves are not synchronously involved in the two-phase commit protocol. We must never have a situation where a manager is waiting for a reply. All managers must be ready to process read and write requests at all times. Unfortunately we cannot avoid this in our somewhat naïve implementation here.

The coordinator has all the objects it wishes to write stored in its local `Store` structure. Before we come to the code for the `commit` function we need an auxiliary function to rearrange the data the transaction wishes to write. Assume that a transaction wants to write two objects `{{T1,K1},V1}` and `{{T2,K2},V2}`. Furthermore, assume that logical table `T1` is replicated on nodes `N1` and `N2`, and that table `T2` is only resident at node `N1`. We then wish to produce a data structure of the form:

```
[{N1, [{K1, V1}, {K2, V2}]}, {N2, [{K1, V1}]}]
```

which is organised as a list of {Node, Objectlist} tuples. This is done by the following function:

```
arrange([], Ack) ->
    Ack;
arrange([Obj|Tail], Ack) ->
    {{Tab,_},_} = Obj,
    trans ! {self(), {get_nodes, Tab}},
    receive
        {trans, _, {reply, []}} ->
            exit({abort, no_table});
        {trans, _, {reply, undefined}} ->
            exit({abort, bad_table});
        {trans, _, {reply, Ns}} ->
            arrange(Tail, into(Ns, Obj, Ack))
    end.

into([], _, Ack) ->
    Ack;
into([Node|Tail], Obj, Ack) ->
    into(Tail, Obj, into2(Node, Obj, Ack)).

into2(Node, Obj, [{Node, Os} |Tail]) ->
    [{Node, [Obj |Os]}|Tail];
into2(Node, Obj, [H|T]) ->
    [H|into2(Node, Obj, T)];
into2(Node, Obj, []) ->
    [{Node, [Obj]}].
```

For each object, the arrange/2 function queries the local server for the list of nodes that is associated with the logical table of the object. If the local server has received a nodedown message and rearranged its table information in such a way so that a requested table is not resident on any nodes, then the transaction aborts before the two-phase commit protocol is initiated.

The code for the client commit/1 function to coordinate the commitment of the transaction is:

```
commit({Store, Ts}) ->
    Objs = db:to_list(Store),
    Data = arrange(Objs, []),
    Nodes = elems(1, Data),
    case ask_commit(Data, Nodes, Ts) of
        commit ->
            send_all(Nodes, {self(), {do_commit, Ts}}),
            committed;
```

```
                {abort, Reason} ->
                    send_all(Nodes, {self(), {do_abort, Ts}}),
                    exit({abort, Reason})
            end.

        send_all([Node|Tail], Msg) ->
            {trans, Node} ! Msg,
            send_all(Tail, Msg);
        send_all([], _) ->
            ok.
```

The coordinator first arranges the data to be written on a per node basis. A list of the nodes involved in the transaction is computed with the `elems/2` function:

```
elems(I, []) -> [];
elems(I, [H|T]) -> [element(I, H) | elems(I, T)].
```

Then the transaction asks all participants if they can commit. Together with the `ask_commit` message the coordinator sends a list of all nodes that participate in the transaction. The participants will need this list if the coordinator should fail in the middle of the two-phase commit protocol. The `ask_commit/3` function is as follows:

```
ask_commit([], Nodes, Ts) ->
    rec_replies(Nodes, Ts, commit);
ask_commit([{Node, Os}|Tail], Nodes, Ts) ->
    monitor_node(Node, true),
    {trans, Node} ! {self(), {ask_commit, Os, Nodes, Ts}},
    ask_commit(Tail, Nodes, Ts).

rec_replies([], Ts, Ret) ->
    Ret;
rec_replies([Node|Tail], Ts, Ret) ->
    receive
        {trans, Node, {reply, accept}} ->
            monitor_node(Node, false),
            rec_replies(Tail, Ts, Ret);
        {trans, Node, {reject, Reason}} ->
            monitor_node(Node, false),
            rec_replies(Tail, Ts, {abort, Reason});
        {nodedown, Node} ->
            rec_replies(Tail, Ts, {abort, {noconnection, Node}})
    end.
```

If all participants reply with an `accept` message, the `ask_commit/3` function returns the atom `commit`, and the coordinator sends a `do_commit` message to all participants, otherwise, if a single manager replies with a `reject` message, the coordinator sends a `do_abort` message to all participants.

The transaction managers that are involved in the transaction receive a list of objects and a list of nodes together with the `ask_commit` message. The server must then check all the objects according to the time-order rules.

The corresponding server code is:

```
{From, {get_nodes, Tab}} ->
    reply(From, db:lookup(Tabinfo, Tab));
{From, {ask_commit, Objs, Nodes, Ts}} ->
    case check(Objs, Ts, Tstamps) of
        accept ->
            reply(From, accept),
            await_decision(S, Objs, Nodes, From, Commitlist, Ts);
        reject ->
            reject(From, conflict),
            do_abort(From, Commitlist, Ts)
    end;
```

This calls two auxiliary functions. Before a manager can commit a transaction, it must check the data to be written with the `check/3` function:

```
check([], Ts, Tstamps) ->
    accept;
check([{K,V}|Tail], Ts, Tstamps) ->
    case db:lookup(Tstamps, K) of
        {Tsr, Tsw} when Tsw =< Ts, Tsr =< Ts  ->
            db:insert(Tstamps, K, {Tsr, Ts}),
            check(Tail, Ts, Tstamps);
        undefined ->
            db:insert(Tstamps, K, {Ts, Ts}),
            check(Tail, Ts, Tstamps);
        {Tsr, Tsw} ->
            reject
    end.
```

When a manager has cast its vote, it enters the `await_decision/6` function in order find out what happened to the transaction:

```
await_decision(S, Objs, Nodes, From, Commitlist, Ts) ->
    receive
        {nodedown, Node} when node(From) == Node  ->
            resolve(S, Objs, Commitlist, node(From), Nodes, From),
            self() ! {nodedown, Node};
        {From, {do_commit, Ts}} ->
            do_commit(From, Objs, S, Commitlist, Ts);
        {From, {do_abort, Ts}} ->
            do_abort(From, Commitlist, Ts)
    end.

do_commit(From, Objs, S, Cl, Ts) ->
    lists:map({trans, do_insert2}, [S], Objs),
    db:insert(Cl, From, {commit, Ts}).

do_insert2({K,V}, S) ->
    db:insert(S,K,V).

do_abort(From, Commitlist, Ts) ->
    db:insert(Commitlist, From, {abort, Ts}).
```

When a manager has cast an `accept` vote for a specific transaction it does not know what the outcome of the transaction will be. It suffices for a single manager voting `reject` for the outcome of the entire transaction to be rejected. The period of time after a manager has voted `accept` until it receives the decision for the outcome of the transaction, is called the manager's *uncertainty period.* If the node where the coordinator runs fails while a manager is in its uncertainty period, the manager does not know what to do with the pending transaction.

When a manager is in its uncertainty period and receives a `nodedown` message from the node where the coordinator resides, we must call the `resolve/6` function in order to find out what really happened to the transaction. We must also re-send the `nodedown` message to ourselves to ensure that `reconfigure/2` gets called.

```
resolve(S, Objs, Cl, Node, Nodes, From) ->
    Ns = lists:delete(Node, lists:delete(node(), Nodes)),
    resolve(S, Objs, Cl, Ns, From).

resolve(S, Objs, Cl, [Node|Tail], From) ->
    monitor_node(Node, true),
    {trans, Node} ! {self(), {what_happend, From}},
    rec_response(S, Objs, Cl, [Node|Tail], From);
```

```
resolve(S, Objs, Cl, [], From ) -> %% no one knows
    Ts = {now(), node()},          %% we have no ts
    do_commit(From, Objs, S, Cl, Ts).

rec_response(S, Objs, Cl, [Node|Tail], From) ->
    receive
        {nodedown, Node} -> %% One more death
            self() ! {nodedown, Node},
            resolve(S, Objs, Cl, Tail, From);
        {trans, Node, {abort, Ts}} ->
            monitor_node(Node, false),
            do_abort(From, Cl, Ts);
        {trans, Node, {commit, Ts}} ->
            monitor_node(Node, false),
            do_commit(From, Objs, S, Cl, Ts);
        {trans, Node, _}  -> %% Pending or undefined
            monitor_node(Node, false),
            resolve(S, Objs, Cl, Tail, From);
        {From, {what_happend, From}} ->
            reply(From, pending),
            rec_response(S, Objs, Cl, [Node|Tail], From)
    end.
```

Together with the `ask_commit` message a list of nodes is sent. This list of nodes includes all nodes that participated in the transaction. In order to find out what happened to the transaction we can query these nodes. Then one of two things can happen:

- We visit a node which considers the transaction to be either committed or aborted. In this case we make the same decision.
- All currently active transaction managers consider the transaction to be pending. If this is the case, we decide to commit the transaction. Since they will be running the same code as we do, they will eventually come to the same conclusion!

We have so far ignored a complex case that cannot necessarily be resolved at run-time. Consider a set of nodes, such that nodes $N1$ and $N2$ reside on one local area network and nodes $N3$ and $N4$ reside on another local area network. Suppose a coordinator resides at node $N1$ and the network connection between the two local area networks fails after the coordinator sends a `do_abort` message to node $N2$ but before the message is sent to $N3$ and $N4$. In this case we have a partitioned network with two autonomous systems running, and which are unaware of each other. This situation cannot be easily remedied. The code in `resolve/7` commits the transaction. One solution would be to write the data of the transaction to a special file and resolve the conflict by manual intervention. Our code does not handle the case with partitioned networks.

Finally we need some code in the server to deal with the **what_happened** message:

```
{From, {what_happened, Pid}} ->
    reply(From, db:lookup(Commitlist, Pid))
```

Note that `rec_response/5` must be prepared to answer any **what_happened** messages that might arrive. If a node fails, several other nodes might have pending transactions with the coordinator at the failing node. If we are not prepared to respond to the `what_happened` while checking what happened, the system might deadlock! This is why we cannot use an RPC to find out what happened to a pending transaction.

12.3.2 Using transactions

Recall why we wanted to have a transaction system in the first place. We wanted to increment a counter stored in the database by first reading the value and the inserting a new incremented value. To do this within a transaction we have the following code:

```
increment(Key) ->
    T = trans:t_begin(),
    case catch increment(T, Key) of
        committed ->
            committed;
        {'EXIT', {abort, conflict}} ->
            random:sleep(),
            increment(Key);
        {'EXIT', Other} ->
            exit(Other)
    end.

increment(T, Key) ->
    case trans:read(T, Key) of
        undefined ->
            trans:write(T, 0);
        Val ->
            trans:write(T, Val+1)
    end,
    trans:commit(T).
```

If we use the `increment/1` function to do the job, we can be assured that the increment operation does not interfere with other processes. In particular, we can be assured that the problem of lost updates is handled by the transaction system. If a conflict should occur, a call to `exit({abort, conflict})` will be done. In this case, we let the transaction sleep for a while, and then restart it.

12.3.3 Discussion

We have deliberately ignored a number of issues in our transaction manager and tried to keep the size of the program small.[6] But we have developed a fault-tolerant distributed transaction manager, which is not a trivial task.

One of the things we have ignored is how to configure the database. We need a mechanism to attach a node to a currently executing set of transaction managers.

We have also ignored how to store the data in the managers on disc.

Since the servers continuously insert time stamp information and each server also inserts information about all committed transactions into the commit-list, the store will continuously grow. This information must be purged from the store at regular intervals. This can be done by looking at the time stamps. We can easily find the smallest active time stamp in the system, and then remove all commitment information and time stamps that are smaller than the smallest active transaction.

So there are a number of unresolved issues, but the purpose of this chapter is only to indicate how to build a distributed transaction system. A full-scale transaction system is beyond the scope of this book.

[6] Although it might appear as the opposite to the reader.

Chapter 13

Operating Systems

This chapter describes the standard ERLANG operating system and shows how various operating system components can be built using ERLANG.

13.1 Overview of the Standard ERLANG OS

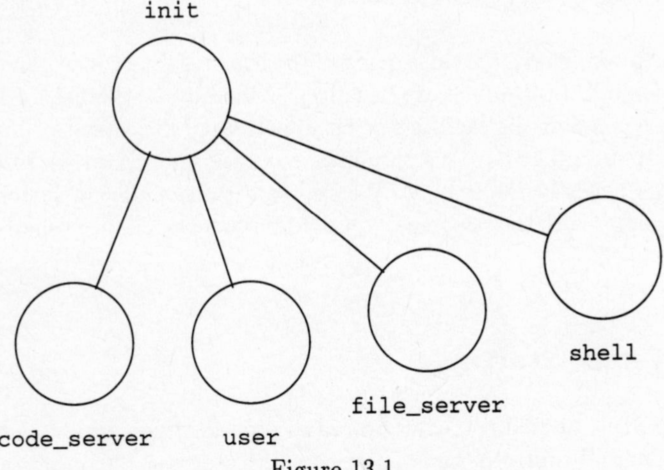

Figure 13.1

When ERLANG is run a small operating system (OS) is started. This OS provides the mechanisms for loading and running applications, an interface to the user and a file system. The parts and structure of this OS are shown in Figure 13.1. The system has five registered processes:

`init`
: This is the initial process which is created when the system is run. It starts the other parts of the system.

`code_server`
: This process handles the loading and purging of code. It also handles multiple versions of code.

`user`
: This process provides an interface to the user. Input and output requests to the user are processed here.

`file_server`
: This process provides an interface to the external file system. All file system requests are processed here.

`shell`
: This process is a simple interactive command interpreter which allows the user to compile, load and run applications and to inspect and control the system.

These parts of the system are described in greater detail in the following sections. The OS described here is a small one which provides applications with a basic environment upon which they can build their own specialised environments. Considering the diversity of applications which have been run in ERLANG a generalised OS would be very large and complex, yet still not able to cater for all needs.

The ERLANG *language* provides many of the features, like concurrency and interprocess communication, which are usually provided by OS kernels. Also, in some cases, we use some of the facilities of an underlying OS instead of implementing these directly in ERLANG. This simplifies our task and allows us to concentrate on the higher levels of the system. We still call it an operating system, however, because, together with the language, it provides the functionality usually associated with an OS.

13.2 System Startup

When ERLANG is started it creates an initial process which evaluates the function `init:boot` and all control is then passed to this process. This process now starts the rest of the system.

The code-handling BIFs in ERLANG are not designed to be used directly by an application but from a code server which is used by applications for handling code. Before anything else is run `init:boot` loads the code server, defined in module `code`, and starts the server processes. To implement the *autoload* facility a suitable version of the module `error_handler` is needed (see Section 7.6) which interacts with the code server when a call is made to an undefined function. The function `init:boot` loads in the default `error_handler` which does this. Users can modify this behaviour by using their own private error handlers for specific processes (see Section 7.6), which is dangerous, or by loading in their own module `error_handler` to replace the default one, which is *very* dangerous.

The `init` process, the `code_server` process and the `error_handler` module are the *kernel* of this operating system. At this stage the system is considered to be up and running. The process `init` will now process the command line arguments (for systems which have these) and then:

- Start the default servers `user`, `file_server` and `shell`.[1]
- Start any servers or evaluate any functions requested by the user in the command line arguments.
- Save the rest of the arguments for the user.

The processes `user` and `file_server` are started by `init` before starting any user servers, evaluating user functions or starting the shell. This is to ensure that an application sees a consistent environment. The present `init` does not supervise the servers it has started. It could, however, be modified to do this. Section 8.4 describes how this can be done.

13.3 Code Management

ERLANG supports both dynamic[2] loading of code on running systems and the use of multiple versions of the same module. The basic building block for code is the module. Currently, the system can contain two versions of a module at one time:

Latest version
: This is the version that all *new fully qualified* calls made to a function within a module will evaluate.

Old version
: No new fully qualified calls will execute the old version, but code already executing the old version of a module will continue using the old version when doing internal calls.

For a description of how multiple versions of code can be used see the examples in Section 9.3. In this section we describe *how* this is implemented and managed.

13.3.1 BIFs for code replacement

The following BIFs allow the user to build systems which permit dynamic code replacement:

[1] The user can specifically request that this not be done.

[2] By dynamic loading of code we mean that the code is loaded and linked at run-time unlike languages such as C where code is statically linked prior to loading.

erlang:load_module(Module, Binary)
Loads the ERLANG module in binary data object **Binary**. If code for this module already exists, moves the latest code to the old and replaces all references to exported functions so they point to the new code.

erlang:delete_module(Module)
Moves the latest version of the code for **Module** to the old code buffer and deletes all references to exported functions of **Module**.

erlang:module_loaded(Module)
Tests if **Module** is loaded. Does not attempt to load the module.

erlang:check_process_code(Pid, Module)
Tests if the process **Pid** is executing an old version of Module.

erlang:purge_module(Module)
Removes old code associated with **Module**. **erlang:check_process_code** must be called before using **erlang:purge_module** to check that no processes are executing old code for this module.

erlang:pre_loaded()
Returns a list of all modules that are preloaded into the ERLANG system.

Note that these BIFs are all optional (see Appendix B). Users should *not* use them directly but instead use the module **code** which is described in Appendix C or implement their own application-specific code handler.

13.3.2 Purging code

When a new version of a module is loaded, the current old version of that module is lost and the current latest version becomes the new old version.

We must check that there are no processes left which run the old version when it is removed. This is called *purging* code. The function **code:purge** ensures this by killing all processes which are evaluating any functions in the old version. It does this by the following means:

- Get a list of all currently executing processes with the BIF **processes**. All processes that are executing old code will be in this list as no new processes can be spawned which execute old code in any module.
- For each process in this list, call **erlang:check_process_code** and, if a process is evaluating a function in the old version of the module, kill it by sending it an **EXIT** signal. The **EXIT** signal sent is **kill** which is untrappable, even if the process is trapping **EXIT**s.
- When we are sure that there are no processes executing old code in the module we call **erlang:purge_module** to move the latest version to the old version.

An application-specific code server could choose to handle this differently, for example, by not killing processes executing old code but asking some manager process what should be done with them. The manager, for example, might decide not to allow purging of the code, or to notify the processes executing old code to call the new version (see Section 9.3). By being able to change the default mechanism code handling can be changed to meet specific needs.

13.3.3 Loading a module

Before we can safely load a new module we must ensure that the module has been purged. When this has been done we obtain the object code for the module throgh the file system using `{ok, Bin} = file:read_file(Filename)` and then evaluate `erlang:load_module(Module, Bin)` which makes the current latest version the old version and loads in a new latest version of the module. An error is generated if there is an old version of the module when `erlang:load_module/2` is evaluated.

Since the actual obtaining of object code is separated from the loading of the object code, it is easy to write application specific routines to obtain object code. For example when a node runs on a host without a file system, or with a file system different from the one that contains the application code, a pseudo file system like the one demonstrated in Section 11.9 can be started. Since all code loading is done through the file system, the code server will never notice that the code it is loading is fetched transparently from a remote node.

It is also possible to obtain new object code throgh for example a serial port on the target host. This may sometimes be a option when running ERLANG on small embedded systems with a serial `tty` as its only communications means.

A final note to be made about loading code and booting is that since all code is loaded into the run-time systems through ERLANG ports, someone has to load the ERLANG code which is used to load the code ! This initial boot code is preloaded into the runtime system, and the BIF `erlang:pre_loaded/0` can be used to see which modules are preloaded.

13.4 The Input/Output System

This part of the OS provides applications with formatted input/output (IO). It is a server-based system consisting of a standard interface, utility libraries and default servers. This section describes the design and interaction of the different parts.

The IO system is designed to work with any server which obeys the standard protocol. This allows an application using the IO interface to be used with any IO server.

`io_lib`
: This contains formatting functions for converting terms to lists of characters and converting input characters to tokens for the ERLANG parser.

`parse`
: This is the parser which converts a list of tokens into the internal representation of the input form or term.

The standard interface defined in the module `io` consists of:

`put_chars(Device, Chars)`
: Writes the characters in the list `Chars`. This is translated into the request `{put_chars,Chars}`.

`write(Device, Term)`
: Writes the printed representation of `Term`. This is translated into the request `{put_chars,io_lib,write,[Term]}`.

`format(Device, FormatString, FormatArgs)`
: Formats the items in `Args` as specified by `Format`. This is translated into the request `{put_chars,io_lib,format,[Format,Args]}`.

`nl(Device)`
: Writes a new line. This is translated into the request `{put_chars,"\n"}`.

`get_chars(Device, Prompt, Count)`
: Fetches `Count` characters, prompting with `Prompt`. This is translated into the request `{get_until,Prompt,io,collect_chars,[Count]}`.

`get_line(Device, Prompt)`
: Fetches a line, prompting with `Prompt`. This is translated into the request `{get_until,Prompt,io,collect_line,[]}`.

`read(Device, Prompt)`
: Reads a term, prompting with `Prompt`.

`parse_exprs(Device, Prompt)`
: Reads a sequence of expressions, prompting with `Prompt`.

`parse_form(Device, Prompt)`
: Reads an ERLANG form (something which is valid in an ERLANG source file), prompting with `Prompt`.

`requests(Device, Requests)`
: Performs the list of requests in one atomic operation to the standard output.

Only a brief description is given here. Note that:

- The argument `Device` in each function is optional. If a device has been given then it will be used, otherwise input will be taken from standard input and output written to standard output. Standard input and output are provided by the registered process `user`.
- All functions return `{error,What}` if an error occurs, output functions return the atom `ok` to show success and input functions return `eof` if an end of file is encountered.

- All input functions have a 'prompt' argument. In a concurrent environment it is impossible to guarantee that two requests sent from a client to a server are handled consecutively by the server. Each input operation has a prompt included with it to ensure that the prompt and the input request are treated together by the server. The prompt is ignored when it is not applicable (for example the file server).
- The three input functions `read`, `parse_exprs` and `parse_form` all translate into the request `{get_until,Prompt,io,scan,[]}`. The tokens returned by `io:scan` are parsed by the caller.

13.4.2 The file server

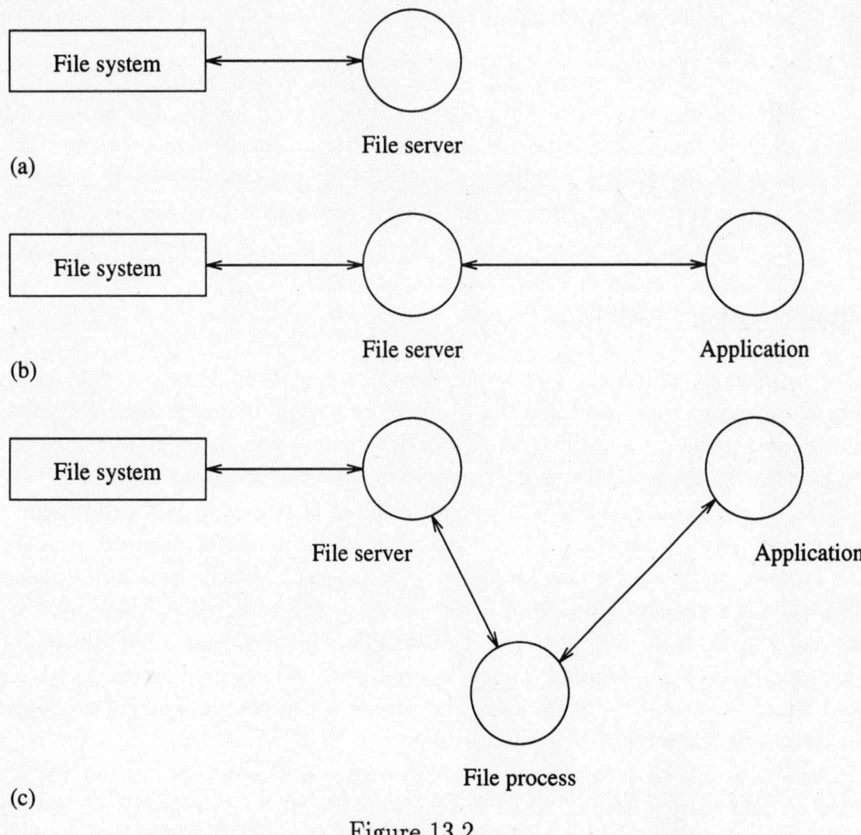

Figure 13.2

The file server provides ERLANG applications with a hierarchical file system. It presents a different set of problems to the user server, although they have basically the same interface. The current implementation of the server uses the file system of the host operating system and does not implement its own file system. This has been done to allow the ERLANG system to share files with other applications runnning on the underlying host operating system.

The file server is an ERLANG server, registered with the name **`file_server`**, connected through a port (see Section 9.4) to the file system of the underlying OS (see Figure 13.2(a)). The server process sends commands to the file system to do all operations on files within the system.

When a process needs to open a file it sends an open request to the file server (see Figure 13.2(b)). The server then tries to open the file through the external file system. If this succeeds the file server starts a process representing the file to handle operations on this file (see Figure 13.2(c)). The Pid of this process is returned to the application where it is used as the device (see Section 13.4.1) for IO operations. All access requests to a file are sent to the file process where they are handled. The file process communicates with the external file system through the file server.

The file server must ensure that there are no files left opened by applications which have terminated. The file process is linked to both the file server and the application process which opened the file. If the process which opened the file terminates before the file has been closed the file process detects this and closes the file. After the file has been closed the file process for that file also terminates.

13.4.3 The user server

The user server, which is registered under the name **`user`**, is responsible for handling all standard input and standard output requests. It is a process connected to a port (see Section 9.4) which 'is' the user terminal and must handle IO requests from ERLANG applications as well as asynchronous input from the user.

The server waits in a loop. If an IO request is received it is processed. Any unsolicited input from the port is saved; this allows type-ahead in the user server. Concurrency causes problems for the server – we must be able to handle concurrent requests. If a request were completely to block the user server then once a read request arrived from any process (for example, the shell) no other process could perform any IO until the read request was satisfied. This would severely restrict the concurrent nature of the language. The problem is a consequence of multiplexing all IO to a single stream.

Our solution is to recognise that there are *two different* types of request – read requests and write requests. Write requests are atomic and do not block the server. A read request, however, waits until there is sufficient input before it is completed, potentially blocking the server for a long period of time. During a read request we allow write requests from other processes[3] to be handled, continuing the read after each output has completed. Other read requests arriving are buffered and handled

[3]The process requesting the read is, of course, blocked and cannot request a write.

one at a time.

Program 13.2 is the code for the function `get_until` which does this. Before any input has been received by a `get_until` request we allow it to be interrupted by an output request. This is implemented by processing input in two stages. The first stage, the function `get_until1`, is called before there is any input. This waits for either input from the port or output requests for other processes. Output requests are processed immediately. When input arrives from the port we go to the second stage, the function `get_until2`, which repeatedly calls the user function until it has collected all the characters it needs. The function `prompt` writes the prompt to the port, while the function `unprompt` is used to indicate that this read has been interrupted by output. When the read is resumed the prompt is written again.

13.5 The Standard Shell

A simple command interpreter is included in the standard ERLANG distribution to allow the user to interact with the system. The example in Section 8.3 shows how to write such a shell. It is a simple *read–eval–print*[4] loop where the user can enter expressions which are evaluated by the shell and the result is printed.

The shell described here is more complex, with the following features:

- A history mechanism, which saves the last 20 expressions entered and the values returned. It is possible to re-evaluate an expression or to use the returned value of an expression.
- Variables can be bound in expressions and then used later. As a variable can never be rebound to a new value, there is also a mechanism to 'forget' the binding of a variable. This avoids inventing new names.
- Sometimes we do not wish to wait for an expression evaluation to terminate, when, for example, we start a long-lived process. There is an explicit mechanism to run expressions *in the background* and continue execution of the shell.
- A module `c`, which contains functions which are intended for interactive use. Examples of these functions are compiling and loading modules, and printing information about current processes and loaded modules.

There are many ways in which the shell could be extended:

- The current command could be aborted. To be more precise, the process which was started to evaluate the expression could be killed.
- Command line editing.
- Settable options, for example, the length of history list saved.
- More useful functions.

[4]An expression is read, evaluated and then its value is printed.

```
get_until(Prompt, Mod, Func, As, Port, Buf) ->
    prompt(Port, Prompt),
    get_until1(Prompt, Mod, Func, As, Port, Buf).

get_until1(Prompt, Mod, Func, As, Port, []) ->
    receive
        {Port,{data,Bytes}} ->
            get_until2(catch apply(Mod, Func, [[],Bytes|As]),
                       Mod, Func, As, Port);
        {From,ReplyAs,{put_chars,Chars}} when pid(From) ->
            get_until1_out({put_chars,Chars}, From, ReplyAs,
                           Prompt, Mod, Func, As, Port);
        {From,ReplyAs,{put_chars,M1,F1,A1}} when pid(From) ->
            get_until1_out({put_chars,M1,F1,A1}, From, ReplyAs,
                           Prompt, Mod, Func, As, Port);
        {'EXIT',_,What} ->
            {exit,What}
    end;
get_until1(Prompt, Mod, Func, As, Port, Buf) ->
    get_until2(catch apply(Mod, Func, [[],Buf|As]),
               Mod, Func, As, Port).

get_until1_out(Req, From, ReplyAs, Prompt, Mod, Func, As, Port) ->
    unprompt(Port, Prompt),
    io_request(Req, From, ReplyAs, Port, []),
    prompt(Port, Prompt),
    get_until1(Prompt, Mod, Func, As, Port, []).

get_until2({more,Cont}, Mod, Func, As, Port) ->
    receive
        {Port,{data,Bytes}} ->
            get_until2(catch apply(Mod, Func, [Cont,Bytes|As]),
                       Mod, Func, As, Port);
        {'EXIT',_,What} ->
            {exit,What}
    end;
get_until2({done,Result,Buf}, Mod, Func, As, Port) ->
    {ok,Result,Buf};
get_until2(Other, Mod, Func, As, Port) ->
    {error,{error,get_until},[]}.
```

Program 13.2

It is, however, doubtful if it is worthwhile adding more to this shell since larger applications will define their own user interfaces. Most non-trivial applications will probably make use of a graphical user interface (see Chapter 17) rather than the type of shell described in this section.

13.5.1 Eval

The central part of the shell is the expression evaluator, which takes a representation of an expression (or rather an expression sequence) in the form returned by the parser and tries to evaluate it. We give the code for `eval` without really defining the representation of ERLANG expressions. It is straightforward to extract the format from the code as each different form is explicitly handled.

```
expr({atom,A}, Bs) -> {value,A,Bs};
expr({number,N}, Bs) -> {value,N,Bs};
expr({char,C}, Bs) -> {value,C,Bs};
expr({var,V}, Bs) ->
    case binding(V, Bs) of
        {value,Val} -> {value,Val,Bs};
        unbound -> exit(unbound)
    end;
expr({string,S}, Bs) -> {value,S,Bs};
expr(nil, Bs) -> {value,[],Bs};
expr({cons,H0,T0}, Bs0) ->
    {value,H,Bs1} = expr(H0, Bs0),
    {value,T,Bs2} = expr(T0, Bs0),
    {value,[H|T],merge_bindings(Bs1, Bs2)};
expr({tuple,Es0}, Bs0) ->
    {Vs,Bs} = eval_list(Es0, Bs0),
    {value,list_to_tuple(Vs),Bs};
expr({arith,Op,L0,R0}, Bs0) ->
    {value,L,Bs1} = expr(L0, Bs0),
    {value,R,Bs2} = expr(R0, Bs0),
    {value,eval_arith(Op, L, R),merge_bindings(Bs1, Bs2)};
expr({arith,Op,A0}, Bs0) ->
    {value,A,Bs} = expr(A0, Bs0),
    {value,eval_arith(Op, A),Bs};
```

Program 13.3(a)

Program 13.3(a) gives the code for `eval:expr/2`, which takes an expression and tries to evaluate it. The first argument is the parsed form of the expression

```
expr({bif,Name,As0}, Bs0) ->
    {As,Bs} = eval_list(As0, Bs0),
    {value,bif(Name, As),Bs};
expr({call,[],Name,As0}, Bs0) ->     %No local functions
    exit(undef);
expr({call,Mod,Name,As0}, Bs0) ->
    {As,Bs} = eval_list(As0, Bs0),
    {value,apply(Mod, Name, As),Bs};
expr({match,Lhs,Rhs0}, Bs0) ->
    {value,Rhs,Bs1} = expr(Rhs0, Bs0),
    case match(Lhs, Rhs, Bs1) of
        {match,Bs} ->
            {value,Rhs,Bs};
        nomatch ->
            exit(badmatch)
    end;
expr({block,Es}, Bs) ->
    seq(Es, Bs);
expr({'if',Cs}, Bs) ->
    if_clauses(Cs, Bs);
expr({'case',E,Cs}, Bs0) ->
    {value,Val,Bs} = expr(E, Bs0),
    case_clauses(Val, Cs, Bs);
expr({'catch',Expr}, Bs0) ->
    case catch expr(Expr, Bs0) of
        {value,Val,Bs} ->
            {value,Val,Bs};
        Other ->
            {value,Other,Bs0}
    end;
expr({send,T0,M0}, Bs0) ->
    {value,T,Bs1} = expr(T0, Bs0),
    {value,M,Bs2} = expr(M0, Bs0),
    {value,T ! M,merge_bindings(Bs1, Bs2)};
expr({value,Val}, Bs) ->                %Special case
    {value,Val,Bs};                     % straight values.
expr(E, Bs) ->                          %Not Yet Implemented
    exit({'NYI',E}).
```

Program 13.3(a)(cont)

to evaluate and the second argument is a list of the current variable bindings. `eval:expr` returns `{value,Value,Bindings}` if the expression can be evaluated,

```
match(Pat, Term, Bs) ->
    catch match1(Pat, Term, Bs).

match1({atom,A}, A, Bs) ->
    {match,Bs};
match1({number,N}, N, Bs) ->
    {match,Bs};
match1({char,C}, C, Bs) ->
    {match,Bs};
match1({var,'_'}, _, Bs) ->             %Anonymous variable matches
    {match,Bs};                         % everything, no new bindings
match1({var,Name}, Term, Bs) ->
    case binding(Name, Bs) of
        {value,Term} -> {match,Bs};
        {value,V} -> throw(nomatch);
        unbound -> {match,add_binding(Name, Term, Bs)}
    end;
match1({string,S}, S, Bs) ->
    {match,Bs};
match1(nil, [], Bs) ->
    {match,Bs};
match1({cons,H,T}, [H1|T1], Bs0) ->
    {match,Bs} = match1(H, H1, Bs0),
    match1(T, T1, Bs);
match1({tuple,Elts}, Tuple, Bs) when length(Elts) == size(Tuple) ->
    match_list(Elts, Tuple, 1, Bs);
match1(_, _, _) ->
    throw(nomatch).

match_list([E|Es], Tuple, I, Bs0) ->
    {match,Bs} = match1(E, element(I, Tuple), Bs0),
    match_list(Es, Tuple, I+1, Bs);
match_list([], _, _, Bs) ->
    {match,Bs}.
```

Program 13.3(b)

otherwise it generates a fault by calling `exit`. There is a separate clause in `expr` for each type of expression and we can see how `expr` follows the standard evaluation mechanism of ERLANG. Care must be taken to ensure that the variable bindings are correct when evaluating subexpressions. The only expression which is not

```
eval_arith('+', A1, A2) when number(A1), number(A2) ->
    A1 + A2;
eval_arith('-', A1, A2) when number(A1), number(A2) ->
    A1 - A2;
eval_arith('*', A1, A2) when number(A1), number(A2) ->
    A1 * A2;

. . .

eval_arith('bsl', A1, A2) when integer(A1), integer(A2) ->
    A1 bsl A2;
eval_arith('bsr', A1, A2) when integer(A1), integer(A2) ->
    A1 bsr A2;
eval_arith(Op, A1, A2) ->
    exit(badarith).

eval_arith('+', A) when number(A) ->
    A;
eval_arith('-', A) when number(A) ->
    -A;
eval_arith('bnot', A) when integer(A) ->
    bnot A;
eval_arith(Op, A) ->
    exit(badarith).
```

Program 13.3(c)

handled here is `receive`, which is difficult to implement correctly in this fashion.[5]

Program 13.3(b) is the code for `match`, which performs all match operations. Only `match` can add new variables to the binding list. The function `match` takes three arguments, a pattern, a term to match and the initial variable bindings. If the match succeeds `{match,NewBindings}` is returned, otherwise it returns `nomatch`. `NewBindings` contains the initial variable bindings updated with those generated by the match.

If we detect that the match has failed (different type of term or variables have different values) then we abort the entire match operation immediately. To simplify the code we enclose the match function in a `catch` and use `throw` to exit in the event of an error (see Section 7.1). This makes it unnecessary to have code to handle unwinding every recursive call of `match1`.

[5]We cannot remove messages from the input buffer to inspect them and then be certain that they are put back correctly; other messages may have been sent to us in the meantime.

```
%% if_clauses(Clauses, Bindings)

if_clauses([{clause,G,B}|Cs], Bs) ->
    case guard(G, Bs) of
        true ->
            seq(B, Bs);
        false ->
            if_clauses(Cs, Bs)
    end;
if_clauses([], Bs) ->
    exit(if_clause).

%% case_clauses(Value, Clauses, Bindings)

case_clauses(Val, [{clause,[P],G,B}|Cs], Bs0) ->
    case match(P, Val, Bs0) of
        {match,Bs} ->
            case guard(G, Bs) of
                true ->
                    seq(B, Bs);
                false ->
                    case_clauses(Val, Cs, Bs0)
            end;
        nomatch ->
            case_clauses(Val, Cs, Bs0)
    end;
case_clauses(Val, [], Bs) ->
    exit(case_clause).
```

Program 13.3(d)

Program 13.3(c) contains the code for evaluating arithmetic expressions. The arguments to the operator have been evaluated by `expr`. In the functions `eval_arith` there is one clause for each operator and a failure clause if the arguments are of the wrong type. Note that not all the cases have been shown.

The code for evaluating the `case` and `if` primitives is shown in Program 13.3(d). We attempt to match the value for each clause (only for `case`) and then try to evaluate the guard. If the guard succeeds we evaluate the expression sequence in the body, otherwise we attempt the next clause. If none of the clauses is chosen we generate a failure using `exit`.

Evaluating guards is shown in Program 13.3(e). For each test or comparison in a guard we evaluate the arguments and then attempt to perform the test or comparison. If a test or comparison fails we do not continue with the remaining

```
guard([{test,Name,As0}|Gs], Bs0) ->
    {As,Bs} = eval_list(As0, Bs0),
    case guard_test(Name, As) of
        true ->
            guard(Gs, Bs);
        false ->
            false
    end;
guard([{comp,Op,Lhs0,Rhs0}|Gs], Bs0) ->
    {value,Lhs,Bs1} = expr(Lhs0, Bs0),
    {value,Rhs,Bs} = expr(Rhs0, Bs1),
    case guard_comp(Op, Lhs, Rhs) of
        true ->
            guard(Gs, Bs);
        false ->
            false
    end;
guard([], Bs) ->
    true.

guard_test(integer, [A]) when integer(A) -> true;
guard_test(float, [A]) when float(A) -> true;

. . .

guard_test(reference, [A]) when reference(A) -> true;
guard_test(port, [A]) when port(A) -> true;
guard_test(_, _) ->
    false.

guard_comp('==', Lhs, Rhs) when Lhs == Rhs -> true;
guard_comp('/=', Lhs, Rhs) when Lhs /= Rhs -> true;

. . .

guard_comp('=:=', Lhs, Rhs) when Lhs =:= Rhs -> true;
guard_comp('=/=', Lhs, Rhs) when Lhs =/= Rhs -> true;
guard_comp(_, _, _) -> false.
```

Program 13.3(e)

```
seq(Seq, Bs) ->
    seq(Seq, Bs, true).

seq([E|Es], Bs0, _) ->
    {value,V,Bs} = expr(E, Bs0),
    seq(Es, Bs, V);
seq([], Bs, V) ->
    {value,V,Bs}.

eval_list(Es, Bs) ->
    eval_list(Es, [], Bs, Bs).

eval_list([E|Es], Vs, BsOrig, Bs0) ->
    {value,V,Bs1} = expr(E, BsOrig),
    eval_list(Es, [V|Vs], BsOrig, merge_bindings(Bs1, Bs0));
eval_list([], Vs, _, Bs) ->
    {reverse(Vs),Bs}.

%% bif(Name, Arguments)
%%  Evaluate the Erlang builtin function Name.

bif(Name, As) ->
    apply(erlang, Name, As).
```

Program 13.3(f)

tests but return `false`; if all complete successfully we return `true`. Note that as the cases for doing the guard tests and comparisons are very similar not all are shown.

Finally, Program 13.3(f) contains some miscellaneous functions. The function `seq` evaluates a sequences of expressions (kept as a list) and returns the value of the last expression. `eval_list` evaluates a list of expressions and returns all the values and tries to merge the bindings. It is used for arguments to functions and BIFs, and the elements of a tuple. To evaluate a BIF we could have written a clause for each BIF, as for the arithmetic operators; instead, we use the fact that all BIFs are exported from the module `erlang` and use `apply`.

No code is given here for handling the bindings, which are kept in a dictionary. The only other function necessary for the bindings is `merge_bindings`, which takes two sets of bindings and merges them into one, checking that the values of variables occurring in both bindings are the same. If an inconsistent value is found then a `badmatch` fault is generated.

As noted before, there is no code for the `receive` primitive. It is difficult to do this in a safe manner by this method.

The operation of wait_time can be understood if we first look at the function insert:

```
insert(Dir, Floor, Now, Stop) ->
    insert(Dir, Floor, Now, [], Stop).

insert(Dir, Floor, Now, Before, []) ->
    lists:reverse([Floor|Before]);
insert(Dir, Floor, Now, Before, [Floor|After]) ->
    lists:reverse(Before, [Floor|After]);
insert(Dir, Floor, Floor, Before, [Next|After]) ->
    lists:reverse(Before, [Next|After]);
insert(up, Floor, Now, Before, [Next|After])
    when Now < Floor, Floor < Next ->
    lists:reverse(Before, [Floor,Next|After]);
insert(down, Floor, Now, Before, [Next|After])
    when Next < Floor, Floor < Now ->
    lists:reverse(Before, [Floor,Next|After]);
insert(Dir, Floor, Now, Before, [Next|After]) ->
    insert(Dir, Floor, Next, [Next|Before], After).
```

In the above Now is the current floor where the lift is, Stop is a list of floors at which the lift must stop and Floor is the floor number where the call request was made. insert(Dir, Floor, Now, Stop) works out where to place Floor in the stop list. Dir is up or down. insert/4 returns a new stop list:

```
> lifts:insert(up, 6, 4, [5,7,9,3]).
[5,6,7,9,3]
> lifts:insert(down, 6, 4, [5,7,9,3]).
[5,7,9,6,3]
```

If the lift is at floor 4 and the stop list is [5,7,9,3], pressing up from the 6th floor will cause the lift to stop on the way up, i.e. the new stop list is [5,6,7,9,3]. Pressing down on the 6th floor causes the lift to stop on the way down and the new stop list is [5,7,9,6,3].

The wait time for a lift is calculated by assuming it takes one time unit to travel between floors and five time units to stop and open and close the lift doors.

wait_time(Dir, Floor, Now, Stop) works out the time to wait for a lift. The arguments have the same meaning as for insert/4.

```
wait_time(Dir, Floor, Now, Stop) ->
    wait_time(Dir, Floor, 0, Now, Stop).
```

```
wait_time(Dir, Floor, T, Now, []) ->
    T + abs(Floor - Now);
wait_time(Dir, Floor, T, Now, [Floor|After]) ->
    T + abs(Floor - Now);
wait_time(up, Floor, T, Now, [Next|After]) when
    Now =< Floor, Floor =< Next ->
    T + Floor - Now;
wait_time(down, Floor, T, Now, [Next|After]) when
    Now >= Floor, Floor >= Next ->
    T + Now - Floor;
wait_time(Dir, Floor, T, Now, [Next|After]) ->
    wait_time(Dir, Floor, T+abs(Now-Next)+5, Next, After).

> lifts:wait_time(up,6,4,[5,7,9,3]).
7
> lifts:wait_time(down,6,4,[5,7,9,3]).
23
```

We have to wait 7 time units for the lift to arrive at floor 6 if we request an up journey and 23 time units for a down journey.

We now have the basic components of the algorithm. All that remains is to add code for what happens if a floor is requested from within the lift.

If a button is pressed within the lift a new stop list is created where the requested floor is inserted in the stop list at the earliest available opportunity. `stop_at(Floor,Now,Stop)` creates such a list:

```
stop_at(Floor, Now, Stop) ->
    stop_at_1(Floor, [], [Now|Stop]).

stop_at_1(Floor, Before, []) ->
    lists:reverse([Floor|Before]);
stop_at_1(Floor, Before, [Floor|After]) ->
    lists:reverse(Before, [Floor|After]);
stop_at_1(Floor, Before, [X,Y|After])
    when X < Floor, Floor < Y ->
    lists:reverse(Before, [X,Floor,Y|After]);
stop_at_1(Floor, Before, [X,Y|After])
    when Y < Floor, Floor < X ->
    lists:reverse(Before, [X,Floor,Y|After]);
stop_at_1(Floor, Before, [H|T]) ->
    stop_at_1(Floor, [H|Before],T).

> lifts:stop_at(6,4,[5,7,9,3]).
[4,5,6,7,9,3]
```

Immediate requests from within the lift are processed in the top loop of the lift controller, as are messages from the environment:

```
top_lift(Lift, {Doing, Now, Stop}) ->
    receive
        {internal, stop, Time, Floor} ->
            Stop1 = stop_at(Floor, Now, Stop),
            top_lift(Lift, {Doing, Now, Stop1});
        {internal, at_floor, N} ->
            case Stop of
                [N|Stop1] ->
                      top_lift(Lift, {Doing, N, Stop1});
                _ ->
                      top_lift(Lift, {Doing, N, Stop})
            end;
        {Id, how_long, Floor, Dir} ->
            ...
            top_lift(Lift, State1)
    end.
```

Here we assume the message `{internal, at_floor, N}` is sent automatically when the lift arrives at or passes floor `N`. This messages causes updating of the stop list and the current floor.

All that remains is to establish the overall process structure. This consists of spawning 3 lift and 12 floor processes. Error recovery code can be added to restart any crashed process. This code is left as an exercise for the reader.

14.2 A Satellite Control System

In this section we construct a system which encapsulates the quintessential aspects of a satellite control system (SCS).[1]

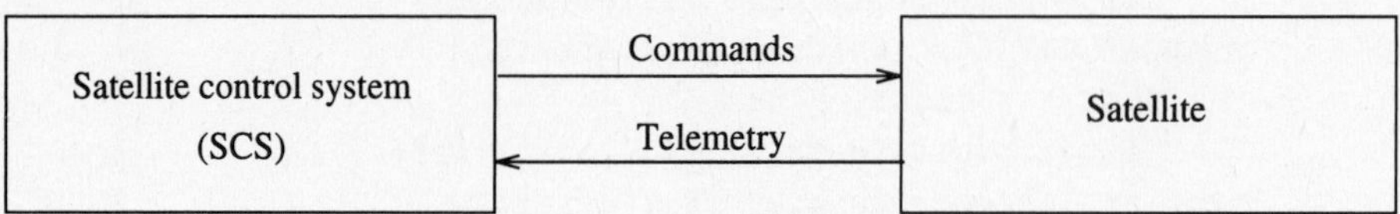

Figure 14.2 A satellite control system

As far as the logical design of an SCS is concerned, a satellite can be considered a 'black box', controlled by sending it commands. The effect of these commands

[1]The SCS described here is loosely based on the control system which was written in Fortran by one of the authors to control the Swedish Viking satellite. Here we show how it could have been done in ERLANG!

can be seen by analysing the telemetry data which the satellite sends back to the control system (see Figure 14.2).

The SCS is responsible for the following tasks:

- Generation and supervision of commands which are sent to the satellite.
- Display of telemetry data for monitoring the performance of the satellite.
- Continuous monitoring of telemetry data to detect possible fault conditions in the satellite.
- Permanent storage of all telemetry data for subsequent analysis.
- Mission planning – this includes orbit determination, manœuvre planning, etc.

Telemetry data contains data which is measured by instruments in the satellite. This data is sent to the ground station. Physical parameters such as temperature and magnetic field strengths are converted to sequences of bytes and are stored in the telemetry data. The data is continuously transmitted as a sequence of fixed-length frames. Raw data corresponding to a particular measurement occupies known positions in these frames.

Conversion between physical units and the representation used in the telemetry requires a knowledge of the conversion algorithm, together with possible calibration factors. While in operation, the satellite continuously sends telemetry data which may or may not be received by the ground station.

Our SCS is built using the following modules:

`convert`
: Used to convert between physical units and raw command or telemetry data formats.

`data_manager`
: Provides access to telemetry data and allows commands to be sent to the satellite.

`data_logger`
: Permanently stores all telemetry data.

`alarm`
: Handles processing of alarm data.

In addition, we give examples of how modules can be written for monitoring the health of the satellite (for example, `monitor_battery`) and performing 'end-to-end' confirmation of commands. Figure 14.3 shows the *logical* structure of the different components in the SCS.

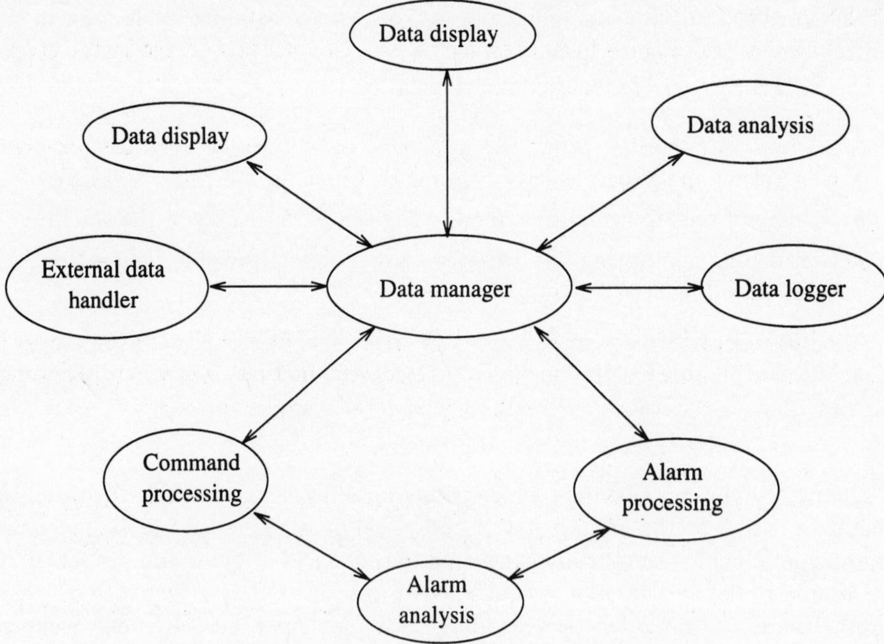

Figure 14.3 Logical structure of the SCS

In Figure 14.3 the functions of the different components are as follows:

`Data display`
: One or more processes which are responsible for real-time display of data received from the satellite.

`Data analysis`
: One or more processes responsible for analysing data received from the satellite.

`Data manager`
: A process which manages all requests for data. This is connected through a port to the external data handler.

`External data handler`
: An external process which interfaces the ERLANG system to the hardware which communicates with the satellite.

`Data logger`
: A process which stores all incoming data from the satellite.

`Command processor`
: One or more processes which interact with an operator to send commands to the satellite. Commands are actually sent using services provided by the data manager.

`Alarm processing`
: One or more processes which monitor data from the satellite for possible fault conditions.

`Alarm analysis`
: Processes which are started to analyse alarm conditions detected by the alarm processing software.

The arrows in Figure 14.3 show the principal flow of data between the different components.

14.2.1 Data conversion

The module `convert` hides knowledge about where and how physical data is stored in the telemetry and command data streams and performs conversion between physical and raw data units. `convert` exports the following functions:

`get_data(Descriptor, Telemetry)`
: Returns the physical data associated with `Descriptor` from the data in `Telemetry`. `Descriptor` can describe one data item or a list of data items.

`encode_cmd(Cmd)`
: Takes a command and returns the list of bytes representing that command.

The code for `convert` hides a lot of complexity, tables of addresses, calibration data, etc. No code is given here.

14.2.2 Data management

We assume that an external process is used to communicate with the satellite through some external hardware. We communicate with this external process using the port mechanism described in Chapter 9. The data management process multiplexes all requests between various ERLANG processes which want to send commands to, or receive data from, the satellite. The data management process is interfaced with the following function calls:

`subscribe(Tag, Descriptor)`
: Requests that the current process be sent a message containing `Tag` together with the data described by `Descriptor` every time new telemetry data is received.

`unsubscribe(Tag)`
: Stops sending the data set referenced by `Tag`.

`send_command(Command)`
: Sends `Command` to the satellite.

`get_data(Descriptor)`
: Sends the data described by `Descriptor` from the last received telemetry frame.

The data manager is shown in Program 14.1.

```
-module(data_manager).
-export([start/1, internal/1, subscribe/2, unsubscribe/1,
         send_command/1, get_data/1]).

start() ->
    register(data_manager, spawn(data_manager, internal,[])).

subscribe(Tag, Data) ->
    data_manager ! {self(), {subscribe, Tag, Data}}.

unsubscribe(Tag) ->
    data_manager ! {self(), {unsubscribe, Tag}}.

send_command(Cmd) ->
    data_manager ! {send_command, Cmd}.

internal() ->
    Port = open_port({spawn, data_handler}),
    server(Port, [], []).

server(Port, Clients, Telemetry) ->
    receive
        {Port,{data, Telemetry1}} ->
            send_to_clients(Clients, Telemetry1),
            server(Port, Clients, Telemetry1);
        {Pid, {subscribe, Tag, Data}} ->
            server(Port, add_request(Pid, Tag, Data, Clients),
                   Telemetry);
        {Pid, {unsubscribe, Tag}} ->
            server(Port, delete_request(Pid, Tag, Clients),
                   Telemetry);
        {send_command, Cmd} ->
            Port ! {command, convert:encode_cmd(Cmd)},
            server(Port, Clients, Telemetry);
        {Pid, {get_data, Desc}} ->
            Pid ! {data_manager,
                       {data, convert:get_data(Desc, Telemetry)}},
            server(Port, Clients, Telemetry);
     end.
```

```
get_data(Descriptor) ->
    data_manager ! {self(), {get_data, Descriptor}},
    receive
        {data_manager, {data, Data}} ->
            Data
    end.
```

Program 14.1

`send_to_clients(Requests, Telemetry)` takes a list of requests and which telemetry data they require, extracts the required data from the telemetry and sends messages to the requesting processes containing the required data.

```
send_to_clients([{Pid, Tag, Descriptor}|T], Telemetry) ->
        Pid ! {data_manager, Tag,
                convert:get_data(Descriptor, Telemetry)},
        send_to_clients(T, Telemetry);
send_to_clients([], Telemetry) ->
        true;
```

The functions `add_request/4` and `delete_request/3` manipulate the request list `Requests`, adding and removing requests for data to/from this list.

Once the data capture process has been started with `data_manager:start()`, any process in the system which wants access to telemetery data can make a request of the form:

```
data_manager:subscribe(Tag, Descriptor)
```

Having made this request, every time a new telemetry frame is received by the data capture process, the requesting process will be sent messages which can be received with:

```
receive
    {data_manager, Tag, Data} ->
        ...
end
```

The `data_manager` process which we have discussed contains no code for error recovery. In a real system we would monitor the behaviour of the clients and remove them from the `Client` list if they terminate. This can be done by setting a link between the server and the clients and trapping any `EXIT` signals originating from the clients; details of this programming technique were covered in the section on reliable servers in Chapter 8. Another problem concerns the safety of the server. In addition to monitoring the behaviour of the clients, we should also monitor the servers and the external port, and restart them if they crash.

Having made the above changes we should be reasonably convinced that the data capture server is correct and will not crash at run-time. For additional security we would also add code to monitor the behaviour of the data manager process, and restart it if it terminates.

Another design decision concerns changing the code for the data manager while the system is running. If we want to be able to do this then the tail recursive calls to `server/3` in the body of the `receives` in the server loop should be changed to `data_manager:server/3` calls. If this change is made new versions of the data manager can be introduced without stopping the system; this technique was described in more detail in Section 9.3. Having started the data manager we can create a number of clients which use its services.

14.2.3 Data logging

A client of the data manager is the data logger which makes a permanent copy of all the telemetry data:

```
-module(data_logger).
-export([start/0, internal/0]).

start() -> spawn(data_logger, internal, []).

internal() ->
    data_manager:subscribe(telemetry, raw, all_raw_data),
    server(file:open('raw.data')).

server(Stream) ->
    receive
        {data_manager, raw, Data} ->
            io:write(Stream, Data),
            server(Stream)
    end.
```

The code for the data logger is simplified: in reality we should check the return codes from the `open` and `write` function calls. We might also want to limit the maximum size of the output data file by splitting it into smaller chunks and building some index files so that we can navigate through the raw data at a later stage.

14.2.4 Data monitoring

During the lifetime of the satellite we monitor certain parameters and take action if these parameters assume abnormal values. For example, the operating instructions for the satellite might advise that the battery temperature and voltage should be measured every two minutes and that action be taken if the battery gets too cold or if the battery voltage falls below a given value.

```
-module(monitor_battery).
-export([start/0, internal/0]).

start -> spawn(monitor_battery, internal, []).

internal() ->
    data_manager:subscribe(battery_info,
        [battery_temperature, battery_voltage]),
    server().

server() ->
    receive
        {data_manager, battery_info, [Temp, Voltage]} ->
            check(Temp, Voltage)
    end,
    server().

check(Temp, Voltage) when Temp < 10.0 ->
    alarm ! {self(),{alarm, {battery_too_cold, Temp}}};
check(Temp, Voltage) when Temp > 60.0 ->
    alarm ! {self(),{alarm,{battery_too_hot, Temp}}};
check(Temp, Voltage) when Voltage < 2.3 ->
    alarm ! {self(),{alarm,{battery_voltage_too_low, Voltage}}};
...
```

The process defined in the module `monitor_battery` sends a message to the `alarm` process if an error condition occurs. In a real system we make several design decisions about the exact nature of the monitoring process. The following points would have to be considered:

- Instantaneous or smoothed data. We may not want to take a decision on the instantaneous value of a data item but rather take the average over some period of time.
- False alarms. We may not wish to raise an alarm on the first occasion when we suspect trouble (sometimes simple loss of data or corrupted data causes 'false' alarm indications), preferring to wait until the evidence that something has gone wrong becomes convincing.
- Table-driven or hard-coded alarm procedures. In our example we 'hard-coded' the tests for an alarm condition. In practice, we make a generic module to handle simple 'out-of-bounds' data and hard-code the more complex cases.

14.2.5 Data display

Data display is a simple case of data monitoring. All we have to do is obtain the incoming data and present it to the operator in some easily understandable form. Here we make extensive use of graphics and use the techniques of Chapter 17 for presentation of data.

14.2.6 Commanding the satellite

Commands to the satellite can come from a number of different sources, which include:

- Operator commands – these are entered on a command console and are obeyed immediately.
- Pre-scheduled commands – these are command sequences which are scheduled to be sent to the satellite at a pre-determined time.
- Alarm processing commands – these are sent when an alarm condition is detected.

Operator commands are sent directly with `data_manager:send_command(Cmd)`.

Pre-scheduled commands can be arranged by spawning a process which is suspended until the required time has elapsed and then sends the required commands when it resumes execution. If one wishes to cancel a set of pre-scheduled commands then the process which is waiting to perform these commands is killed. Alarm processing commands are sent either automatically or manually when alarm conditions are detected.

There are three types of command sending strategy:

- Send and pray – send the command but do not check if it has reached the satellite.
- Send and acknowledge – send the command and check that it has been *received* by the satellite.
- Send and confirm effect of command – send the command, check that it has been received by the satellite and check that it has had the desired physical effect.

`data_manager:send_command` has 'send and pray' semantics. In practice, almost all satellite command decoders are designed to transmit the last received command continuously in the telemetry data. `send_command_and_acknowledge` sends a command and checks the next ten telemetry frames to see if a copy of the command reappears in the telemetry data.

```
send_command_and_acknowledge(Cmd) ->
    data_manager:send_cmd(Cmd),
    data_manager:subscribe(cmd, command_replica),
    Reply = wait_acknowledge(10, Cmd),
    data_manager:unsubscribe(cmd),
    Reply.

wait_acknowledge(0, Cmd) ->
    {command_not_acknowledged, Cmd}
wait_acknowledge(N, Cmd) ->
    receive
       {data_manager, cmd, Cmd}->
           command_sent;
       {data_manager, cmd, _}->
           wait_acknowledge(N-1, Cmd)
    end.
```

While such a procedure suffices for most practical purposes, the fact that certain commands have worked must be inferred by analysing other parameters in the telemetry data.

For example, after sending a 'battery heater on' command, one checks that the main bus voltage and current both change by an appropriate amount and that the battery temperature increases. Note that what an 'appropriate amount' is, and how much temperature increase should be expected, may be data which has to calculated in real-time using some program which simulates the expected behaviour of the satellite.

14.2.7 Alarm processing

The registered process `alarm` is responsible for processing alarm data. We alert the operator if an alarm has occurred. The following strategy is assumed:

- Alert the operator, suggest a possible solution to the problem and the maximum time the operator has in which to take action.
- Set a timeout, the maximum time allowed for the operator to take action.
- If the operator enters a command then cancel the timeout.
- If the timeout occurs and the operator has not yet given a command perform the default corrective action.

The server loop of a simple alarm processing module is written as follows:

```
server(Index, Pending) ->
    receive
        {Pid, {alarm, What}} ->
             {Suggest, MaxTime} = analyse:alarm(What),
                  operator:alert(Index,What,Suggest,MaxTime),
                  schedule_timeout(MaxTime, Index),
                  server(Index+1, [{Index, What}|Pending]);
        {operator, {response, Index, Cmds}} ->
                  do_command(Cmds),
                  server(Index, remove_pending(Index,Pending));
        {timeout, Index} ->
                  What = get_alarm(Index, Pending),
                  DefaultCmds = analyse:default_action(What),
                  do_cmds(DefaultCmds),
                  server(Index, remove_pending(Index,Pending))
    end.

schedule_timeout(MaxTime, Index) ->
    spawn(alarm, send_message, [self(), MaxTime, Index]).

send_message(Pid, Time, Index) ->
    receive
    after Time ->
        Pid ! {timeout, Index}
    end.
```

In the above code fragment `Pending` is a list of tuples `{Index, What}` representing alarms which are waiting operator action.

We could imagine a more complex scenario:

- A monitoring process detects that the battery temperature is too low. It sends an alarm message to the alarm process.
- The alarm process calls code in `analyse` to work out what to do. If the battery state of charge is high turn on the battery heater, if it is low turn off any non-essential items in the payload.
- The alarm process suggests what action should be taken and gives the operator a maximum time in which to make a decision.
- The operator makes a decision, or a timeout occurs and the default corrective action is taken.
- Commands are sent to the satellite.
- The system monitors the battery temperature to see if the corrective action has suceeded.

All the above activities can easily be programmed as a set of concurrent communicating processes, analysing alarms, monitoring the success of a corrective action, waiting for a certain event, etc.

14.2.8 Mission planning

The SCS is responsible not only for real-time control of the satellite but also for mission planning and support. Typical mission planning involves time-consuming and complex tasks like orbit determination and manœuvre planning. These in turn use 'standard' software packages (typically involving hundreds of thousands of lines of Fortran). Such packages are best left unchanged[2] and interfaced to the system using the standard port mechanism described in Chapter 9. Assuming that we are running on an operating system which supports multiprocessing with different priority levels, we can easily arrange that the ERLANG system runs at a high priority and takes care of the real-time control aspects of the system, and that background tasks (such as orbit determination) are run at a lower priority as external processes to the ERLANG system. This has the added advantage that failures in large packages are detectable as `EXIT` signals from ports so that the system can restart the external processes if they fail.

Using the port mechanism, all the 'foreign' code in the external packages can be interfaced to the system to appear as if it had been written in ERLANG. The ability to mix different languages, reusing old code where appropriate, into a uniform framework simplifies the overall design of the system since it presents the system designer with a uniform and consistent view of the system.

[2] If it works don't touch it!

`Address1` and `Address2` (i.e. starts the transmission of speech between these two addresses).

`disconnect(Address1, Address2)`
: Removes a connection in the speech switch.

`start_tone(Address, Type)`
: Starts sending a tone of type `Type` to a telephone at hardware address `Address`. This means that the tone will be heard in the telephone handset. Type is one of `dial`, `ring`, `busy` or `fault`.

`analyse(Number)`
: Analyses a dialled number (which is a list of digits). This returns `invalid` if the number dialled is not a valid telephone number, `get_more_digits` if the number is not complete[4] or `{address, Pid, Address}` if `Number` corresponds to a line in the switch (in this example we ignore calls which do not terminate in our own exchange). `Pid` is the process identity of the process controlling the telephone corresponding to the dialled number, and `Address` is its hardware address.

Each process controlling a telephone can receive the following messages from the telephone:

`off_hook`
: The handset has been lifted from the telephone.

`on_hook`
: The handset has been put back onto the telephone.

`{digit, Digit}`
: The digit `Digit` has been dialled.[5]

We also need to define the messages between the A and B sides of the call.

`{seize, Pid}`
: We ask the process controlling a telephone if we may make a new call to that telephone. We send our own process identity `Pid` so that the other process knows to which process it should send its reply.

`seized`
: A reply to the `{seize, Pid}` message above indicating that a new call has been accepted.

`rejected`
: A reply to the `{seize, Pid}` message above indicating that a new call has been rejected.

---

[4] Many countries have variable length telephone numbers, thus we cannot know in advance how many digits are going to correspond to a telephone number, but must perform a new analysis every time a digit is received.

[5] Nowadays this will probably have been done using a push-button telephone which sends tones to the exchange. How these tones are received by the exchange is beyond the scope of this chapter.

```
write(fd,(char*) programmer,sizeof(struct Person));
/* assume we succeed with malloc and write */
```

If the above code runs on machine A then the following code could be run on machine B to read the data written by A:

```
struct Person *programmer;

programmer = (struct Person*) malloc(sizeof(struct Person));
read(fd,(char*)programmer,sizeof(struct Person));
/* assume we succeed with malloc and read */
```

This works provided computers A and B are of the same type. If the two computers use a different byte ordering for the representation of integers then, in our example, the integer 32 which was sent will not be received as 32. Moreover, if the receiving computer represents characters in a different way, the bit-pattern that on computer A means the character 'a' may not represent that character on computer B.

Not only can different computers represent the basic data types differently but also different implementations of the *same* computer language could have different representations of both primitive and structured data types. If the programs which communicate are written in different programming languages the problem gets worse.

One solution to this is to use a common language to describe all data types which are involved in acts of communication between the two machines and to adopt a set of rules for serialising an instance of a type into a sequence of bytes which can be sent on a communications channel. In the above case, the serialising process was easy – we just sent the structure exactly as it was represented in memory. This is also where the problem arises: computer B may not represent an integer in memory in the same way as computer A. One widely adopted solution to this is to describe the data in a machine-independent way, or to decide in the application level that all integers must occupy four bytes and have a predefined byte order, and so on for all data types which the application is expected to process. This is *very* error-prone.

A better solution is to adopt a common language to describe the data types. One such language is ASN.1. The widespread use of a standardised type description language would reduce the number of strange home-brewed data transport formats currently in use. The price is reduced performance.

Currently ASN.1 is used mainly within the OSI framework in the representation and applications layers. It could also be used, however, in less complicated contexts where the entire OSI environment is not present. An example is the Simple Network Management Protocol SNMP [10] which uses ASN.1-based messages on top of UDP/IP datagrams to manage and monitor computer networks.

It should be noted that if we use distributed ERLANG to communicate between different computers the entire problem domain of different data representation is

Chapter 16

An ASN.1 Compiler

ASN.1 is a type description language defined and standardised by the CCITT[1] in the X.208 [12] and X.209 [13] standards. It is becoming widely used for the specification of communications protocols. ASN.1 is used in virtually all of the layer seven protocols within the OSI [24] computer communications protocols and is also the main building block of the OSI presentation layer.

This chapter describes a fairly complicated ERLANG application, an ASN.1 to ERLANG cross-compiler. We start with a discussion of ASN.1, what it is and why it is. We continue with a description of the compiler and finally give an example of a non-trivial application developed with the aid of the compiler.

16.1 Background

ASN.1 is a *type description language* which is used to define types in a manner similar to the typing facilities found in imperative programming languages such as Pascal or C. The following C code could be used to create an instance of a data type and write it to some communication channel:

```
struct Person {
    unsigned int age;
    char name[25];
};

struct Person *programmer;
programmer = (struct Person*) malloc(sizeof(struct Person));
programmer->age = 32;
strcpy(programmer->name,"A. Hacker");
```

[1]The CCITT (International Telegraph and Telephone Consultative Committee) is the organisation responsible for international telecommunication standards.

Recall that the code for `make_call_to_B` was as follows:

```
make_call_to_B(Address, B_Pid, B_Address) ->
    receive
        seized ->
            tele_os:start_tone(Address, ring),
            ringing_A_side(Address, B_Pid, B_Address);
        rejected ->
            tele_os:start_tone(Address, busy),
            wait_on_hook(Address, busy);
        {seize, Pid} ->
            Pid ! rejected,
            make_call_to_B(Address, B_Pid, B_Address)
    after 1000 ->
          tele_os:start_tone(Address, fault),
          wait_on_hook(Address, fault)
    end.
```

Observe that:

- The ERLANG code and the SDL diagram have exactly the same structure.
- The ERLANG code is more detailed than the SDL diagram; for example, the code uses explicit names and arguments in all messages and functions.

The ERLANG code is a refinement of the SDL specification. SDL gives a clear overview of the functionality whereas the ERLANG code gives sufficient detail to execute the program.

Note that after rejecting other calls (when this process has received a **`seize`** message) we make a recursive call to `make_call_to_B`. This is done in SDL by returning to the same state using a state symbol containing a '-' character.

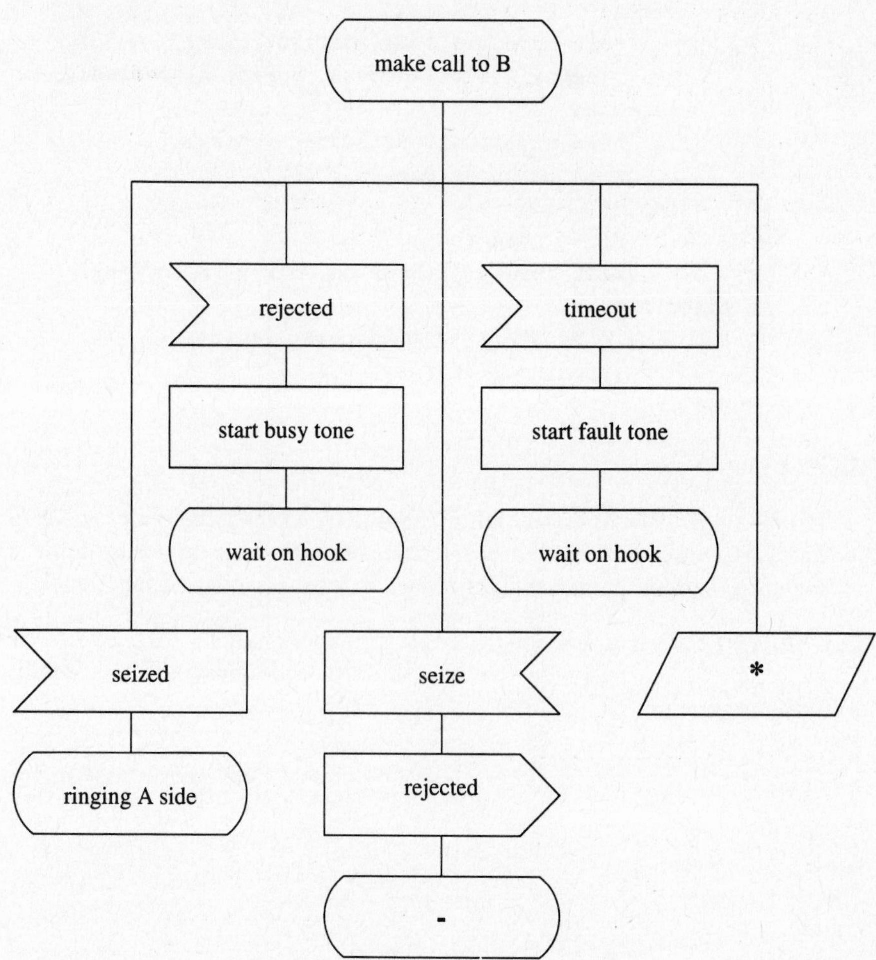

Figure 15.7 SDL: making a call to B

Output symbol. Sends a message.

Input symbol 'Consumes' a message. This corresponds to a pattern in a receive primitive.

Save symbol. Unlike ERLANG, SDL discards messages which do not match any input symbol. In SDL a save symbol is used to save explicitly messages which do not match. A '*' in a save symbol means save all non-matching messages.

Task symbol. Performs some action.

These symbols are connected with lines which show the flow of control.

The function representing the idle state of the telephony example may be represented in SDL as shown in Figure 15.6. Note that in ERLANG we explicitly 'throw away' unwanted messages in this state, but in SDL this is the default semantics.

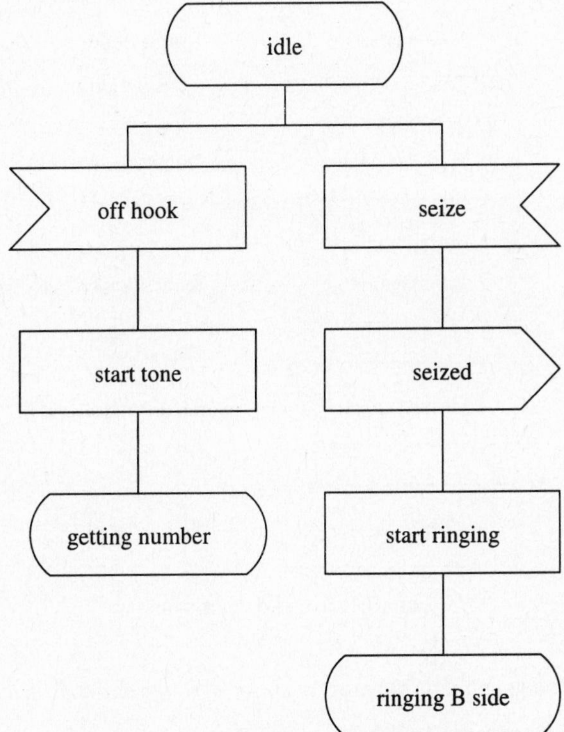

Figure 15.6 SDL: the idle state

The function `make_call_to_B` could be represented in SDL as shown in Figure 15.7. Here we see that we need to use the save symbol to save explicitly messages which we do not wish to receive in this state.

15.4 SDL

SDL [11] (Specification and Description Language) is a specification language which is widely used in the telecommunications industry to specify the behaviour of switching systems. SDL has a textual representation and a graphical representation. This section shows how specifications in SDL can be programmed in ERLANG with very little effort.

SDL has a processed-based model of concurrency with asynchronous message passing between processes. This maps in an obvious manner onto ERLANG. The corresponding mapping of SDL onto non-concurrent languages such as C or C++ or onto a language with a different model of concurrency, such as Ada, is a more difficult task.

In the graphical representation of SDL the symbols in Figure 15.5 are used.[7]

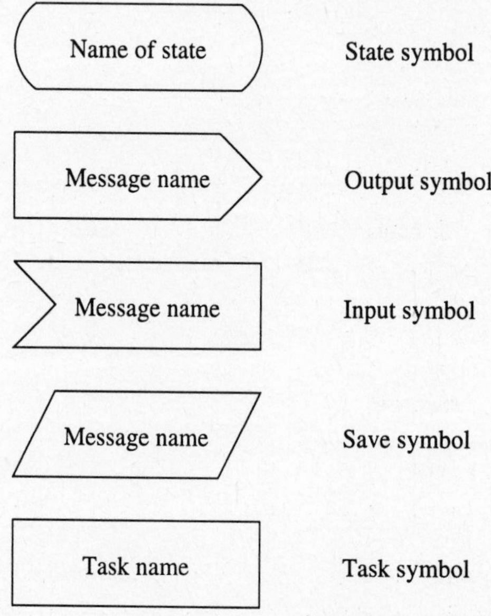

Figure 15.5 SDL symbols

The subset of the graphical representation of SDL we show here has the following parts:

State symbol A process waits for an input message (which is called a signal in SDL, but we will use 'message' here to avoid confusion). This corresponds to the `receive` primitive.

[7]The SDL in this example has been simplified for clarity – see [11] for full details.

```
other_connections(_,_,[]) ->
        no;
other_connections(A,_, [{A,_,_} | _ ]) ->
        yes;
other_connections(A,_, [{_,A,_} | _ ]) ->
        yes;
other_connections(_,A, [{A,_,_} | _ ]) ->
        yes;
other_connections(_,A, [{_,A,_} | _ ]) ->
        yes;
other_connections(A,B, [_ | T]) ->
    other_connections(A,B,T).

delete_connection(A,B, []) ->
        no;
delete_connection(A,B, [{A,B,Pid} | T]) ->
        {yes, T};
delete_connection(A,B, [{B,A,Pid} | T]) ->
        {yes, T};
delete_connection(A,B, [H | T]) ->
    {Result, Rest} = delete_connection(A,B, T),
    {Result, [H | Rest]}.

delete_process(Pid, []) -> [];
delete_process(Pid, [{A,B,Pid} | T]) ->
    hw:disconnect(A,B),
    delete_process(Pid,T);

delete_process(Pid, [H | T]) ->
    [H | delete_process(Pid,T)].
```

The function `start_switch()` is used to spawn and register the server. Functions `connect(A, B)` and `disconnect(A, B)` send messages to the switch server requesting action in the switch.

The server first checks that the action requested is consistent, i.e. it does not conflict with existing connections in the switch. When a connection is made, the server stores the connection and the Pid of the process 'owning' the connection (i.e. the process which evaluated `connect(A, B)`) and sets up a link to this process. Since the server traps `EXIT` signals, it will receive an `EXIT` signal if the process owning a connection terminates. When an `EXIT` signal is received, the server checks through its list of connections and, if it finds a connection owned by the process from which the `EXIT` was received, removes the connection. When a connection is disconnected normally (when the function `disconnect(A, B)` is evaluated) the process link to the server is removed.

```
wait_on_hook(Address, Type) ->
    case get_event() of
        on_hook ->
            case Type of
                none ->
                    true;
                _ ->
                    tele_os:stop_tone(Address)
            end,
            idle(Address);
        _ ->
          wait_on_hook(Address, Type)
    end.

get_event() ->
    receive
        {seize, A_Pid} ->
            A_Pid ! rejected,
            get_event();
        Other ->
            Other
    end.

get_event_or_time_out(Time) ->
    receive
        {seize, A_Pid} ->
            A_Pid ! rejected,
            get_event();
        Other ->
            Other
    after Time ->
            timeout
    end.

max_time_before_answer() ->
    90000.
max_time_between_digits() ->
    30000.
```

```
ringing_A_side(Address, B_Pid, B_Address) ->
    case get_event_or_time_out(max_time_before_answer()) of
        on_hook ->
            B_Pid ! cleared,
            tele_os:stop_tone(Address),
            idle(Address);
        answered ->
            tele_os:stop_tone(Address),
            tele_os:connect(Address, B_Address),
            speech(Address, B_Pid, B_Address);
        timeout ->
            B_Pid ! cleared,
            tele_os:stop_tone(Address),
            tele_os:start_tone(Address, fault),
            wait_on_hook(Address, fault);
        _ ->
            ringing_A_side(Address, B_Pid, B_Address)
    end.

speech(Address, Other_Pid, Other_Address) ->
    case get_event() of
        on_hook ->
            Other_Pid ! cleared,
            maybe_disconnect(Address, Other_Address, Other_Pid),
            idle(Address);
        cleared ->
            maybe_disconnect(Address, Other_Address, Other_Pid),
            wait_on_hook(Address, none);
        _ ->
           speech(Address, Other_Pid, Other_Address)
    end.

maybe_disconnect(Address, not_used, Other_Pid) ->
    unlink(Other_Pid),
    true;
maybe_disconnect(Address1, Address2, Other_Pid) ->
    tele_os:disconnect(Address1, Address2).
```

```
getting_number(Address, Number) ->
    case get_event_or_time_out(max_time_between_digits()) of
        {digit, Digit} ->
            maybe_remove_tone(Address, Number),
            Number1 = lists:append(Number, [Digit]),
            case tele_os:analyse(Number1) of
                get_more_digits ->
                    getting_number(Address, Number1);
                invalid ->
                    tele_os:start_tone(Address, fault),
                    wait_on_hook(Address, fault);
                {address, B_Pid, B_Address} ->
                    B_Pid ! {seize, self()},
                    make_call_to_B(Address, B_Pid, B_Address)
            end;
        on_hook ->
            maybe_remove_tone(Address, Number),
            idle(Address);
        timeout ->
            maybe_remove_tone(Address, Number),
            tele_os:start_tone(Address, fault),
            wait_on_hook(Address, fault);
        _ ->
            getting_number(Address, Number)
    end.

maybe_remove_tone(Address, []) -> tele_os:stop_tone(Address);
maybe_remove_tone(_,_)         -> true.

make_call_to_B(Address, B_Pid, B_Address) ->
    receive
        seized ->
            tele_os:start_tone(Address, ring),
            ringing_A_side(Address, B_Pid, B_Address);
        rejected ->
            tele_os:start_tone(Address, busy),
            wait_on_hook(Address, busy);
        {seize, Pid} ->
            Pid ! rejected,
            make_call_to_B(Address, B_Pid, B_Address)
    after 1000 ->
        tele_os:start_tone(Address, fault),
        wait_on_hook(Address, fault)
    end.
```

eliminated, thus there is no need for a data description language when we use ERLANG. We use ASN.1 from ERLANG when we wish to communicate with some other system which speaks ASN.1.

16.2 About ASN.1

The primitive data types of ASN.1 are booleans, integers, reals, enumerated, bit-strings, byte strings and a variety of character strings. These types can be combined to make the following structured data types:

- `SEQUENCE` — similar to C structs, or Pascal records.
- `SET` — as a `SEQUENCE` but unordered.
- `SEQUENCE OF` — similar to a C or Pascal array.
- `SET OF` — as above but unordered.
- `CHOICE` — similar to a C union or Pascal variant record.

With these constructs various structured data types can be defined. For example, the ASN.1 data type `Apdu` is defined by the following ASN.1 specification:

```
Apdu ::= [PRIVATE 1] SEQUENCE {
     num INTEGER,
     data CHOICE {
         stringdata [0] OCTET STRING,
         intdata [1] INTEGER (0..48) } }
```

Types can be given names with the ASN.1 assignment operator '::=', and these names can be used to define other types. The type `Apdu` defined in the example above, is a structure which has two fields, one `INTEGER` and one `CHOICE`, where the latter can be either an `OCTET STRING` or an `INTEGER`. The two components of the `SEQUENCE` can be distinguished by the identifiers `num` and `data` and the components of `CHOICE` by `stringdata` and `intdata`. This type also has a tag, namely `[PRIVATE 1]`, [2] and the components of the `CHOICE` part also have tags.

The tags are used to identify the data on the decoding side. For example, the tag `[PRIVATE 1]` encodes into the byte `225` so when a decoder receives the byte `225` it can associate it with the type `Apdu`. The tags provide a way to associate a type with a small number which is sent as the first byte in every instance of that type on a communications channel.

Inner tags are used to distinguish components in a specific context. In the above example the first component of the CHOICE structure has tag `[0]` which is encoded as `128` and the second component as `129`. When a decoder decodes the `CHOICE` it inspects the first byte of the data and takes different action depending upon whether the first byte is `128` or `129`.

[2] **`PRIVATE`** is a reserved word of ASN.1.

Creating an instance of this Apdu type involves assigning a value to the two component fields in the SEQUENCE. To do this in ERLANG we represent ASN.1 values by tuples of size 2 where the first element is the name of the ASN.1 type and the second element the value of that type instance. If the type is a structured type, as in our Apdu example, then the components of the instance are a list, where each component is again a tuple of size 2: the first element of each tuple is the component identifier and the second element is the value of the component. For example, in order to create an instance of Apdu in an ERLANG program we could write:

```
ApduValue  = {'Apdu',[{num,7},
                      {data,{stringdata ,[88,77,66,55] }}]}
```

An ASN.1 encoder works on these type instances and produces a sequence of bytes which can be sent to a communications channel or supplied as raw data to a lower protocol layer if we are operating inside a protocol stack.

The serialisation of the above type will have the byte 225 as its first byte. Immediately following the tag comes a sequence of bytes informing the decoder of the length of the instance. This is sometimes referred to as tag length value (TLV) encoding. We will write the TLV encoding as an ERLANG tuple of the form {Tag, Length, List_of_values}.[3] Using this notation, the value of ApduValue given above would be encoded as follows:

```
{225, 13, [{48, 11, [{2,1,[7]}, {128, 6, [{4, 4,[88,77,66,55]}]}]}]}
```

where 255 is the Apdu tag, 48 the SEQUENCE tag, 2 the integer tag, 128 a context tag and 4 the string tag.

On output this structure is 'flattened', i.e. the bytes:

```
225, 13, 48, 11, 2, 1, 7, 128, 6, 4, 4, 88, 77, 66, 55
```

are written to the communication line.

16.3 BER – Basic Encoding Rules

ASN.1 type instances are encoded and decoded using the Basic Encoding Rules (BER) defined by the CCITT in the X.209 standard.

Since all structured types are compositions of the primitive types, we have defined a run-time library which contains encode and decode routines for all the basic types. This library is contained in the ERLANG modules encode and decode. The following routines encode and decode booleans according to the BER.

[3]Note that the encoding routines described hereafter do not use the tuple notation given here but work directly with flat lists of characters – this is for reasons of efficiency.

```
encode_boolean({'BOOLEAN',Val}) ->
    encode_boolean(Val);

encode_boolean('TRUE') ->
    [1,1,255];

encode_boolean('FALSE') ->
    [1,1,0].

decode_boolean([1,1,0]) ->
    'FALSE';

decode_boolean([1,1,_]) ->
    'TRUE'.
```

The boolean value `FALSE` is encoded as the list `[1,1,0]`, where the first `1` is the tag for `BOOLEAN`, the second `1` means that the length of the actual value is 1 byte, and the third digit, `0`, is the actual value. The BER rules state that any non-zero value means `TRUE` and the value zero means `FALSE`. The primitive types can be combined into structured types, as in:

```
Btype ::= [PRIVATE 2] SEQUENCE {
    a BOOLEAN,
    b BOOLEAN }
```

An instance of `Btype` could be written in ERLANG as:

```
{'Btype',[{a,'TRUE'},{b,'FALSE'}]}
```

This would encode into the following structure:

```
{226, 8, [{48, 6, [{1, 1, [255]}, {1, 1,[0]}]}]}
```

where `226` is the tag of `Btype` since `[PRIVATE 2]` is encoded as `226`; `8` is the number of bytes that remain of the instance of the `Btype`; `48` is the tag defined in ASN.1 to represent `SEQUENCE`; and `6` is the number of bytes that remain of the instance of the `SEQUENCE`; the structure concludes with the two booleans.

The modules `encode` and `decode` also contain code for encoding *all* the primitive ASN.1 types (`INTEGER`, `OCTET STRING`,...). This code is not given here.

It is perhaps worth mentioning that research is being done to develop other and more efficient encoding rules. We may wish to optimise different applications for different goals. For example, one application might send a million integers to another application. The ASN.1 solution of wrapping each of these integers with a tag incurs a considerable run-time overhead – it may be desirable to have different encoding standards which satisfy the dual goals of generality and efficiency (ASN.1 is very general but somewhat inefficient).

16.4 Implementation

16.4.1 Tokenising

In order to parse ASN.1 we need a tokeniser which transforms a sequence of characters into a sequence of tokens. The tokeniser is written as follows, where the argument is a list containing all the characters in the file.

```
tokenise([H|T]) when $a =< H , H =< $z ->
    {X, T1} = get_name(T, [H]),
    [{identifier, X}|tokenise(T1)];

tokenise([H|T]) when $A =< H , H =< $Z ->
    {X, T1} = get_name(T, [H]),
        case reserved_word(X) of
            {true,Word} ->
                [{reserved_word, Word}|tokenise(T1)];
            false ->
                case pre_defined(X) of
                    false ->
                        [{typereference,X} |tokenise(T1)];
                    {true,Word} ->
                        [{preDefined, Word}|tokenise(T1)]
                end
        end;

tokenise([$:,$:,$=|T]) ->
    [implies|tokenise(T)];

tokenise([${|Tail]) ->
        [lbrace|tokenise(Tail)];

....
```

16.4.2 Parsing

First we have to decide what the output of the parser should be. We have chosen to represent the intermediate code as a dictionary where the values associated with each property may also be a dictionary. So for example:

```
Easy ::= SEQUENCE {
    i INTEGER,
    b BOOLEAN }
```

is represented by the following parse tree:

```
[{typename,'Easy'},
    {definition,[{typename,'SEQUENCE'}, {attributes,[
        [{position,1},{id,i},{typename,'INTEGER'}],
        [{position,2},{id,b},{typename,'BOOLEAN'}]]}]}]
```

The job of the parser is first to verify that the input data represents correct ASN.1 syntax and then store the parse tree for each parsed type in a small database.

A recursive descent parser will suit our purposes here. Slightly simplified, this could contain code similar to the following:

```
parse([{typereference,Type},implies,{reserved_word,'SEQUENCE'},
      lbrace | Tail]) ->
     {Attributes,Tail2} = collect_attributes(Tail),
     Def = [{typename,Type},{definition,
                                 [{typename,'SEQUENCE'},
                                  {attributes,Attributes}]}],
     {Def,Tail2};
parse([{typereference,Type},implies,
      {reserved_word,'INTEGER'} | Tail ]) ->
     {IntProps,Tail2} = collect_properties('INTEGER',Tail),
     Def = [{typename,Type},{definition,IntProps}],
     {Def,Tail2};
...
```

Here we use clause head pattern matching and match as many tokens as are needed on the output of the tokeniser in order to decide which kind of code we are actually parsing. Once we are sure of what we are parsing, we commit to that choice and call auxiliary functions to collect the remaining parts of the type definition.

```
collect_attributes(Tokens) ->
   collect_attributes(Tokens,[]).

collect_attributes([],_) ->
   throw({asn1_error,{unexpected end of tokens',[]}});
collect_attributes([rbrace|Tail],Result) ->
   {Result,Tail};
```

```
collect_attributes([{identifier,Id},comma,
                    {reserved_word,'INTEGER'}|Tail],Result) ->
   {IntProps,Tail2} = collect_properties('INTEGER',Tail),
   Def = [{id,Id},{typename,'INTEGER'},{props,IntProps}],
   collect_attributes(Tail2,[Def|Result]);
....
```

As we can see, the entire list of tokens is passed around as an argument to all the functions of the parser. This is particularly useful when an error occurs. For example the last clause of the `collect_attributes/1` function is written:

```
collect_attributes(Tokens,_) ->
    throw({asn1_error,{'Unexpected token',Tokens}}).
```

The entire parser is enclosed within a `catch`. If an error occurs, we `throw` an error descriptor containing the remaining list of tokens where the error occurred. The top level of the parser calculates the position of the error relative to the original unparsed list of tokens. It is the responsibility of the function which performs the `throw` to diagnose the error and the responsibility of the top level to calculate the position of the error and present it in a readable way.

16.4.3 Code generation

Once the ASN.1 code has been parsed, the data structures which were the output of the parser are stored in a database where a code generating routine can extract them and generate ERLANG code which can encode and decode an instance of the type. An instance of the above-mentioned type `Easy` could resemble the following:

```
EasyValue = {'Easy',[{i,55},{b,'TRUE'}]}.
```

We wish to produce a routine that is specialised for the `Easy` type so we can write

```
Bytes = encode(EasyValue),
```

and have the output of that encode routine be a list of bytes. We also wish to produce a decoding routine. Slightly simplified, the output of the code generator for the `Easy` type would look like the following:

```
encode_Easy({'Easy',Val}) ->
    encode_Easy(Val);
```

```
encode_Easy(Val) ->
    Bytes1 = encode_Easy_attributes(list_to_tuple(Val)),
    Len1 = encode:elength(length(Bytes1)),
    Tag1 = 48,
    lists:concat([[Tag1],Len1,Bytes1]).

encode_Easy_attributes(Val) ->
    {i,Val1} = element(1,Val),
    L1 = encode:encode_integer(Val1),
    {b,Val2} = element(2,Val),
    L2 = encode:encode_boolean(Val2),
    lists:concat([L1,L2]).
```

where the generated code contains calls to the predefined library encoding routines for the primitive types: in this example `INTEGER` and `BOOLEAN`.

```
decode_Easy(Bytes) ->
    Parts = list_to_tuple(asn1_lib:partition(Bytes2)),
    {'Easy',decode_Easy_attributes(Parts)}.

decode_Easy_attributes(Parts) ->
    Bytes1 = element(1,Parts),
    Term1 = {i,decode:decode_integer(Bytes1)},
    Bytes2 = element(2,Parts),
    Term2 = {b,decode:decode_boolean(Bytes2)},
    [Term1,Term2].
```

16.4.4 Applying the generated code

If we wish to encode an instance of an ASN.1 type from within an ERLANG program, then we need to supply the name of the module where the generated code is defined. Either the user supplies this information or we look it up in the database which was created when we compiled our ASN.1 definitions to discover which module should be used for a particular ASN.1 type. We also use the convention that the generated code in a module has the same name as the ASN.1 module which defined that type.

The user could also supply the name of the module and use the generic `encode` function which is defined in the module `asn1`.

```
encode(Module,Term) ->
    Type = element(1,Term),
    Call = list_to_atom(lists:concat(['encode_',Type])),
    apply(Module,Call,[Term]).
```

specifications only describe one part of the protocol.[5] In our example the order of messages is embedded in the application code.[6]

16.5.3 The VTFTP server

The server must run on each and every machine in the network which wishes to provide this service. The server is in a loop which spawns processes for each connection.

```
server() ->
    Handler = spawn(vtftp_server,handler,[self()]),
    receive
        {Handler,i_have_channel_now} ->
            server()
    end.
```

The functions `communic:obtain_channel/1` and `communic:accept_channel/1` are functions which manage communications to the outside world.

`accept_channel/1` suspends the caller until an external request for a channel is received. `obtain_channel/1` allocates a virtual channel once communication has been established. `server/0` ensures that a handler process exists for each external channel. The handler function is spawned once per connection, waits in a loop and exits when it either receives garbage or when the communication process exits.

```
handler(Controller) ->
    %%% we wait in the next statement until an external request for
    %%% a channel is made ...
    Channel = communic:accept_channel(Controller),
    Controller ! {self(),i_have_channel_now},
    handler2(Channel).

handler2(Channel) ->
    Action = read_channel(Channel),
    process(Channel,Action),
    handler2(Channel).

process(Channel,close_this_channel_now) ->
    Channel ! {self(),close},
    exit(normal);
```

[5] A construct in ASN.1 called MACROS tries to solve this problem but makes a poor job of it.

[6] This is not generally thought of as good programming practice!

```
process(Channel,{'Mess',{get,[{file,Filename},{mode,Mode}]}}) ->
    case file:open(list_to_atom(Filename),read) of
        {error,_} ->
            M = {'Mess',{error,[{errCode,accessViolation}]}},
            Channel ! {self(),{deliver,encode(M)}};
        File ->
            M = {'Mess',{op,ok}},
            Channel ! {self(),{deliver,encode(M)}},
            pack_and_send(1, File, Channel)
    end;

process(Channel,{'Mess',{ls,Dir}}) ->
    case catch file:list_dir(Dir) of
        {ok,List} ->
            Reply = {'Mess',{lsResponse,List}};
        _ ->
            Reply = {'Mess',{error,[{errCode,noDirectory}]}}
    end,
    Channel ! {self(),{deliver,encode(Reply)}};

process(Channel,{'Mess',{cd,Where}}) ->
    case file:set_cwd(Where) of
        ok ->
            Reply = {'Mess',{op,ok}};
        _ ->
            Reply = {'Mess',{error,[{errCode,noDirectory}]}}
    end,
    Channel ! {self(),{deliver,encode(Reply)}};

process(Channel,_) ->
    Reply = {'Mess',{error,[{errCode,illegalOperation}]}},
    Channel ! {self(),{deliver,encode(Reply)}}.
```

The controller evaluates `pack_and_send/3` which reads the file, partitions it into 512-byte packets and sends it:

```
pack_and_send(BlockNumber,File,Channel) ->
    case io:get_chars(File,'',512) of
        eof ->
            T = {'Mess',{op,eof}},
            Channel ! {self(),{deliver,encode(T)}};
        Chars when list(Chars) ->
            T = {'Mess',{data,[{blockNr,BlockNumber},
                                {data,Chars}]}},
            Channel ! {self(),{deliver,encode(T)}},
            pack_and_send(BlockNumber+1,File,Channel);
        Other ->
            T = {'Mess',{error,[{errCode,readError}]}},
            Channel ! {self(),{deliver,encode(T)}},
            file:close(File)
    end.
```

The encode and decode routines which evaluate the ASN.1 library encoders and decoders are as follows:

```
encode(Term) ->
    case catch asn1:encode('Vtftp',Term) of
        {'EXIT',R} ->
            io:format("Encoder can't encode ~w~n",[{R,Term}]),
            exit(crash_bam_boo);
        X ->
            X
    end.

decode(Bytelist) ->
    case catch asn1:decode('Vtftp','Mess',Bytelist) of
        {'EXIT',R} ->
            io:format("Decoder got garbage ~w~n",[R]),
            close_this_channel_now;
        X ->
            X
    end.

read_channel(Channel) ->
    receive
        {Channel,{fromChannel,Bytes}} ->
            decode(Bytes);
        {Channel,_} ->
            close_this_channel_now
    end.
```

This code is equivalent to `ftpd` in a UNIX environment. The server contains several misfeatures and its functionality is far from the real `ftp`. For example, it has no security, poor error recovery and no user authentication.

16.5.4 The VTFTP client

The client is the equivalent of the `ftp` program which is started on a local machine when we wish to send or retrieve files from some host:

```
client_loop(Host,Channel) ->
    Chars = io:get_line('vtftp-> '),
    P = catch parse(string:strip(Chars,right,[10])),
    client_do(P,Host,Channel).

client_do({unix,Com},Host,Channel) ->       %% shell escape
    io:format("~s",[unix:cmd(Com)]),
    client_loop(Host,Channel);

client_do({quit},Host,Channel) when pid(Channel) ->
    Channel ! {self(),close},
    exit(normal);

client_do({quit},Host,Channel) ->
    exit(normal);

client_do({connect,Where},nil,nil)  ->
    case catch communic:obtain_channel(Where),
        {'EXIT',Reason} ->
            io:format("Can't connect ~w~n",[Reason]),
            client_loop(nil,nil);
        S ->
            io:format("Connected ~n",[]),
            client_loop(Where,S)
    end;

client_do({close},Host,Channel) when pid(Channel) ->
    Channel ! {self(),close},
    client_loop(nil,nil);
```

```
client_do({cd,Where},Host,Channel) when atom(Where),pid(Channel) ->
    M = {'Mess',{cd,{dir,atom_to_list(Where)}}},
    Channel ! {self(),{deliver,encode(M)}},
    case read_channel(Channel) of
        close_this_channel_now ->
            Channel ! {self(),close},
            loop(nil,nil);
        {'Mess',{op,ok}} ->
            io:format("cd complete~n",[]),
            client_loop(Host,Channel);
        {'Mess',{error,What}} ->
            io:format("can't cd ~w~n",[What]),
            client_loop(Host,Channel)
        end;

client_do({get,File},Host,Channel) when atom(File), pid(Channel) ->
    statistics(runtime),
    case get_file(Channel,File) of
        {vtftp_error,{noclose,Reason}} ->
            io:format("Can't get file: ~w~n",[Reason]),
            client_loop(Host,Channel);
        close_this_channel_now ->
            io:format("Transfer incomplete ~w",[Reason]),
            io:format("Closing connection~n",[]),
            Channel ! {self(),close},
            client_loop(nil,nil);
        file_transferred ->
            io:format("Transfer complete ~n",[]),
            {_,T} = statistics(runtime),
            case file:file_info(File) of
                {ok,Tup} ->
                    io:format("~w bytes in ~w millisecs~n",
                              [element(1,Tup),T]);
                _ ->
                    true
            end,
            client_loop(Host,Channel)
    end;

client_do({ls}, Host, Channel) ->
    client_do({ls,'.'}, Host, Channel);
```

```
client_do({ls,Dir}, Host, Channel) when pid(Channel) ->
    Directory = atom_to_list(Dir),
    M = {'Mess',{ls,Directory}},
    Channel ! {self(),{deliver,encode(M)}},
    case read_channel(Channel) of
        close_this_channel_now ->
            io:format("Connection broken ~w~n",[Reason]),
            client_loop(nil,nil);
        {'Mess',{lsResponse,Resp}} ->
            io:format("Transfer complete~n",[]),
            print_ls_response(Resp),
            client_loop(Host,Channel);
        {'Mess',{error,What}} ->
            io:format("can't ls ~w~n",[What]),
            client_loop(Host,Channel)
    end;

client_do(_, Host, Channel) ->
    io:format("Que !!~n",[]),
    client_loop(Host, Channel).
```

`client_do/3` uses some auxiliary functions. `get_file/2` sends the actual `get` message to the server and receives the file in 512-byte packets which it writes to a local file:

```
get_file(Channel,File) ->
    case file:file_info(File) of
        {ok,_} ->
            {vtftp_error,{noclose,'File already exists'}};
        _ ->
            M = {'Mess',{get,[{file,atom_to_list(File)},
                              {mode,octet}]}},
            Channel ! {self(),{deliver,encode(M)}},
            case read_channel(Channel) of
                close_this_channel_now ->
                    close_this_channel_now;
                {'Mess',{error,Reason}} ->
                    {vtftp_error,{noclose,Reason}};
                {'Mess',{op,ok}} ->
                    Localfile = file:open(File,write),
                    get_file2(Channel,LocalFile);
                _ ->
                    close_this_channel_now
            end
    end.
```

```
get_file2(Channel,{error,open}) ->
    close_this_channel_now;

get_file2(Channel,File) ->
    case read_channel(Channel) of
        close_this_channel_now ->
            file:close(File),
            close_this_channel_now;
        {'Mess',{error,Reason}} ->
            file:close(File),
            close_this_channel_now;
        {'Mess',{data,[_,{data,Chars}]}} ->  %% ignore block number
            io:put_chars(File,Chars),
            get_file2(Channel,File);
        {'Mess',{op,eof}}  ->
            file:close(File),
            file_transferred;
        Other ->
            close_this_channel_now
    end.

print_ls_response([]) ->
    done;
print_ls_response([H|T]) ->
    io:format("~s~n",[H]),
    print_ls_response(T).
```

We also need a very simple parser for input from the user. It uses the library routines in the module `string`, where `string:words/1` returns the number of words in a string and `string:sub_word(Chars,Pos)` returns the `Pos`th subword in `Chars`, i.e. `string:sub_word("Peter Paul and Mary",3)` will return `"and"`.

```
parse([$!|Tail]) ->
    {unix,Tail};
parse(Chars) when list(Chars) ->
    Words = string:words(Chars),
    list_to_tuple(lists:reverse(trans(Chars,1,Words,[])));
parse(_) -> false.

trans(Chars,Pos,Max,R) when Pos == Max+1 ->
    R;
trans(Chars,Pos,Max,R) ->
    Elem = list_to_atom(string:sub_word(Chars,Pos)),
    trans(Chars,Pos+1,Max,[ Elem | R]).
```

This code could be improved by adding security features, such as using a privileged communications channel, adding a top directory to the server, making it impossible to change directory above that directory, etc. It should also be possible to `put` files at the server site. The code could also benefit from enhanced error recovery. Note that the parameters `mode` and `blockNr` are unused. They appear because similar parameters are present in the UNIX TFTP[7] protocol which was the original inspiration for our example.

The reader should take care to note the correspondence between the ASN.1 type definitions in Figure 16.1 and the ERLANG code. For example, in the client code for `ls` (list directory) we find the line

```
M = {'Mess',{ls,Directory}},
Channel ! {self(),{deliver,encode(M)}},
```

and in the controller

```
process(Channel,{'Mess',{ls,Dir}}) ->
```

These correspond in an obvious manner to the ASN.1 type definition for the `ls` message which (from Figure 16.1) is:

```
Mess ::= [PRIVATE 10] CHOICE {
        get         [1] Get,
        ls          [2] Directory,
        ...
```

The semantic gap between the ASN.1 type definitions and the ERLANG code which manipulates instances of these types is so small that we could think that we were programming in ASN.1 itself.

The reader is invited to perform this exercise in a conventional programming language in order fully to appreciate the advantages of our approach.

[7]Trivial File Transfer Protocol [25] – mainly used to boot discless machines over a network.

Chapter 17

Graphics

17.1 The User Interface

An important aspect of any computer program is its interaction with the user. This chapter shows how ERLANG programs can be written which interact with the user through a standard graphical user interface (GUI).

The natural way for us to think about a windowing system is as if each window represents a concurrent activity. The activities in one window proceed in parallel with and are unrelated to the activities taking place in other windows (assuming, of course, that the applications running in different windows are not engaged in some form of cooperative activity). Such a view of a windowing system maps in an obvious manner onto a set of concurrent ERLANG processes, where each window is controlled by a single controller process and all controller processes execute concurrently.

Our examples make use of locally developed program called `pxw`, which allows ERLANG to access the X Window System. ERLANG communicates with `pxw` using the port mechanism described in Section 9.4. The `pxw` program, together with the X Window System, is written in C – the interface to these programs is achieved through use of the `graphics` module. This module contains all the code necessary to interface ERLANG programs with the `pxw` program. It also makes the external windowing system appear to the user as if it were a set of ERLANG processes. The details of the module `graphics` are not given here, only the interface.

The interaction between ERLANG and the external windowing software is a good illustration of how ERLANG programs can be written to interact with programs written in other languages, and of how code written in other languages can be made to appear to the user as if it were written in ERLANG.

17.2 Basic Graphics Primitives

The module **graphics** exports the function **create_window/4** which creates a process which controls a graphics window. Evaluating:

```
Win = graphics:create_window(400, 100, "Test", "IconName")
```

creates a process `Win` and associated graphics window which looks like Figure 17.1.

Figure 17.1 An empty window

This is just an 'empty' window – it is 400 units wide and 100 units deep. The name of the window is `Test`. The window responds to all the usual X Windows conventions: it can be moved, collapsed, expanded, resized, etc. When collapsed it has the name `IconName`.

We can create a button by evaluating:

```
graphics:create_button(Win,"Push me",Pid,pushed,10,10,100,30)
```

This causes the display to change as shown in Figure 17.2.

Figure 17.2 Adding a button to the window

If we click on the button the message `{Win, {button_pressed, pushed}}` will be sent to the process `Pid`.

The window seen on the screen behaves exactly like an ERLANG process. The only way to interact with it is by sending a message to the process which controls it. If the controlling process terminates abnormally the window will be removed from the screen. From now on we will refer to the window on the screen as if it were a process.

The module `graphics` exports the following functions which can be used to modify the appearance of the display:

`create_button(Win, Text, Pid, Msg, X, Y, Width, Ht)`
: Creates a button displaying the string `Text` within the window. When the button is pressed the message `Msg` will be sent to the process `Pid`.

`draw_line(Win, Style, Width, Path)`
: Draws a line within the window. `Style` is one of `solid`, `stipple` or `erase` and denotes the visual appearance of the line, `Width` denotes the width of the line, and `Path` is a list of tuples denoting the `X` and `Y` coordinates of the line.

`create_text_box(Win, X, Y, Width, Ht)`
: Creates a text box within the window, and returns the name of the text box.

`write_text_box(Win, Name, String)`
: Causes the character list `String` to be displayed in the text box `Name`.

`create_bitmap(Win, File, X, Y)`
: Displays the bitmap stored in `File`, and returns the name of a region describing the bitmap.

`change_bitmap(Win, Name, File)`
: Changes the bitmap in region `Name` to the bitmap stored in `File`.

`create_edit_box(Win, X, Y, Width, Ht)`
: Creates a region in the window which can be edited, and returns the name of an edit box.

`read_edit_box(Win, Name)`
: Returns the contents of the edit box `Name`.

In the above `X, Y, Width` and `Ht` represent the position and size of the associated object within the window.

In addition to messages to the window the following messages can be received from the window:

- `{Win, {button_pressed, Msg}}` – this message is sent when one of the buttons in the window is pressed.
- `{Win, {mouse_event, X, Y}}` – this message is sent when the mouse button in the window is pressed and is not pointing at a button; `X` and `Y` give the coordinates of the mouse pointer.

We demonstrate the use of these messages in Program 17.1.

```
-module(graphics_demo).
-export([start/0, internal/0]).

start() ->
    spawn(graphics_demo, internal, []).

internal() ->
    S = self(),
    Win = graphics:create_window(200, 270, "Demo","Collapsed demo"),
    graphics:create_button(Win, "one", S, one, 10, 10, 100, 30),
    graphics:create_button(Win, "2", S, {digit, 2}, 150, 10 ,30,30),
    Path = [{10, 50}, {30, 50}, {30, 60}, {60,60}],
    graphics:draw_line(Win, solid, 2, Path),
    Text_box = graphics:create_text_box(Win, 80, 50, 80, 30),
    graphics:write_text_box(Win, Text_box, "hello"),
    BitMap = graphics:create_bitmap(Win, "erlang_logo", 10, 90),
    server(Win, BitMap).

server(Win, BitMap) ->
    receive
        {Win, {button_pressed, one}} ->
            graphics:change_bitmap(Win, BitMap, "mona_lisa");
        {Win, {button_pressed, {digit, 2}}} ->
            graphics:change_bitmap(Win, BitMap, "erlang_logo");
        {Win, {mouse_event, X, Y}} ->
            io:format('graphics_demo mouse event:~w ~w~n',[X, Y])
    end,
    server(Win, BitMap).
```

Program 17.1

Evaluating `graphics_demo:start()` yields the display shown in Figure 17.3(a). After clicking on the button marked 'one' the display changes to that of Figure 17.3(b).

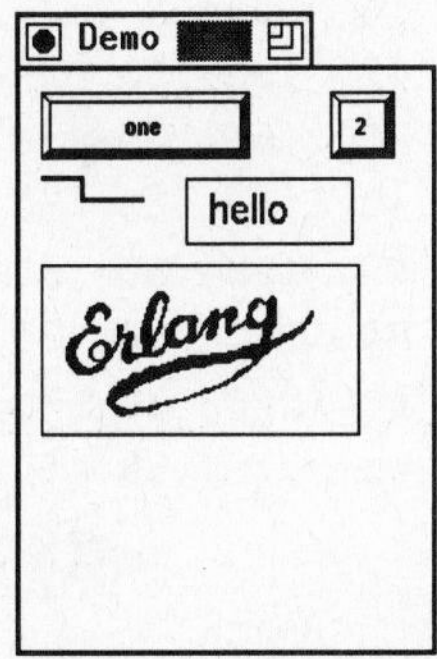

Figure 17.3(a)

Figure 17.3(b)

17.3 A Pocket Calculator

Program 17.2 creates a pocket[1] calculator.

```
-module(calc).
-export([start/0, internal/0]).
-import(graphics, [create_button/8]).

start() ->
    spawn(calc, internal,[]).

internal() ->
    {Win, Output} = draw_calculator(),
    {Txt, State} = calc_logic:start(),
    graphics:write_text_box(Win, Output, Txt),
    calc_loop(Win, Output, State).

draw_calculator() ->
    Width = 125, Ht = 270,
    Win = graphics:create_window(Width, Ht, "Calc", "calculator"),
    S = self(),
    Output = graphics:create_text_box(Win, 10, 10, 100, 30),
    graphics:write_text_box(Win, Output, "reset"),
    create_button(Win, "1", S, {digit, 1}, 10, 50, 30, 30),
    create_button(Win, "2", S, {digit, 2}, 45, 50, 30, 30),
    create_button(Win, "3", S, {digit, 3}, 80, 50, 30, 30),
    create_button(Win, "4", S, {digit, 4}, 10, 85, 30, 30),
    create_button(Win, "5", S, {digit, 5}, 45, 85, 30, 30),
    create_button(Win, "6", S, {digit, 6}, 80, 85, 30, 30),
    create_button(Win, "7", S, {digit, 7}, 10, 120, 30, 30),
    create_button(Win, "8", S, {digit, 8}, 45, 120, 30, 30),
    create_button(Win, "9", S, {digit, 9}, 80, 120, 30, 30),
    create_button(Win, "+", S, plus,       10, 155, 30, 30),
    create_button(Win, "0", S, {digit, 0}, 45, 155, 30, 30),
    create_button(Win, "-", S, minus,      80, 155, 30, 30),
    create_button(Win, "*", S, times,      10, 190, 30, 30),
    create_button(Win, "Clr", S, clear,    45, 190, 30, 30),
    create_button(Win, "/", S, divide,     80, 190, 30, 30),
    create_button(Win, "Off", S, off,      10, 225, 30, 30),
    create_button(Win, "Enter", S, enter,  45, 225, 65, 30),
    {Win, Output}.
```

[1]Assuming your pockets are large enough for a workstation!

```
calc_loop(Win, Output, State) ->
    receive
        {Win, {button_pressed, off}} ->
            exit(die);
        {Win, {button_pressed, Button}} ->
            {Txt, NextState} = calc_logic:calc(Button, State),
            graphics:write_text_box(Win, Output, Txt),
            calc_loop(Win, Output, NextState)
    end.
```

Program 17.2

Figure 17.4

Evaluating `calc:start()` results in Figure 17.4. Note that we have isolated the logic of the calculator from the control – the module `calc` only contains the code necessary for controlling the GUI. All the logic of the calculator is contained in the module `calc_logic`. `calc_logic:start()` returns the tuple `{Txt, State}`, where `Txt` is a character string which should be displayed by the calculator and `State` is a data structure representing the state of the calculator when it is turned on.

`calc_logic:calc(Button, State)` is a function which is called with the `Button` which has been pressed and the current value of the `State` of the calculator. It returns a new value to be displayed and a new state for the calculator.

The use of two modules `calc` and `calc_logic` cleanly separates the control of the graphics object from the internal logic of the calculator. This is an example of good program design. Modules and their interfaces should be designed on a need-to-know basis, separating issues wherever possible. A consequence of the above design is that we do not even know (from the point of view of the graphics control of the program) if the calculator is a reverse Polish or conventional infix operator calculator.[2] This decision is left to the designer of the module `calc_logic`.

17.4 A Prompter

Prompters are used to ask questions. So, for example, evaluating:

```
prompter:ask("What is your favourite programming language?")
```

causes a window to be created which looks like Figure 17.5.

[2]Careful examination of the calculator will reveal a certain bias!

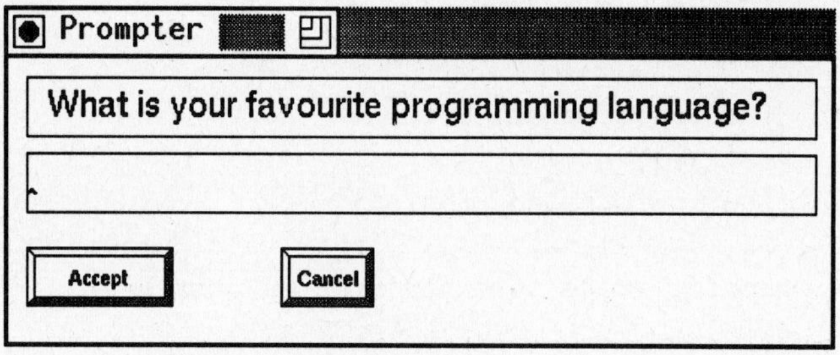

Figure 17.5 A Prompter

When the user replies by entering the word `Erlang` in the text region of the window and clicking on the 'accept' button `ask` returns `{reply, "Erlang"}`; if the user clicks the 'cancel' button `ask` returns `cancel`. A process evaluating `ask` is suspended until a reply is received from the prompter.

The module `prompter` also exports the function `ask1(Question)` which does not wait for a reply from the prompter. Use of `ask1` allows a process to ask several different questions which can then be answered (and processed) in an arbitrary order. For example:

```
Q1 = ask1("Name"),
Q2 = ask1("Address"),
Q3 = ask1("Hobby"),
receive
    {Q1, ...} ->
        ...
    {Q2, ...} ->
        ...
end
```

causes three prompters to be displayed simultaneously – the user is not forced to complete the dialogue in any particular order but can interact with the prompters in any desired order. This kind of behaviour, while simple to express in a concurrent programming language, is difficult to program in a conventional sequential programming language.

The code for the prompter is shown in Program 17.3.

```
-module(prompter).
-export([ask/1, ask1/1, internal/2]).

ask(Question) ->
    Pid = ask1(Question),
    receive
        {Pid, Reply} ->
            Reply
    end.
```

```
ask1(Question) ->
    spawn(prompter, internal, [self(), Question]).

internal(Pid, Question) ->
    Width = 450, Ht = 150,
    S = self(),
    Win = graphics:create_window(Width, Ht, "Prompter","Question?"),
    Box = graphics:create_text_box(Win, 10, 10, 430, 30),
    graphics:write_text_box(Win, Box, Question),
    Edit = graphics:create_edit_box(Win, 10, 50, 430, 30),
    graphics:create_button(Win, "Accept", S, accept, 10, 100,80,30),
    graphics:create_button(Win, "Cancel", S, cancel, 150,100,50,30),
    Pid ! {self(), server(Win, Edit)},
    exit(Win, die).

server(Win, Edit) ->
    receive
        {Win, {button_pressed, accept}} ->
            {reply, graphics:read_edit_box(Win, Edit)};
        {Win, {button_pressed, cancel}} ->
            cancel
    end.
```

Program 17.3

17.5 A TV Simulation

This section illustrates a graphics-based simulation of a TV camera and monitor. We start by making a model of a TV monitor. Assume that the process `Monitor` represents a TV monitor. Evaluating `monitor:start(Win, X, Y)` starts the process representing the monitor. `Win` represents a window where the monitor is to be displayed, and `X` and `Y` are coordinates within that window. When the monitor is started it is turned 'off' and looks like Figure 17.6(a). Once the monitor has been created it can be told to display the picture `Pict` by sending it the command `{on, Pict}`. Figure 17.6(b) shows the result of sending such a message. The code for manipulating the monitor is given in Program 17.4.

Figure 17.6(a) Figure 17.6(b)

```
-module(monitor).
-export([start/3, internal/3]).

start(Win, X, Y) ->
    spawn(monitor, internal, [Win, X, Y]).

internal(Win, X, Y) ->
    Monitor=graphics:create_bitmap(Win,"tv_monitor.large",X,Y),
    Display=graphics:create_bitmap(Win,"no_picture.large",X+6,Y+6),
    server(Win, Display, none).

server(Win, Display, Source) ->
    receive
        {technician, {source, NewSource}} ->
            server(Win, Display, NewSource);
        {Source, {on, Picture}} ->
            graphics:change_bitmap(Win, Display, Picture),
            server(Win, Display, Source);
        {Source, off} ->
            graphics:change_bitmap(Win, Display,"no_picture.large"),
            server(Win, Display, Source)
    end.
```

Program 17.4

The message `{technician, {source, S}}` can be sent to the monitor process, to define a source `S` for the 'on' and 'off' messages.

Signals to the monitor are carried by connectors – in reality a connector could be a coaxial cable or an optical fibre. Assume the call `connector:start(Win, Path)` creates a process representing such a connector. `Win` represents a window, and `Path` a list of `{X, Y}` coordinates. Evaluating `connector:start` with path set to describe some wiggly line results in the creation of an object such as Figure 17.7(a). The code for the connector is given in Program 17.5.

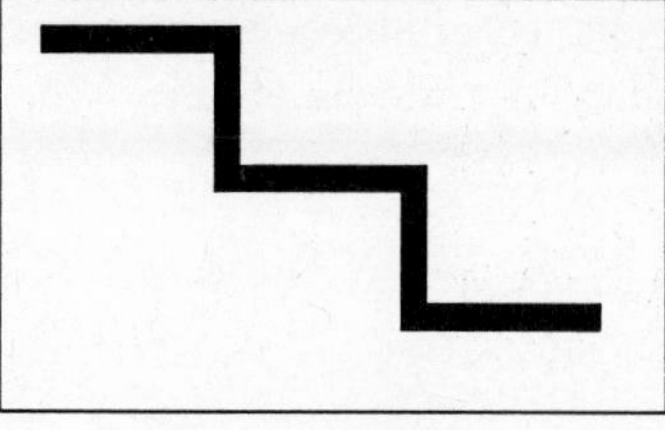

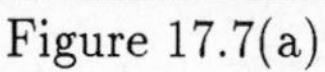
Figure 17.7(a)

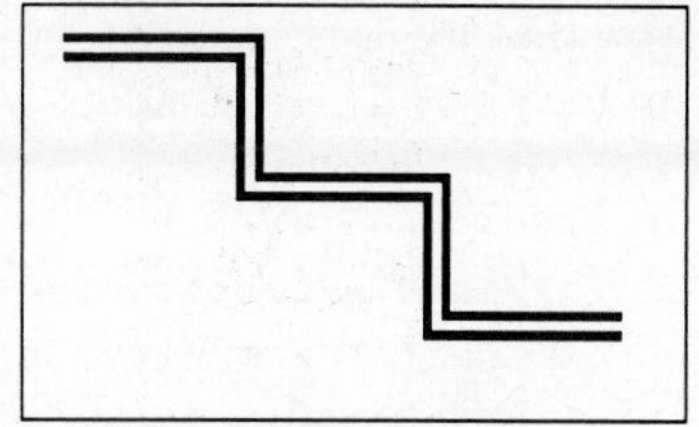

Figure 17.7(b)

```
-module(connector).
-export([start/2, internal/2]).

start(Win, Path) ->
    spawn(connector, internal, [Win, Path]).

internal(Win, Path) ->
    graphics:draw_line(Win, solid, 10, Path),
    server(Win, Path, off, none, none).

server(Win, Path, State, Source, Dest) ->
    receive
        {technician, {connect, Source1, Dest1}} ->
            server(Win, Path, State, Source1, Dest1);
        {Source, off} ->
            graphics:draw_line(Win, solid, 10, Path),
            Dest ! {self(), off},
            server(Win, Path, off, Source, Dest);
        {Source, Signal} ->
            graphics:draw_line(Win, erase, 4, Path),
            Dest ! {self(), Signal},
            server(Win, Path, Signal, Source, Dest)
    end.
```

Program 17.5

The connector process passes a signal between its source and destination processes. These are represented by the local variables `Source` and `Dest` in the server loop of Program 17.5. The values of these variables are set by sending the message `{technician, {connect, Source, Dest}}` to the connector process. All other messages from `Source` which arrive at the connector process are sent to `Dest`. If the connector process receives a message which is not the atom `off` from `Source`, it changes the display to represent the fact that it is now transmitting data (Figure 17.7(b)).

Now that we have created a monitor and connector object we can try connecting them together. This we can do with the following code fragment:

```
Win = graphics:create_window(...),
Monitor = monitor:start(Win, 100, 10),
Path = [{10,40}, {100,40}],
Connector = connector:start(Win, Path),
Monitor !   {technician, {source, Connector}},
Connector ! {technician, {connect, self(), Monitor}},
```

The messages `{technician, ... }` are used to ensure that the output from the connector process appears as the input to the monitor process.

Executing this code fragment results in Figure 17.8(a). If we now send the message `Connector ! {self(), {on, "face2.large"}}` the connector becomes transparent, indicating that it is 'on'. It then sends a message to the monitor which in turn causes it to display the requested picture. The display then looks like Figure 17.8(b).

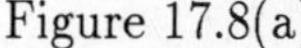
Figure 17.8(a)

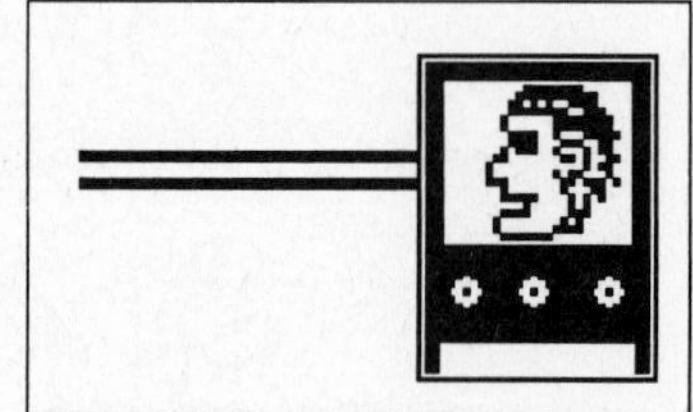

Figure 17.8(b)

We now make a camera process. This has a camera and two buttons, 'on' and 'off'. The code for the camera process is given in Program 17.6.

```
-module(camera).
-export([start/4, internal/4]).

start(Win, X, Y,  BitMap) ->
    spawn(camera, internal, [Win, X, Y, BitMap]).

internal(Win, X, Y, Picture) ->
    S = self(),
    graphics:create_bitmap(Win, Picture, X, Y),
    graphics:create_bitmap(Win, "tv_camera_L.large", X+60, Y),
    graphics:create_button(Win, "on", S, on, X + 60, Y+90,30,30),
    graphics:create_button(Win, "off", S, off, X + 93, Y+90,30,30),
    server(Win, Picture, none).
```

```
server(Win, Picture, Dest) ->
    receive
        {technician, {dest, D}} ->
            server(Win, Picture, D);
        {Win, {button_pressed,on}} ->
            Dest ! {self(), {on, Picture}},
            server(Win, Picture, Dest);
        {Win, {button_pressed,off}} ->
            Dest ! {self(), off},
            server(Win, Picture, Dest);
    end.
```

Program 17.6

We now join the output from the camera to the input of the connector and the output of the connector to the input of the monitor, resulting in Figure 17.9(a).

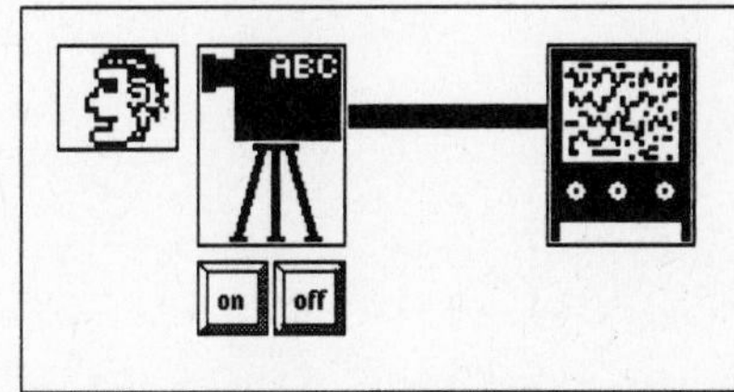

Figure 17.9(a)

Figure 17.9(a) was created with the code fragment:

```
Camera = camera:start(Win, 10, 10, "face2.large"),
Monitor = monitor:start(Win, 220,10),
Path = [{135,40}, {220,40}],
Connector = connector:start(Win, Path),
Camera    ! {technician, {dest, Connector}},
Monitor   ! {technician, {source, Connector}},
Connector ! {technician, {connect, Camera, Monitor}},
```

Again, the `{technician, ... }` messages cause the output from the camera to be sent to the input of the connector and the output of the connector to be sent to the input of the monitor.

Pressing the 'on' button on the camera results in Figure 17.9(b).

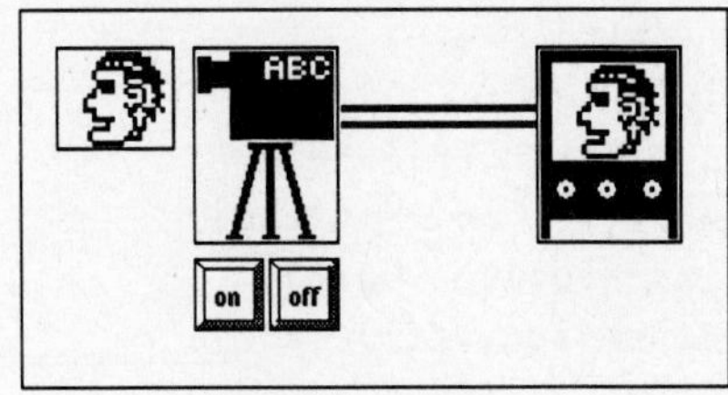

Figure 17.9(b)

This completes our simulation program.

Chapter 18

Object-oriented Programming

In this chapter we look at the basic concepts involved in object-oriented design and programming (OOD and OOP) and see how they relate to ERLANG.

18.1 Basic Concepts

Several authors have tried to identify the most important concepts, but there appears to be no general consensus as to which properties are important. The issue is confused by authors giving subtly different meanings to the same terms. The interested reader can refer to [8], [16], [17], [19] and [26] for more details.

We give a list of concepts which are considered important and a brief description of their meaning:

Abstraction. A description of the essential characteristics of an object.

Behaviour. How an object acts and reacts, in terms of its state changes and message passing.

Class. A set of objects which share a common structure and a common behaviour. We call a class from which another class inherits its *superclass*, and similarly, a class which inherits from one or more other classes a *subclass*.

Concurrency. The property which distinguishes those objects which have a separate thread of control, called *active* objects.

Dynamic memory. The system frees the programmer from the task of allocating and deallocating objects.

Encapsulation. Hiding all details of an object which are not part of its essential characteristics.

Hierarchy. An ordering of abstractions. In the object-oriented model *inheritance* is the most important kind of hierarchy. It defines the relationship between classes where one class shares the structure and behaviour of other classes.

Message. Something which is 'sent' to an object to make it react.

Method. Part of a class which defines the behaviour of an object when a message is received.

Modularity. Decomposition of a system into a set of loosely coupled units.

Object. Something which has state, behaviour and an identity. The structure and behaviour of an object are defined by its class. Usually the terms 'instance' (of a class) and 'object' are interchangeable.

Persistence. The property of an object which continues to exist after its creator has died.

State. A description all of the properties of the object.

Typing. The enforcement of the class of an object such that objects of different classes may not be interchanged, except, perhaps, in well-defined ways.

18.2 Mapping to ERLANG

Some of the concepts mentioned in the previous section are implemented directly in ERLANG (for example, concurrency and dynamic memory), while other concepts have natural counterparts (for example, modules). There are concepts which can be implemented in ERLANG in a number of different ways depending on the context in which they are used. Objects, abstraction and encapsulation are examples of this and are discussed later in this section.

Finally there are some concepts in OOP which have no direct counterpart in ERLANG, but which can be easily programmed. For example, ERLANG has no notion of classes or inheritance though a class and inheritance mechanism can be simulated, as shown in the next section.

18.2.1 Abstraction

Abstraction is important in any system. There are many ways of implementing abstraction in ERLANG, the most common being by the use of modules. As we cannot define our own data types we use a module to define interface functions which operate on an unspecified type. The application can use the abstraction by always accessing the data structure through the interface functions.

Section 3.3.2 defines a *set* in terms of the operations which can be performed on the set and an example of how sets could be implemented using lists. If an application always uses the interface when manipulating sets then it is possible to change the actual implementation *without* affecting the application. For example, we could instead use ordered lists[1] in a module `ordsets` or perhaps even AVL trees (see Section 4.6).

[1] An ordered list is one whose elements are sorted according to comparison ordering (see Section 2.5.6).

Using the module `sets` (or `ordsets`) gives another benefit. These two modules *define* the data type of a set to be a list (or ordered list). This allows the use of list operations on sets as long as we use the set interface to modify the set. This would, of course, limit our choice of implementation of a set, but it does give the power of having both an abstract interface and an explicit data type.

18.2.2 Objects and encapsulation

A central issue in discussing ERLANG and object-oriented programming is the representation of an object. Objects can be represented in many ways. Which way we choose depends on how these objects are to be used:

- As explicit data structures.
- As processes.

ERLANG data structures are 'non-destructive' so we need no special protection mechanism to prevent unauthorised updating of an object. We can freely pass such an object around and allow it to be inspected but not modified. If we wish to encapsulate data structures together with functions which specify behaviour then we can use the module system as described previously.

A process can be thought of as an object since it satisfies all the criteria of an object:

- It has a state defined by the values of its local data and the code it is evaluating.
- The behaviour is determined by its response to messages.
- It has a unique identity, the Pid.
- It provides secure encapsulation since its state and internal data can *only* be affected by message passing.
- Abstraction is provided through the message interface. No knowledge of the actual internal implementation is visible.
- A process's existence is determined by the code which it executes, not by the existence of its creator, which means that it can be persistent.
- Processes provide true concurrent objects for those applications which need them.

As the representation of objects is not fixed, we are free to choose a representation for each type of object which is most convenient *for that type*. For example, active objects can most naturally be represented as processes which provide the concurrency and true message passing required. Static objects, however, can be represented by data structures or by processes, depending on how they are to be used. Also, there are no restrictions on the mixing of representations of objects within an application; different representations can coexist within one system.

18.3 An Object-oriented Interface

In this section we look at how to model a traditional OO interface concentrating on the issues of defining classes and inheritance. We make the following assumptions:

- Each class is implemented by a module whose name is the same as the class name.
- An instance of a class is an ERLANG process and the instance identifier is the Pid of that process.
- Sending a message to an object is implemented by sending a message to the object process.

The general format of a 'class' module is given in Program 18.1. Two exported functions are required: **superclass**, which returns the superclasses of the class and **method**, which is called to evaluate a method. The function **method** has a clause for each method it can handle and returns **{result,MethodResult}** when there is a method and `no_method` if there is no method.

```
-module(ClassName).
-export([superclass/0,method/1]).

superclass() ->
    ...

method(Method1) ->
    ...
method(Method2) ->
    ...
...
method(_) ->
    no_method.
```

Program 18.1

When an object process receives a message it calls the function **dispatch** to find and evaluate the correct method to handle the message. We show the function **dispatch** for the cases where we have *single inheritance* where there is only one superclass, and *multiple inheritance* where there can be many superclasses.

In both cases the function `dispatch` does not explicitly handle the case where there is no method for a message. This would result in an error which would cause the process to terminate. This could be interpreted as a design or programming error as an unknown message is sent to the object. Better control for this type of error could be implemented by having a special class which is the superclass of all classes which have no other superclasses. This class would then provide a method to trap unknown messages.

18.3.1 Single inheritance

Here, each class has only one superclass and the function **superclass** returns the name of the superclass. The function dispatch is given in Program 18.2. It first tries to evaluate the method in the current class. If this fails it gets the superclass and evaluates dispatch for that class to find the method.

```
dispatch(Method, Class) ->
    case apply(Class, method, [Method]) of
        {result,R} ->
            {result,R};
        no_method ->
            SuperClass = apply(Class, superclass, []),
            dispatch(Method, SuperClass)
    end.
```

Program 18.2

18.3.2 Multiple inheritance

Each class in this model can have many superclasses so the function **superclass** returns a list of superclasses. Here the function dispatch, shown in Program 18.3, first tries to evaluate the method in the current class. If this fails it gets the list of superclasses and evaluates dispatch_super on that list of classes to find the method. The function dispatch_super evaluates dispatch on each class in the list until the method has been found. This version of dispatch tries to find the method by traversing the superclasses to the base class in a depth-first manner.

18.3.3 Discussion

We have now shown the general schema of an OO interface which runs 'on top' of standard ERLANG. While relatively small and simple, it gives a powerful object-oriented system with many features:

- Complete encapsulation of objects.
- A hierarchial class system with inheritance.
- Single or multiple inheritance with the possibility of having mixin classes.[2]
- Interactive modification of classes.

[2] A class which is not intended to be used on its own but mixed together with another class to produce new subclasses.

```
dispatch(Method, Class) ->
    case apply(Class, method, [Method]) of
        {result,R} ->
            {result,R};
        no_method ->
            SuperClasses = apply(Class, superclass, []),
            dispatch_super(Method, SuperClasses)
    end.

dispatch_super(Method, [Class|Classes]) ->
    case dispatch(Method, Class) of
        {result,R} ->
            {result,R};
        no_method ->
            dispatch_super(Method, Classes)
    end;
dispatch_super(Method, []) ->
    no_method.
```

Program 18.3

- The messages sent between objects are real messages between concurrent objects.

One benefit of *not* having an OO mechanism with classes and inheritance *built in* to the language is the ability to modify the OO system to suit the application using it. For example, adding daemons to the basic message handling is relatively simple and would allow classes to be 'informed' of messages which they do not wish to handle directly.

The system presented here requires the programmer to write the OO part directly in ERLANG which hides the some of the OO features. We could, for example, define our own syntax which could be analysed, checked and then transformed into standard ERLANG to be compiled by the system. This would present a much cleaner interface than the one given here and allow classes to be defined in a more OO manner while still being able to use ERLANG code within a method. Such a system, while not difficult, is beyond the scope of this chapter.

18.4 Object-oriented Programming

We have seen in the preceding sections that an OOP system can be simply implemented directly in ERLANG without any special constructs or syntax being necessary. We have also shown the ease with which such constructs could be added to the basic ERLANG system *without* having to make any real changes to the syntax or semantics of the language.

While the OO style is suited for some problems, other programming styles seem especially suited for many concurrent applications and are supported by ERLANG. For example state×event driven programming can be written in ERLANG by representing the current state by the function being evaluated. A large problem is then easily split into many smaller functions, or even modules, each waiting for and processing its own events. The progression from state to state is then explicit and clear and the relationship between a state, an event and the actions to be taken is distinct. See the description in Section 5.2.3 and the telephony application in Chapter 15 for an example of this. The centralised dispatching of messages in traditional OO systems tends to hide this.

While an OO system can be very good at providing abstractions and hierarchy, it makes it difficult to find out just *where* and *by whom* a message is processed. In a very objected-oriented system (for example, Smalltalk) the processing of a message can wander up and down the class hierarchy before finally being completed. In a system where *time* is important, especially a real-time system, this can be very dangerous as it is critical to know exactly who does what.

18.5 Object-oriented Design

OOD methods have become increasingly popular for the design of large-scale industrial software projects. In this section we discuss how OOD relates to ERLANG.

The major step in OOD is to identify the different objects which will occur in the system and to specify their behaviour. While for some systems the concurrent behaviour can be ignored, in real-world systems, where the objects are things like people, cars or telephones, concurrency is a central part of the problem. Potentially each object in such a system can perform operations in parallel with other objects and this must be taken into account when modelling the system. There is no clear way to specify the system without concurrency.

When these concurrent objects in the real world have been identified and the communication between them specified, the most natural way of modelling them is to have one concurrent object in the model for each such object in the real world. If such a model is then programmed in ERLANG we can continue with this one-to-one mapping by assigning one ERLANG process to each concurrent object in the model. To do this in a language like C++ [26], which lacks concurrency, requires support from an operating system.

The one-to-one correspondence between concurrent activities in the real world and objects in our model is extremely important, since in ERLANG we can represent each concurrent object by one process. This one-to-one mapping ensures a small 'semantic gap' between the real world, its model (design) and the implementation of the model (program).

It is important to realise that the objects ERLANG provides are true concurrent objects. While traditional OO systems use terms like 'sending a message' the actual operation involved is most like a traditional procedure call. This misleading terminology is very unfortunate since it tends to hide the distinction between active and passive objects. In systems where all objects are passive this may lead to the system not behaving as expected because real messages are not sent, but in designing and programming concurrent systems this can be fatal as the distinction is fundamental.

Bibliography

[1] Adelson-Velskii, G.M. and Landis E.M., "An algorithm for the organisation of information", *Doklady Akademia Nauk SSSR, 146*, (1962), 263–266; English translation in *Soviet Math, 3*, 1259–63.

[2] Ahlberg, I., Bauner, J-O. and Danne, A., "Prototyping cordless using declarative programming", International Switching Symposium, October 25–30, 1992, Yokohama.

[3] Armstrong, J. L., Virding, S. R. and Williams, M. C., "Use of Prolog for developing a new programming language", The Practical Application of Prolog, 1–3 April 1992, Institute of Electrical Engineers, London.

[4] Agha, Gul A., *Actors: A Model of Concurrent Computation in Distributed Systems*, MIT Press, 1986.

[5] Bal, H. *Programming Distributed Systems*, Prentice Hall 1990.

[6] Birell ,A D, Nelsson, B. J. "Implementing remote procedure calls" *ACM Trans. Comp. Syst.*, 2, (1) 1984.

[7] Bernstein, P., Hadzilacos ,V., Goodman, N. *Concurrency Control and Recovery in Database Systems*, Addison-Wesley 1987

[8] Booch, G., *Object-oriented Design with Applications*, Benjamin-Cummings Publishing Company, 1991.

[9] Bratko, I., *Prolog Programming for Artificial Intelligence*, Addison-Wesley, 1986, pp. 241–245.

[10] Case, Jeffrey D., Feodor, Mark S., Shoffstall, Martin L. and Davin, James R., "A Simple Network Management Protocol", Request For Comment 1098, April 1989.

[11] CCITT *Specification and Description Language (SDL)*, Recommendation X.100, Geneva, Switzerland.

[12] CCITT *Specification of Abstract Syntax Notation One (ASN.1)*, Recommendation X.208, Geneva, Switzerland.

[13] CCITT *Specification of Basic Encoding Rules (BER for Abstract Syntax One (ASN.1)*, Recommendation X.209, Geneva, Switzerland.

[14] Gray, Jim and Reuter, Andreas *Transaction Processing Concepts and Techniques*, Morgan Kaufmann Publishers, 1993.

[15] Clocksin, W. F. and Mellish, C. S., *Programming in Prolog*, Springer-Verlag, 1981.

[16] Coed, P. and Yourdon, E., *Object-oriented Analysis*, Yourdon Press, 1991.

[17] Coed, P. and Yourdon, E., *Object-oriented Design*, Yourdon Press, 1991.

[18] Eriksson, D., Persson, M. and Ödling, K., "A switching software architecture prototype using a real-time declarative language", International Switching Symposium, October 25–30, 1992, Yokohama.

[19] Jacobson, I., Christerson, M., Jonsson, P. and Övergaard, G., *Object-oriented Software Engineering*, Addison-Wesley, 1992.

[20] Lamport, L., "Time, clocks and the ordering of events in a distributed system" *Comm. ACM*, 21(7), July, 1978.

[21] Liskov, B. "Linguistic support for efficient asynchronous calls in distributed systems". Proceedings of the SIGPLAN, 1988.

[22] Foster, I. and Taylor, S., *STRAND: New Concepts in Parallel Processing*, Prentice Hall, 1989.

[23] "SunOs 4.0 reference manual V. 10" 1987 Sun Microsystems, Inc.

[24] Open Systems Interconnection: Basic reference model. International Oganization for Standardization and Electrotechnical Committee, 1984.

[25] Sollins, K. R., "The TFTP Protocol (Revision 2)", Request For Comment 783, June 1981.

[26] Stroustrup, B., *The C++ Programming Language*, 2nd edition, Addison-Wesley, 1991.

[27] Ullman, J. D., *Principles of Database and Knowledgebase Systems*, Computer Science Press, 1988.

[28] Wikström, Å., *Functional Programming Using Standard ML*, Prentice Hall, 1987.

[29] Wirth, N., *Algorithms + Data Structures = Programs*, Prentice Hall, 1976, pp. 215–226.

[30] Kunz, T. "The influence of different workload descriptions on a heuristic load balancing scheme". *IEEE Trans. Software Eng.*, 17, (7), July, 1991 pp. 725-730.

Appendix A

ERLANG Reference Grammar

The ERLANG reference grammar which follows is an adaptation of an LALR(1) grammar for ERLANG.

This grammar differs from a strict LALR(1) grammar in the treatment of the production for the non-terminal "match_expr". In this case the expression to the left-hand side of the "=" symbol could be a pattern *or* an expression – the ambiguity is resolved in the semantic phase of the ERLANG compiler.

Type	Precedence	Operator
Nonassoc	0	'catch'.
Right	200	'='.
Right	200	'!'.
Left	300	add_op.
Left	400	mult_op.
Nonassoc	500	prefix_op.

```
Line Non-terminal         Productions
1    add_op               := "+"
                          |  "-"
                          |  "bor"
                          |  "bxor"
                          |  "bsl"
                          |  "bsr"
2    comp_op              := "=="
                          |  "/="
                          |  "=<"
                          |  "<"
                          |  ">="
                          |  ">"
                          |  "=:="
```

```
                                | ”=/=”
3    mult_op                    := ”*”
                                | ”/”
                                | ”div”
                                | ”rem”
                                | ”band”
4    prefix_op                  := ”+”
                                | ”-”
                                | ”bnot”
5    basic_type                 := ”atom”
                                | ”number”
                                | ”string”
                                | ”var”
                                | ”true”
6    pattern                    := basic_type
                                | pattern_list
                                | pattern_tuple
7    pattern_list               := ”[” ”]”
                                | ”[” pattern pattern_tail ”]”
8    pattern_tail               := ”|” pattern
                                | ”,” pattern pattern_tail
                                | ε
9    pattern_tuple              := ”{” ”}”
                                | ”{” patterns ”}”
10   patterns                   := pattern
                                | pattern ”,” patterns
11   expr                       := basic_type
                                | list
                                | tuple
                                | function_call
                                | expr add_op expr
                                | expr mult_op expr
                                | prefix_op expr
                                | ”(” expr ”)”
                                | ”begin” exprs ”end”
                                | ”catch” expr
                                | case_expr
                                | if_expr
                                | receive_expr
                                | match_expr
                                | send_expr
12   list                       := ”[” ”]”
                                | ”[” expr expr_tail ”]”
```

```
13  expr_tail              := "|" expr
                           |  "," expr expr_tail
                           |  ϵ
14  tuple                  := "{" "}"
                           |  "{" exprs "}"
15  function_call          := "atom" "(" parameter_list ")"
                           |  "atom" ":" "atom" "(" parameter_list ")"
16  parameter_list         := exprs
                           |  ϵ
17  case_expr              := "case" expr "of" cr_clauses "end"
18  cr_clause              := pattern clause_guard clause_body
19  cr_clauses             := cr_clause
                           |  cr_clause ";" cr_clauses
20  if_expr                := "if" if_clauses "end"
21  if_clause              := guard clause_body
22  if_clauses             := if_clause
                           |  if_clause ";" if_clauses
23  receive_expr           := "receive" "after" expr clause_body "end"
                           |  "receive" cr_clauses "end"
                           |  "receive" cr_clauses "after" expr clause_body "end"
24  match_expr             := expr "=" expr
25  send_expr              := expr "!" expr
26  exprs                  := expr
                           |  expr "," exprs
27  guard_expr             := basic_type
                           |  guard_expr_list
                           |  guard_expr_tuple
                           |  guard_call
                           |  "(" guard_expr ")"
                           |  guard_expr add_op guard_expr
                           |  guard_expr mult_op guard_expr
                           |  prefix_op guard_expr
28  guard_expr_list        := "[" "]"
                           |  "[" guard_expr guard_expr_tail "]"
29  guard_expr_tail        := "|" guard_expr
                           |  "," guard_expr guard_expr_tail
                           |  ϵ
30  guard_expr_tuple       := "{" "}"
                           |  "{" guard_exprs "}"
31  guard_exprs            := guard_expr
                           |  guard_expr "," guard_exprs
32  guard_call             := "atom" "(" guard_parameter_list ")"
33  guard_parameter_list   := guard_exprs
```

<table>
<tr><td></td><td></td><td>| ε</td></tr>
<tr><td>34</td><td>bif_test</td><td>:= "atom" "(" guard_parameter_list ")"</td></tr>
<tr><td>35</td><td>guard_test</td><td>:= bif_test</td></tr>
<tr><td></td><td></td><td>| guard_expr comp_op guard_expr</td></tr>
<tr><td>36</td><td>guard_tests</td><td>:= guard_test</td></tr>
<tr><td></td><td></td><td>| guard_test "," guard_tests</td></tr>
<tr><td>37</td><td>guard</td><td>:= "true"</td></tr>
<tr><td></td><td></td><td>| guard_tests</td></tr>
<tr><td>38</td><td>function_clause</td><td>:= clause_head clause_guard clause_body</td></tr>
<tr><td>39</td><td>clause_head</td><td>:= "atom" "(" formal_parameter_list ")"</td></tr>
<tr><td>40</td><td>formal_parameter_list</td><td>:= patterns</td></tr>
<tr><td></td><td></td><td>| ε</td></tr>
<tr><td>41</td><td>clause_guard</td><td>:= "when" guard</td></tr>
<tr><td></td><td></td><td>| ε</td></tr>
<tr><td>42</td><td>clause_body</td><td>:= "->" exprs</td></tr>
<tr><td>43</td><td>function</td><td>:= function_clause</td></tr>
<tr><td></td><td></td><td>| function_clause ";" function</td></tr>
<tr><td>44</td><td>attribute</td><td>:= pattern</td></tr>
<tr><td></td><td></td><td>| "[" farity_list "]"</td></tr>
<tr><td></td><td></td><td>| "atom" "," "[" farity_list "]"</td></tr>
<tr><td>45</td><td>farity_list</td><td>:= farity</td></tr>
<tr><td></td><td></td><td>| farity "," farity_list</td></tr>
<tr><td>46</td><td>farity</td><td>:= "atom" "/" "number"</td></tr>
<tr><td>47</td><td>form</td><td>:= "-" "atom" "(" attribute ")"</td></tr>
<tr><td></td><td></td><td>| function</td></tr>
</table>

Non-terminal	Line Numbers
add_op	*1 11 27
attribute	*44 47
basic_type	*5 6 11 27
bif_test	*34 35
case_expr	11 *17
clause_body	18 21 23 38 *42
clause_guard	18 38 *41
clause_head	38 *39
comp_op	*2 35
cr_clause	*18 19
cr_clauses	17 *19 19 23
expr	*11 11 12 13 17 23 24 25 26
expr_tail	12 *13 13
exprs	11 14 16 *26 26 42
farity	45 *46
farity_list	44 *45 45

Appendix B

Built-in Functions

Appendix B contains descriptions of ERLANG's *built-in functions*. BIFs are, by convention, regarded as being in the module `erlang`. Thus both of the calls `atom_to_list('Erlang')` and `erlang:atom_to_list('Erlang')` are considered identical.

BIFs may fail for a variety of reasons. All BIFs fail if they are called with arguments of incorrect type. For example, `atom_to_list/1` will fail if it is called with an argument which is not an atom. If this type of failure is not caught (or the BIF is not called within a guard – see below), it will cause the process making the call to *exit* and an `EXIT` signal with reason `badarg` will be sent to all processes which are linked. The other reasons why BIFs may fail are given together with the description of each BIF.

A few BIFs may be used in guard tests (a complete list is given in the table in Section 2.5.5). For example:

```
tuple_5(Something) when size(Something) == 5 ->
    is_tuple_size_5;
tuple_5(_) ->
    is_something_else.
```

Here the BIF `size/1` is used in a guard. If `size/1` is called with a tuple it will return the size of the tuple (i.e. how many elements there are in the tuple). In the example above `size/1` is used in a guard which tests if its argument `Something` is a tuple *and*, if it is a tuple, whether it is of size 5. In this case calling size with an argument other than a tuple will cause the *guard to fail* and execution will continue with the next guard. Suppose `tuple_5/1` is written as follows:

```
tuple_5(Something) ->
    case size(Something) of
        5 -> is_tuple_size_5;
         _ -> is_something_else
    end.
```

In this case `size/1` is not in a guard. If `Something` is not a tuple `size/1` will fail and cause the *process to fail*, with reason `badarg` (see above).

Some of the BIFs in this chapter are optional to ERLANG implementations, i.e. not all implementations will contain these BIFs. These BIFs cannot be called by their names alone, but must be called using the module name `erlang`. For example, `erlang:load_module(xyz)`.

The descriptions which follow indicate which BIFs can be used in guards and which BIFs are optional.

B.1 The BIFs

abs(Number)

Returns an integer or float which is the arithmetic absolute value of the argument `Number` (integer or float).

```
> abs(-3.33).
3.3300000000000000e+00
> abs(-3).
3
```

This BIF is allowed in guard tests.
Failure: `badarg` if the argument is not an integer or a float.

alive(Name,Port)

The `alive/2` BIF publishes the name *Name* as a symbolic name of our node. This must be done if we want to communicate with other nodes, or want other nodes to be able to communicate with us. Once this BIF returns the system is a *node.* The argument `Port` must be a port (a driver or an external port program) that can understand the internal ERLANG distribution protocol.

This BIF designates the given port as a special 'distribution' port.

Optional BIF.
Failure: `badarg` If the `net_kernel` is not running or if the parameters `Port` and `Name` ar not a port and an atom, respectively.

apply(Module, Function, ArgumentList)

Returns the result of applying `Function` in `Module` to `ArgumentList`. The applied function must have been exported from the `Module`. The `arity` of the function is the length of the `ArgumentList`.

```
> apply(lists, reverse, [[a, b, c]]).
[c, b, a]
```

BIFs themselves can be applied by assuming they are exported from the module `erlang`.

```
> apply(erlang, atom_to_list, ['Erlang']).
[69,114,108,97,110,103]
```

Failure: `error_handler:undefined_function/3` is called if `Module` has not exported `Function/Arity`.[1] If the `error_handler` is undefined, or the user has redefined the default `error_handler` so that replacement is undefined, an error with reason `undef` will be generated.

apply({Module, Function}, ArgumentList)

Equivalent to `apply(Module, Function, ArgumentList)`.

atom_to_list(Atom)

Returns a list of integers (ASCII value) which corresponds to the textual representation of the argument `Atom`.

```
> atom_to_list('Erlang').
[69,114,108,97,110,103]
```

Failure: `badarg` if the argument is not an atom.

binary_to_list(Binary)

Converts a binary data object into a list of integers between 0 and 255 corresponding to the memory `Binary` represents.
Failure: `badarg` if `Binary` is not a binary data object.

binary_to_list(Binary, Start, Stop)

Converts a portion of the binary `Bin` into a list of characters, starting at position `Start`, and stopping at position `Stop`. The first position of the binary has position 1.

[1]The error handler can be redefined (see BIF `process_flag/2`).

Failure: `badarg` if `Binary` is not a binary data object, if not both `Start` and `Stop` are integers or if `Start` or `Stop` are out of range.

binary_to_term(Binary)

Returns an ERLANG term corresponding to a binary. The binary should have the same format as a binary produced with `term_to_binary/1` on page 335. Failure: `badarg` if the argument is not a binary or the argument has an incorrect format.

erlang:check_process_code(Pid, Module)

Returns `true` if the process `Pid` is executing an old version of Module.[2] Otherwise returns `false`.

```
> check_process_code(Pid, lists).
false
```

Optional BIF.
Failure: `badarg` if `Pid` is not a process or `Module` is not an atom.

concat_binary(ListOfBinaries)

Concatenates the list of binaries `ListOfBinaries` into one binary.
Failure: `badarg` if `ListOfBinaries` is not a well-formed list or if any of its arguments is not a binary.

date()

Returns today's date as `{Year, Month, Day}`

```
> date().
{1995,11,29}
```

erlang:delete_module(Module)

Moves the current version of the code of `Module` to the old version and deletes the export references of `Module`. Returns `undefined` if the module does not exist,

[2]The current call of the process is executing code for an old version of the module, or the processes has references to an old version of the module.

otherwise `true`.

```
> delete_module(test).
true
```

Optional BIF.

disconnect_node(Node)

Removes the connection to `Node`
Optional BIF.

element(N, Tuple)

Returns the `N`th element (numbering from 1) of `Tuple`.

```
> element(2, {a, b, c}).
b
```

Failure: `badarg` if `N` $<$ 0 or `N` $>$ `size(Tuple)` or if the argument `Tuple` is not a tuple. Allowed in guard tests.

erase()

Returns the process dictionary and deletes it.

```
> put(key1, {1,2,3}), put(key2, [a, b, c]), erase().
[{key1,{1,2,3}},{key2,[a, b, c]}]
```

erase(Key)

Returns the value associated with `Key` and deletes it from the process dictionary. Returns `undefined` if no value is associated with `Key`. `Key` can be any ERLANG term.

```
> put(key1, {merry, lambs, are, playing}),
  X = erase(key1), {X, erase(key1)}.
{{merry,lambs,are, playing},undefined}
```

exit(Reason)

Stops execution of current process with reason `Reason`. Can be caught. `Reason` is any ERLANG term.[3]

```
> exit(foobar).
** exited: foobar **
> catch exit(foobar).
{'EXIT',foobar}
```

exit(Pid, Reason)

Sends an `EXIT` message to the process `Pid`. Returns `true`.

```
> exit(Pid, goodbye).
true
```

Note that the above is not necessarily the same as:

```
Pid ! {'EXIT', self(), goodbye}
```

If the process with process identity `Pid` is *trapping exits* the two alternatives above are the same. *However*, if `Pid` is *not trapping exits*, the `Pid` will itself exit and propagate `EXIT` signals in turn to its linked processes.

If the reason is given as `kill`, for example, `exit(Pid, kill)`, an untrappable `EXIT` signal will be sent to the process `Pid`. In other words, the process `Pid` will be unconditionally killed.

Returns `true`.
Failure: `badarg` if `Pid` is not a Pid.

float(Number)

Returns a float by converting `Number` to a float.

```
> float(55).
5.5000000000000000e+01
```

Allowed in guard test.
Failure: `badarg` if the argument is not a float or an integer.

[3]The return value of this function is obscure.

float_to_list(Float)

Returns a list of integers (ASCII values) corresponding to Float.

```
> float_to_list(7.0).
[55,46,48,48,48,48,48,48,48,48,48,48,48,48,48,48,48,48,
 101,43,48,48]
```

Failure: badarg if the argument is not a float.

get()

Returns the process dictionary as a list of {Key, Value} tuples.

```
> put(key1, merry), put(key2, lambs),
  put(key3, {are, playing}), get().
[{key1,merry},{key2,lambs},{key3,{are, playing}}]
```

get(Key)

Returns a value associated with Key in the process dictionary. Returns undefined if no value is associated with Key. Key can be any ERLANG term.

```
> put(key1, merry), put(key2, lambs),
  put({any, [valid, term]}, {are,playing}),
  get({any, [valid, term]}).
{are, playing}
```

erlang:get_cookie()

ERLANG has built in support for authentication by magic cookies. Every distributed ERLANG system has a magic cookie. This is a secret atom. In order to be able to communicate with a node, one must know the magic cookie of the node. This BIF returns the magic cookie of our own node.
Optional BIF.

get_keys(Value)

Returns a list of keys which correspond to Value in the process dictionary.

```
> put(mary, {1,2}), put(had, {1,2}), put(a, {1,2}),
  put(little, {1,2}), put(dog, {1,3}), put(lamb, {1,2}),
  get_keys({1,2}).
[mary,had,a,little,lamb]
```

group_leader()

All ERLANG processes have a group leader. Processes do not belong to a process group, but every process has an other Pid associated with it. This Pid, which is called the group leader of the process, is returned by this BIF.

When a process is spawned the group leader of the spawned process will be the same as that of the process which evaluated the `spawn` statement. Initially on system startup, `init` is, as well as its own group leader, the group leader of all processes.

group_leader(Leader, Pid)

Sets `Pids` group leader to be `Leader`. This is typically used by a shell to ensure that all IO that which is produced by processes started from the shell is sent back to the shell. This way all IO can be displayed at the `tty` where the shell is running. Failure: `badarg` if not both `Leader` and `Pid` are Pids.

halt()

Halts the ERLANG system.

```
> halt().
unix_prompt%
```

erlang:hash(Term, Range)

Returns a hash value for `Term` in the range `0..Range`.

hd(List)

Returns the first item of `List`.

```
> hd([1,2,3,4,5]).
```

```
1
```

Allowed in guard tests.
Failure: `badarg` if `List` is the empty list `[]`, or is not a list.

integer_to_list(Integer)

Returns a list of integers (ASCII values) corresponding to `Integer`.

```
> integer_to_list(77).
[55,55]
```

Failure: `badarg` if the argument is not an integer.

is_alive()

Returns `true` if we are alive, `false` otherwise.
Optional BIF.

length(List)

Returns the length of `List`.

```
> length([1,2,3,4,5,6,7,8,9]).
9
```

Allowed in guard tests.
Failure: `badarg` if the argument is not a list or is not a well-formed list.

link(Pid)

Makes a link to process (or port) `Pid` if such a link does not already exist. A process cannot make a link to itself. Returns `true`.
Failure: `badarg` if the argument is not a Pid or port. Sends the `EXIT` signal `noproc` to the process evaluating `link` if the argument is the Pid of a process which does not exist.

list_to_atom(AsciiIntegerList)

Returns an atom whose textual representation is that of the integers (ASCII values) in `AsciiIntegerList`.

```
> list_to_atom([69,114,108,97,110,103]).
'Erlang'
```

Failure: `badarg` if the argument is not a list of integers, or if any integer in the list is not an integer or is less than `0` or greater than [illegible].

list_to_binary(AsciiIntegerList)

Converts `AsciiIntegerList` into a binary data object. This is not the same as `term_to_binary(AsciiIntegerList)`.

This BIF builds a binary object containing the bytes in `AsciiIntegerList` as opposed to `term_to_binary(AsciiIntegerList)` which builds a binary object containing the bytes of the external term format of the *term* `AsciiIntegerList`. Failure: `badarg` if the argument is not a list of integers, or if any integer in the list is not an integer or is less than `0` or greater than `255`.

list_to_float(AsciiIntegerList)

Returns a float whose textual representation is that of the integers (ASCII values) in `AsciiIntegerList`.

```
> list_to_float([50,46,50,48,49,55,55,54,52,101,43,48]).
2.2017763999999999e+00
```

Failure: `badarg` if the argument is not a list of integers or if `AsciiIntegerList` contains a bad representation of a float.

list_to_integer(AsciiIntegerList)

Returns an integer whose textual representation is that of the integers (ASCII values) in `AsciiIntegerList`.

```
> list_to_integer([49,50,51]).
123
```

Failure: `badarg` if the argument is not a list of integers or if `AsciiIntegerList` contains a bad representation of an integer.

list_to_pid(AsciiIntegerList)

Returns a process identifier whose textual representation is that of the integers (ASCII values) in `AsciiIntegerList`. Note that this BIF is intended for use in debugging and in the ERLANG operating system and *should not be used in application programs.*

```
> list_to_pid("<0.4.1>").
<0.4.1>
```

Failure: `badarg` if the argument is not a list of integers or `AsciiIntegerList` contains a bad representation of a process identifier.

list_to_tuple(List)

Returns a tuple which corresponds to `List`. `List` can contain any ERLANG terms.

```
> list_to_tuple([mary, had, a, little, {dog, cat, lamb}]).
{mary,had,a,little,{dog,cat,lamb}}
```

Failure: `badarg` if `List` is not a list or is not well formed, i.e. is terminated with anything except the empty list.

erlang:load_module(Module, Binary)

If `Binary` contains the object-code for module `Module` this BIF loads the object-code, and if code for this module already exists, it moves the present code to the old and replaces all export references so they point to the new code. Returns either `{module,Module}` where `Module` is the name of the module which has been loaded, or `{error, Reason}` if loading fails. `Reason` is one of:

`badfile` if the object-code in `Binary` is of an incorrect format.
`not_purged` if `BInary` contains a module which cannot be loaded since old code for this module already exists (see BIFs `purge_module` and `delete_module`).

In normal ERLANG implementations code handling (i.e. loading, deleting and replacing of modules) is done by the module `code`. *This BIF is intended for use by the implementation of the module* `code` *and should not be used elsewhere*
Optional BIF.
Failure: `badarg` if `Module` is not an atom or if `Binary` is not a binary.

make_ref()

Returns a world-wide unique reference.

```
> make_ref().
#Ref
```

erlang:math(Function, Number [, Number])

Returns a float which is the result of applying `Function` (an atom) to one or two numerical arguments. The functions which are available are implementation-dependent and may include: `acos`, `acosh`, `asin`, `asinh`, `atan`, `atanh`, `atan2`, `cos`, `cosh`, `erf`, `erfc`, `exp`, `lgamma`, `log`, `log10`, `pow`, `sin`, `sinh`, `sqrt`, `tan` or `tanh`. *This BIF is intended for use by the implementation of the module* `math` *and should not be used elsewhere.*

```
> erlang:math(sin, math:pi()/6).
0.500000
```

Optional BIF.
Failure: `badarg` if `Function` is not an atom, is an incorrect atom, or if the argument(s) is (are) not number(s).

erlang:module_loaded(Module)

Returns the atoms `true` if the module contained in atom `Module` is loaded, otherwise returns `false`. Does not attempt to load the module. *This BIF is intended for use by the implementation of the module* `code` *and should not be used elsewhere.*

```
> module_loaded(lists).
true
```

Optional BIF.
Failure: `badarg` if the argument is not an atom.

monitor_node(Node, Flag)

Can be used to monitor nodes. An ERLANG process evaluating the expression `monitor_node(Node,true)` will be notified with a `{nodedown, Node}` message if `Node` should fail, if the network connection to `Node` should fail or if the process unsuccessfully tries to do any operations on `Node`. A process evaluating `monitor_node(Node,true)` twice, will receive two `nodedown` messages upon the failure of `Node`.

If `Flag` is `false`, the process will receive one `nodedown` message less upon the failure of `Node`.
Optional BIF.

node()

Returns the name of our own node. If we are not a networked node, but a local ERLANG system, the atom `nonode@nohost` is returned.

Allowed in guard tests.

node(Arg)

Returns the node where `Arg` resides. `Arg` can be a Pid, reference or a port.

```
> node(self()).
'klacke@super.eua.ericsson.se'
```

Allowed in guard tests. Failure: `badarg` if the argument is not a Pid, port or a reference.

nodes()

Returns a list of all nodes we are currently connected to.

Allowed in guard test.

now()

The BIF returns an integer representing current time as microseconds. The value is derived from (and thus its accuracy limited by the precision of) the system clock, and will on most systems represent the time since Jan. 1, 1970, 00:00:00 Coordinated Universal Time (UTC).

Failure to initialise, or unreasonable changes to the setting of, the system clock will of course adversely affect the returned value; however, it is guaranteed that consecutive calls during one invocation of ERLANG will always return increasing values.

open_port(PortName, PortSettings)

Returns a port which is the result of opening a new ERLANG port. A port can be seen as an external ERLANG process. `PortName` is one of:

`{spawn, Command}`
: Starts an *external* program. `Command` is the name of the external program which will be run. `Command` runs outside the ERLANG workspace.

`Atom`
: `Atom` is assumed to be the name of an external resource. A transparent connection between ERLANG and the resource named by the atom is established. The behaviour of the port depends upon the type of the resource. If `Atom` represents a file then a single message is sent to the ERLANG process containing the entire contents of the file. Sending messages to the port causes data to be written to the file.

`{fd, In, Out}`
: Allow an ERLANG process to access any currently opened file descriptors used by ERLANG. File descriptor `In` can be used for standard input and file descriptor `Out` for standard output. Very few processes need to use this, only various servers in the ERLANG operating system (`shell` and `user`).

`PortSettings` is a list of settings for the port. Valid values are:

`{packet, N}`
: Messages are preceded by their length, which is sent in `N` bytes with the most significant byte first. Valid values for `N` are 1, 2 or 4.

`stream`
: Output messages are sent without packet lengths – a private protocol must be used between the ERLANG process and the external object.

`use_stdio`
: Only valid for `{spawn, Command}`. Makes spawned (UNIX) process use standard input and output (i.e. file descriptors 0 and 1) for communicating with ERLANG.

`nouse_stdio`
: The opposite of above. Use file descriptors 3 and 4 for communicating with ERLANG.

The default is `stream` for *all* types of port and `use_stdio` for spawned ports.
Failure: `badarg` if bad format of `PortName` or `PortSettings`, or if the port cannot be opened.

pid_to_list(Pid)

Returns a list which corresponds to the process `Pid`. Note that this BIF is intended for use in debugging and in the ERLANG operating system and should not be used in application programs.[4]

```
> pid_to_list(whereis(init)).
[60,48,46,48,46,49,62]
```

Failure: `badarg` if the argument is not a Pid

erlang:pre_loaded()

Returns a list of the ERLANG modules which are preloaded in the system. Since all code loading is done through the file system someone has to load the file system. Thus, in order to be able to boot, the code for file IO, init and networking has to be preloaded into the system.

process_flag(Flag, Option)

Sets certain flags for the process which calls this function. Returns the old value of the flag.

`process_flag(trap_exit, Boolean)` When `trap_exit` is set to `true`, `EXIT` signals arriving at a process are converted to `{'EXIT', From, Reason}` messages which can be received as ordinary messages. If `trap_exit` is set to `false`, the process exits if it receives an `EXIT` signal other than `normal` and propagates the `EXIT` signal to its linked processes. Application processes should normally not trap exits.

`process_flag(error_handler, Module)` This is used by a process to redefine the error handler which deals with undefined function calls and undefined registered processes. *Inexperienced users are not recommended to do this* since code autoloading is dependent on the correct operation of the error handling module.

`process_flag(priority, Level)`
This sets the process priority. `Level` is an atom. All implementation should support two priority levels, `normal` and `low`. The default is `normal`.

Failure: `badarg` if `Flag` is not a atom or is not a recognised flag value, or if `Option` is not a term recognised for `Flag`.

[4] On the other hand this might be a good BIF to use if you want to win the Obfuscated ERLANG Contest.

process_info(Pid)

Returns a *long* list containing information about the process `Pid`. This BIF is only intended for debugging. Use for any other purpose is *strongly discouraged*. The list returned contains the following tuples (the order of these tuples in the list is not defined, nor are all the tuples mandatory).

`{registered_name, Atom}`
: Atom is the registered name of the process (if any).

`{current_function, {Module, Function, Arguments}}`
: `Module`, `Function`, `Arguments` are the current function call of the process.

`{initial_call, {Module, Function, Arity}}`
: `Module`, `Function`, `Arity` are the initial function call with which the process was spawned.

`{status, Status}`
: `Status` is the status of the process. `Status` is one of `waiting`, `running` or `runnable`.

`{messages, MessageQueue}`
: `MessageQueue` is a list of the messages to the process which have not yet been processed.

`{links, ListOfPids}`
: `ListOfPids` is a list of process identities with processes to which the process has a link.

`{dictionary, Dictionary}`
: `Dictionary` is the dictionary of the process.

`{error_handler, Module}`
: `Module` is the error handler *module* used by the process (e.g. for undefined function calls).

`{trap_exit, Boolean}`
: `Boolean` is `true` if the process is trapping exits, otherwise it is `false`.

`{stack_size, Size}`
: `Size` is the stack size of the process in stack words.

`{heap_size, Size}`
: `Size` is the heap size of the process in heap words.

`{reductions,Number}`
: `Number` is the number of reductions executed by the process.

Failure: `badarg` if the argument is not a Pid.

process_info(Pid, Key)

Returns only the information associated with `Key`, where `Key` can be either of the items listed for `process_info/1`.

Example:

```
1> process_info(self(), links).
{links,[<0.9.1>]}
```

Failure: badarg if the argument is not a Pid or if Key is not one of the atoms listed for process_info/1.

processes()

Returns a list of all processes on the current node.

```
> processes().
[<0.0.1>,<0.1.1>,<0.2.1>,<0.3.1>,<0.4.1>,<0.6.1>]
```

erlang:purge_module(Module)

Removes old code for Module. check_process_code/2 should be called before using this BIF to check that no processes are executing old code for this module.

In normal ERLANG implementations code handling (i.e. loading and deleting and replacing of modules) is done by the module code. *This BIF is intended for use by the implementation of the module* code *and should not be used elsewhere.* Optional BIF.

Failure: badarg if Module does not exist.

put(Key, Value)

Adds a new Value to the process dictionary and associates it with Key. If a value is already associated with Key this value is deleted and replaced with the new Value. Returns any value previously associated with Key, or undefined if no value was associated with Key. Key and Value can be any (valid) ERLANG terms. Note that values stored when put is evaluated within the scope of a catch will not be 'retracted' if a throw is evaluated or an error occurs.

```
> X = put(name, walrus), Y = put(name, carpenter),
  Z = get(name), {X,Y,Z}.
{undefined,walrus,carpenter}
```

register(Name, Pid)

Registers the `Name` as an alias for the process identity `Pid`. Processes with such aliases are often called *registered processes.*

Returns `true`.

Failure: `badarg` if `Pid` is not an active process, if the `Name` has previously been used or if the process is already registered (i.e. already has an alias) or if `Name` is not an atom.

registered()

Returns a list of names which have been registered as aliases for processes.

```
> registered().
[code_server,file_server,init,user,my_db]
```

round(Number)

Returns an integer by rounding `Number`.

```
> round(5.5).
6
```

Failure: `badarg` if the argument is not a float (or an integer).

erlang:set_cookie(Node,Cookie)

In order to communicate with a remote node, we must use this BIF to set the magic cookie of that node. If we send a message to a remote node at which we have set the wrong cookie, or not have set the cookie at all, the message we send will be transformed into a message of the form `{From, badcookie, To, Message}` and delivered to the `net_kernel` process at the receiving end.

An important special case for this BIF is when the `Node` argument is the node identity of our own node. In this case the magic cookie of our own node is set to be `Cookie`, as well as the cookie of all other nodes except the ones which already has a cookie which is not the atom `nocookie` are set to be `Cookie`.

Optional BIF.

Failure: `badarg` if not both `Node` and `Cookie` are atoms.

self()

Returns the process identity of the calling process.

```
> self().
<0.16.1>
```

Failure: `badarg` if the current process has exited.

setelement(Index, Tuple, Value)

Returns a tuple which is a copy of the argument `Tuple` with the element given by integer argument `Index` (the first element is the element with index 1) replaced by argument `Value`.

```
> setelement(2, {10, green, bottles}, red).
{10,red,bottles}
```

Failure: `badarg` if `Index` is not an integer or `Tuple` is not a tuple, or if `Index` is less than 1 or greater than the size of `Tuple`.

size(Object)

Returns a integer which is the size of the argument `Object` where `Object` is a tuple or binary.

```
> size({morni, mulle, bwange}).
3
```

Allowed in guard tests.
Failure: `badarg` if `Object` is not a tuple or a binary.

spawn(Module, Function, ArgumentList)

Returns the process identity of a new process started by applying `Module:Function` to `ArgumentList`. Note that the new process thus created will be placed in the systems scheduler queue and will be run at some later time.

`error_handler:undefined_function(Module, Function, ArgumentList)` is evaluated by the new process if `Module:Function/Arity` does not exist[5] (`Arity` is the length of the `ArgumentList`). If the `error_handler` is undefined, or the user has redefined the default `error_handler` so that replacement is undefined, a failure with reason `undef` will arise.

[5]The error handler can be redefined (see BIF `process_flag/2`).

```
> spawn(speed, regulator, [high_speed, thin_cut]).
<0.13.1>
```

Failure: badarg if Module and/or Function is not an atom or if ArgumentList is not a list.

spawn(Node, Module, Function, ArgumentList)

Works exactly as spawn/3, except that the process is spawned at Node. If Node does not exist, a useless Pid is returned.
Optional BIF.
Failure: see spawn/3.

spawn_link(Module, Function, ArgumentList)

This BIF is identical to the following code being executed in an *atomic operation*:

```
Pid = spawn(Module, Function, ArgumentList),
link(Pid),
Pid.
```

This is necessary since the created process might run immediately and fail *before* the call to link/1.
Failure: see spawn/3.

spawn_link(Node, Module, Function, ArgumentList)

Works exactly as spawn_link/3, except that the process is spawned at Node. If an attempt is made to spawn a process on a non-existing node a useless Pid will be returned and in the case of spawn_link an 'EXIT' signal will be delivered to the process which evaluated the spawn_link/4 BIF.
Optional BIF.
Failure:see spawn/3.

split_binary(ListOfBinaries, Pos)

Builds two new binaries, as if Bin had been split at Pos. Returns a tuple consisting of the two new binaries. For example:

```
1> B = list_to_binary("0123456789").
#Bin
2> size(B).
10
3> {B1,B2} = split_binary(B,3).
{#Bin,#Bin}
4> size(B1).
3
5> size(B2).
7
```

statistics(Type)

Returns information about the system. `Type` is an atom which is one of:

`runtime`
: Returns `{Total_Run_Time, Time_Since_Last_Call}`.

`wall_clock`
: The atom `wall_clock` can be used in the same manner as the atom **`runtime`** except that real-time is measured as opposed to run-time or CPU time.

`reductions`
: Returns `{Total_Reductions, Reductions_Since_Last_Call}`.

`garbage_collection`
: Returns `{Number_of_GCs, Word_Reclaimed, 0}`. This information may not be valid for all implementations.

`run_queue`
: Returns the length of the run queue, i.e the number of processes that are scheduled to run.

All times are in milliseconds.

```
> statistics(runtime).
{1690,1620}
> statistics(reductions).
{2046,11}
> statistics(garbage_collection).
{85,23961,0}
```

Failure: `badarg` if `Type` is not one of the atoms shown above.

term_to_binary(Term)

Returns a binary which corresponds to an external representation of the ERLANG term `Term`. This BIF can for example be used to store ERLANG terms on disc or to send terms out through a port in order to communicate with systems written in languages other than ERLANG.

throw(Any)

Non-local return from a function. If executed within a `catch`, `catch` will return the value `Any`.

```
> catch throw({hello, there}).
{hello,there}
```

Failure: `no_catch` if not executed within a catch.

time()

Returns the tuple `{Hour, Minute, Second}` which is the system's notion of the current time. Time zone correction is implementation-dependent.

```
> time().
{9,42,44}
```

tl(List)

Returns `List` stripped of its first element.

```
> tl([geesties, guilies, beasties]).
[guilies,beasties]
```

Failure: `badarg` if `List` is the empty list `[]` or is not a list. Allowed in guard tests.

trunc(Number)

Returns an integer by truncating `Number`.

```
> trunc(5.5).
5
```

Failure: `badarg` if the argument is not a float or an integer.

tuple_to_list(Tuple)

Returns a list which corresponds to `Tuple`. `Tuple` may contain any valid ERLANG terms.

```
> tuple_to_list({share, {'Ericsson_B', 119}}).
[share,{'Ericsson_B',190}]
```

Failure: `badarg` if the argument is not a tuple.

unlink(Pid)

Removes a link (if any) from the calling process to another process given by argument `Pid`. Returns `true`. Will not fail if not linked to `Pid` or if `Pid` does not exist. Returns `true`.
Failure: `badarg` if the argument is not a valid Pid.

unregister(Name)

Removes the alias given by the atom argument `Name` for a process. Returns the atom `true`.

```
> unregister(db).
true
```

Failure: `badarg` if `Name` is not the alias name of a registered process.
Users are advised not to unregister system processes.

whereis(Name)

Returns the process identity for the aliased process `Name` (see `register/2`). Returns `undefined` if no such process has been registered.

```
> whereis(user).
<0.3.1>
```

Failure: `badarg` if the argument is not an atom.

B.2 BIFs Sorted by Type

Some BIFs may occur in two subsections.

B.2.1 Working with processes and ports

`check_process_code(Pid, Mod)`	Checks if a process is running an old version of code.
`exit(Reason)`	Exits.
`exit(Pid, Reason)`	Sends an exit to another process but does not exit.
`group_leader()`	Returns Pid of our group leader.
`group_leader(Leader, Pid)`	Sets `Pids` group leader.
`link(Pid)`	Creates a link from `self()` to Pid.
`open_port(Request)`	Opens a port.
`process_flag(Flag, Option)`	Sets process flags.
`process_info(Pid)`	Returns information about a process.
`processes()`	Returns a list of all processes.
`register(Name, Pid)`	Registers an alias for a process.
`registered()`	Returns a list of all process aliases.
`self()`	Returns own identity.
`spawn(Mod, Func, Args)`	Creates a new process.
`spawn_link(Mod, Func, Args)`	Creates a new process and link to it.
`unlink(Pid)`	Removes any link from `self()` to Pid.
`unregister(Name)`	Removes the alias for a process.
`whereis(Name)`	Returns the Pid corresponding to an alias.

B.2.2 Object access and examination

`element(Index, Tuple)`	Gets an element in a tuple.
`hd(List)`	Returns the head of a list.
`length(List)`	Returns the length of a list.
`setelement(N, Tuple, Item)`	Sets an element in a tuple.
`size(Tuple)`	Returns the size of a tuple.
`tl(List)`	Returns the tail of a list.

B.2.3 Meta programming

`apply(Mod, Func, Args)`	Applies `Mod:Func` to `Args`.
`apply({Mod, Func}, Args)`	Applies `Mod:Func` to `Args`.

B.2.4 Type conversion

`abs(Number)`	Returns the absolute value of a number.
`atom_to_list(Atom)`	Converts an atom to a list of ASCII values.
`float(Integer)`	Converts an integer to a float.
`float_to_list(Float)`	Converts a float to a list of ASCII values.
`integer_to_list(Integer)`	Converts an integer to a list of ASCII values.
`list_to_atom(List)`	Converts a list of ASCII values to an atom.
`list_to_float(List)`	Converts a list of ASCII values to a float.
`list_to_integer(List)`	Converts a list of ASCII values to an integer.
`list_to_pid(List)`	Converts a list of ASCII values to a Pid.
`list_to_tuple(List)`	Converts a list to a tuple.
`pid_to_list(Pid)`	Converts a Pid to a list of ASCII values.
`round(Float)`	Convert a float to an integer.
`tuple_to_list(Tuple)`	Converts a tuple to a list.
`trunc(Float)`	Converts a float to an integer.

B.2.5 Code handling

`check_process_code(Pid, Mod)`	Checks if a process is running an old version of code.
`delete_module(Module)`	Removes the current version of code for a module.
`load_module(FileName)`	Loads code in a file.
`module_loaded(Module)`	Checks if a module is loaded.
`purge_module(Module)`	Removes the old code for a version.

B.2.6 Per process dictionary

`erase()`	Returns and erases the process dictionary.
`erase(Key)`	Erases a key–value pair from the dictionary.
`get()`	Returns the process dictionary.
`get(Key)`	Gets a value associated with a key.
`get_keys(Value)`	Gets a list of all values associated with a key.
`put(Key, Value)`	Puts a key – value pair into the dictionary and returns the old value.

B.2.7 System information

`date()`	Returns today's date.
`node()`	Returns the node identity.
`processes()`	Returns a list of all active Pids.
`process_info(Pid)`	Returns a list containing information about a process.
`registered()`	Returns a list of all process aliases.
`statistics(Type)`	Returns statistics about the ERLANG system.

B.2.8 Distribution

`alive(Name,Port,Settings)`	Makes the system distributed.
`disconnect_node(Node)`	Disconnects `Node`.
`get_cookie()`	Returns own magic cookie.
`is_alive()`	Checks whether the system is distributed.
`node()`	Returns our own node identity.
`node(Arg)`	Return node identity where `Arg` originates.
`monitor_node(Node, Flag)`	Monitor the well-being of `Node`.
`nodes()`	Returns a list of the currently connected nodes.
`node_unlink(Node)`	Removes a link to `Node`.
`set_cookie(Node, Cookie)`	Sets `Nodes` magic cookie.
`spawn(Node,M,F,A)`	Creates a new process on `Node`.
`spawn_link(Node,M,F,A)`	Creates a new process on `Node` and links to it.

B.2.9 Miscellaneous

`halt()`	Stops the ERLANG system.
`hash(Term,Range)`	Returns hash value of `Term`.
`make_ref()`	Makes a unique reference.
`math(Function, N1)`	Evaluates a mathematical function with one argument.
`math(Function, N1, N2)`	Evaluates a mathematical function with two arguments.
`now()`	Returns the current time in microseconds.
`time()`	Returns the current time.
`throw(Any)`	Provides a non-local return value for a function.

Appendix C

The Standard Libraries

Appendix C describes some of the functions in ERLANG's standard library modules.

C.1 io

The module io provides generalised input/output. All the functions have an optional parameter Dev which is a file descriptor to be used for IO. The default is standard input/output.

format([Dev], F, Args)	Outputs Args with format F.
get_chars([Dev], P, N)	Outputs prompt P and reads N characters from Dev.
get_line([Dev], P)	Outputs prompt P and reads a line from Dev.
nl([Dev])	Outputs a new line.
parse_exprs([Dev], P)	Outputs prompt P and reads a sequence of ERLANG expressions from Dev. Returns {form, ExprList} if successful, or {error, What}.
parse_form([Dev], P)	Outputs prompt P and reads an ERLANG form from Dev. Returns {form, Form} if successful, or {error, What}.
put_chars([Dev], L)	Outputs the (possibly non-flat) character list L.
read([Dev], P)	Outputs prompt P and reads a term from Dev. Returns {term, T} if successful, or {error, What} if error.
write([Dev], Term)	Outputs Term.

C.2 file

The module `file` provides a standard interface to the file system.

`read_file(File)`	Returns {`ok, Bin`} where `Bin` is a binary data object containing the contents of the file `File`.
`write_file(File, Binary)`	Writes the contents of binary data object `Binary` to the file `File`.
`get_cwd()`	Returns {`ok, Dir`}, where `Dir` is the current working directory.
`set_cwd(Dir)`	Sets the current working directory to `Dir`.
`rename(From, To)`	Renames the file `From` to `To`.
`make_dir(Dir)`	Creates the directory `Dir`.
`del_dir(Dir)`	Deletes the directory `Dir`.
`list_dir(Dir)`	Returns {`ok, L`}, where `L` is a list of all the files in the directory `Dir`.
`file_info(File)`	Returns {`ok, L`}, where `L` is a tuple containing information about the file `File`.
`consult(File)`	Returns {`ok, L`}, where `L` is a list of all the terms in `File`, or {`error, Why`} if error.
`open(File, Mode)`	Opens `File` in `Mode` which is `read`, `write` or `read_write`. Returns a {`ok, File`}, or {`error, What`} if error.
`close(Desc)`	Closes the file with descriptor `Desc`.
`position(Desc, N)`	Sets the position of the file with descriptor `Desc` to `N`.
`truncate(Desc)`	Truncates the file with descriptor `Desc` at the current position.

C.3 lists

The module `lists` provides standard list processing functions. In the following all parameters starting with '`L`' denote *lists*.

`append(L1, L2)`	Returns `L1` appended to `L2`.
`append(L)`	Appends all of the sublists of `L`.
`concat(L)`	Returns an atom which is the concatenation of all atoms in `L`.
`delete(X, L)`	Returns a list where the first occurrence of `X` in `L` has been deleted.
`flat_length(L)`	Equivalent to `length(flatten(L))`.
`flatten(L)`	Returns a flattened version of `L`.
`keydelete(Key, N, LTup)`	Returns a copy of `LTup` except that the first tuple whose `N`th element is `Key` has been deleted.
`keysearch(Key, N, LTup)`	Searches the list of tuples `LTup` for a tuple `X` whose `N`th element is `Key`. Returns `{value, X}` if found, else `false`.
`keysort(N, LTup)`	Returns a sorted version of the list of tuples `LTup`, where the `N`th element is used as a sort key.
`member(X, L)`	Returns `true` if `X` is a member of the list `L`, otherwise `false`.
`last(L)`	Returns the last element of `L`.
`nth(N, L)`	Returns the `N`th element of `L`.
`reverse(L)`	Reverses the top-level elements of `L`.
`reverse(L1, L2)`	Equivalent to `append(reverse(L1), L2)`.
`sort(L)`	Sorts `L`.

C.4 code

The module code is used to load and manipulate compiled ERLANG code.

set_path(D)	Sets the code server search path to the list of directories D.
load_file(File)	Tries to load File.erl using the current path. Returns {error, What} if error, or {module, ModuleName} if the load succeeded.
is_loaded(Module)	Tests if module Module is loaded. Returns {file, AbsFileName} if the module is loaded, or false if the module was not loaded.
ensure_loaded(Module)	Loads Module if it is not loaded. Return value as for load_file(File).
purge(Module)	Purges the code in Module.
all_loaded()	Returns a list of tuples {Module, AbsFileName} of all loaded modules.

Appendix D

Errors in ERLANG

This appendix gives a precise summary of the error handling mechanisms used in ERLANG.

D.1 Match Errors

A match error is encountered when we call a BIF with bad arguments, try to call a function whose arguments don't match, etc.

The behaviour of the system when a match error is encountered can be described by the following pseudocode:

```
if(called a BIF with bad args)then
    Error = badarg
elseif(cannot find a matching function)then
    Error = badmatch
elseif(no matching case statement)then
    Error = case_clause
    ...
if(within the scope of a 'catch')then
    Value of 'catch' = {'EXIT', Error}
else
    broadcast(Error)
    die
endif
```

where 'broadcast(Reason)' can be described as follows:

```
if(Process has Links)then
    send {'EXIT', self(), Reason} signals to all linked
    processes
endif
```

D.2 Throws

The behaviour of 'throw(Reason)' can be described as follows:

```
if(within the scope of a 'catch')then
    Value of 'catch' = Reason
else
    broadcast(nocatch)
    die
endif
```

D.3 Exit signals

The behaviour of ERLANG when an `{'EXIT', Pid, ExitReason}` signal is received can be described by the following pseudocode:

```
if(ExitReason == kill)then
    broadcast(killed) % note we change ExitReason
    die
else
    if(trapping exits)then
        add {'EXIT', Pid, ExitReason}
        to input mailbox
    else
        if(ExitReason == normal) then
            continue
        else
            broadcast(ExitReason)
            die
        endif
    endif
endif
```

If the process with Pid `Sender` executes the primitive `exit(Pid, Why)` then the signal `{'EXIT', Source, Why}` is sent to the process `Pid` *as if* the process `Sender` had died.

If a process terminates normally the message `{'EXIT', Source, normal}` is sent to all linked processes.

`exit(Pid, kill)` sends an *unkillable* exit message – the receiving process unconditionally dies, and the reason for exiting is changed to `killed` and sent to all linked processes (otherwise we might crash system servers – which was not what was intended).

D.4 Undefined Functions

The final class of error concerns what happens when an undefined function or registered process is referred to.

If a call is made to `Mod:Func(Arg0,...,ArgN)` and no code exists for this function then `error_handler:undefined_function(Mod, Func, [Arg0,...,ArgN])` will be called.

D.5 The error_logger

All error messages generated by the ERLANG run-time system are transformed into a message of the following form

```
{emulator,GroupLeader,Chars}
```

and sent to a process registered under the name of `error_logger`. Any user-defined code can run in the `error_logger` process which makes it easy to send the error messages to an other node for processing. The variable `GroupLeader` is the process identifier of the group leader for the process which caused the error. This makes it possible for the `error_logger` to send the error back to the node of the offending process, to have the error printout performed on the terminal connected to that node.

Appendix E

Drivers

This appendix describes how to write a so-called linked-in ERLANG driver. It is possible to link any piece of software into the ERLANG run-time system and have that software executing at the outside end of an ERLANG port.

ERLANG processes send normal messages to the port, and receive normal messages from the port. The run-time system communicates with the linked-in port software by passing pointers. This might be appropriate for port software that is extremely IO intensive. On operating systems that do not support multiprogramming, this may also be the only way to write ERLANG port software.

The advantage of having an ERLANG port as a linked-in driver instead of letting the port software run in a separate process of the local operating system as described in Chaper 9 is that the communication between ERLANG and the port software is considerably faster. The disadvantage is that if the port software is large and complicated it might leak memory or even fail completeley, thus bringing the entire ERLANG system to a halt.

The following is an example of a linked driver that echoes back into the ERLANG system anything it gets. We have the file easy_drv.c

```
#include <stdio.h>
#include "driver.h"


static int erlang_port;
static long easy_start();
static int easy_init(), easy_stop(), easy_read();

struct driver_entry easy_driver_entry = {
    easy_init,easy_start,easy_stop,easy_read,null_func,
    null_func,"easy"
    };

static int easy_init()
```

`ready_output(long port,int fd)`
This function gets called when the driver has told the emulator to check for output for file-descriptor `fd`, and `fd` is ready to write. This is useful if the driver tries to write a large buffer on a file-descriptor that is non-blocking and the write only partially succeeds. The driver can then tell the run-time system to check that particular file-descriptor for output, save the remaining unwritten parts of the buffer and then return. When the file-descriptor is ready to write again, the run-time system will invoke the `ready_output` function.

`driver_name`
Finally the name of the driver, as a character string, will have to be filled in.

All the above functions are automatically called by the ERLANG run-time system, not by the driver code itself. The driver code also needs a way to interact with the run-time system. This can be done through the following three functions:

`driver_output(int port,char *buf,int len)`
If the driver wants to produce output, i.e. send a message to the ERLANG process that is connected to the port, it can invoke this function.

`driver_failure(int port, int failurecode)`
This will close the port.

`driver_select(int port,int fd,int mode,int on)`
This function needs only to be used if the driver creates new file-descriptors which it wants the ERLANG run-time system to monitor. The code which executes in the driver must never do any blocking operations against the underlying operating system.
So for example, in a UNIX implementation, we cannot make the system call `select()` from the driver, but we can let the run-time system do it for us. If a driver has created a file-descriptor `fd` and wants the emulator to check for IO on the file-descriptor and, once input is available, the driver wants to have its `ready_input` function invoked, the driver executes:

```
driver_select(erlang_port, fd, DO_READ, 1);
```

If the driver chooses to close the file-descriptor it must execute

```
driver_select(erlang_port, fd, DO_READ|DO_WRITE, 0);
```

to indicate to the run-time system that it need not bother with `fd` any more. The last parameter on is either 1 or 0, whether we want to turn select on or off.

It is of utmost importance that the code residing in a linked-in driver is correct. If this code crashes, the entire ERLANG system crashes. If this code hangs, due to an operating system call or an error in the driver, the entire ERLANG system hangs. Note that several UNIX system calls are suspending. For example, if a driver does a blocking read on a file-descriptor it will hang the entire ERLANG run-time system until the call to `read` returns.

The file `config.c` contains an array with the addresses of all `driver_entry`'s. This array needs to be edited and a reference to the new driver must be inserted. Then, all that has to be done is to compile the driver and link it into the ERLANG system, using a standard C code linker. How to go about actually linking the driver into the ERLANG run-time system is implementation-dependent. It also depends upon the choice of operating system.

Index